Flash™ 5
Weekend Crash Course™

Flash™ 5
Weekend Crash Course™

Shamms Mortier

IDG Books Worldwide, Inc.
An International Data Group Company
Foster City, CA • Chicago, IL • Indianapolis, IN • New York, NY

Flash™ 5 Weekend Crash Course™
Published by
IDG Books Worldwide, Inc.
An International Data Group Company
919 E. Hillsdale Blvd., Suite 400
Foster City, CA 94404
www.idgbooks.com (IDG Books Worldwide Web site)
Copyright © 2001 IDG Books Worldwide, Inc. All rights reserved. No part of this book, including interior design, cover design, and icons, may be reproduced or transmitted in any form, by any means (electronic, photocopying, recording, or otherwise) without the prior written permission of the publisher.
ISBN: 0-7645-3546-3
Printed in the United States of America
10 9 8 7 6 5 4 3 2 1
1B/RQ/QR/QR/FC
Distributed in the United States by IDG Books Worldwide, Inc.
Distributed by CDG Books Canada Inc. for Canada; by Transworld Publishers Limited in the United Kingdom; by IDG Norge Books for Norway; by IDG Sweden Books for Sweden; by IDG Books Australia Publishing Corporation Pty. Ltd. for Australia and New Zealand; by TransQuest Publishers Pte Ltd. for Singapore, Malaysia, Thailand, Indonesia, and Hong Kong; by Gotop Information Inc. for Taiwan; by ICG Muse, Inc. for Japan; by Intersoft for South Africa; by Eyrolles for France; by International Thomson Publishing for Germany, Austria, and Switzerland; by Distribuidora Cuspide for Argentina; by LR International for Brazil; by Galileo Libros for Chile; by Ediciones ZETA S.C.R. Ltda. for Peru; by WS Computer Publishing Corporation, Inc., for the Philippines; by Contemporanea de Ediciones for Venezuela; by Express Computer Distributors for the Caribbean and West Indies; by Micronesia Media Distributor, Inc. for Micronesia; by Chips Computadoras S.A. de C.V. for Mexico; by Editorial Norma de Panama S.A. for Panama; by American Bookshops for Finland.

For general information on IDG Books Worldwide's books in the U.S., please call our Consumer Customer Service department at 800-762-2974.
For reseller information, including discounts and premium sales, please call our Reseller Customer Service department at 800-434-3422.
For information on where to purchase IDG Books Worldwide's books outside the U.S., please contact our International Sales department at 317-572-3993 or fax 317-572-4002.
For consumer information on foreign language translations, please contact our Customer Service department at 800-434-3422, fax 317-572-4002, or e-mail rights@idgbooks.com.
For information on licensing foreign or domestic rights, please phone +1-650-653-7098.
For sales inquiries and special prices for bulk quantities, please contact our Order Services department at 800-434-3422 or write to the address above.
For information on using IDG Books Worldwide's books in the classroom or for ordering examination copies, please contact our Educational Sales department at 800-434-2086 or fax 317-572-4005.
For press review copies, author interviews, or other publicity information, please contact our Public Relations department at 650-653-7000 or fax 650-653-7500.
For authorization to photocopy items for corporate, personal, or educational use, please contact Copyright Clearance Center, 222 Rosewood Drive, Danvers, MA 01923, or fax 978-750-4470.
Library of Congress Cataloging-in-Publication Data
Mortier R. Shamms.
  Flash 5 Weekend Crash Course / Shamms Mortier
    p. cm.
    ISBN 0-7645-3546-3 (alk. papaer)
  1. Computer amination. 2. Flash (Computer file) 3. Multinedia systems. 4. Websites--Design. I. Title.
TR897.7 .M675 2001
006.6'96--dc21

LIMIT OF LIABILITY/DISCLAIMER OF WARRANTY: THE PUBLISHER AND AUTHOR HAVE USED THEIR BEST EFFORTS IN PREPARING THIS BOOK. THE PUBLISHER AND AUTHOR MAKE NO REPRESENTATIONS OR WARRANTIES WITH RESPECT TO THE ACCURACY OR COMPLETENESS OF THE CONTENTS OF THIS BOOK AND SPECIFICALLY DISCLAIM ANY IMPLIED WARRANTIES OF MERCHANTABILITY OR FITNESS FOR A PARTICULAR PURPOSE. THERE ARE NO WARRANTIES WHICH EXTEND BEYOND THE DESCRIPTIONS CONTAINED IN THIS PARAGRAPH. NO WARRANTY MAY BE CREATED OR EXTENDED BY SALES REPRESENTATIVES OR WRITTEN SALES MATERIALS. THE ACCURACY AND COMPLETENESS OF THE INFORMATION PROVIDED HEREIN AND THE OPINIONS STATED HEREIN ARE NOT GUARANTEED OR WARRANTED TO PRODUCE ANY PARTICULAR RESULTS, AND THE ADVICE AND STRATEGIES CONTAINED HEREIN MAY NOT BE SUITABLE FOR EVERY INDIVIDUAL. NEITHER THE PUBLISHER NOR AUTHOR SHALL BE LIABLE FOR ANY LOSS OF PROFIT OR ANY OTHER COMMERCIAL DAMAGES, INCLUDING BUT NOT LIMITED TO SPECIAL, INCIDENTAL, CONSEQUENTIAL, OR OTHER DAMAGES.

Trademarks: All brand names and product names used in this book are trade names, service marks, trademarks, or registered trademarks of their respective owners. IDG Books Worldwide is not associated with any product or vendor mentioned in this book.

 is a registered trademark or trademark under exclusive license to IDG Books Worldwide, Inc. from International Data Group, Inc. in the United States and/or other countries.

ABOUT IDG BOOKS WORLDWIDE

Welcome to the world of IDG Books Worldwide.

IDG Books Worldwide, Inc., is a subsidiary of International Data Group, the world's largest publisher of computer-related information and the leading global provider of information services on information technology. IDG was founded more than 30 years ago by Patrick J. McGovern and now employs more than 9,000 people worldwide. IDG publishes more than 290 computer publications in over 75 countries. More than 90 million people read one or more IDG publications each month.

Launched in 1990, IDG Books Worldwide is today the #1 publisher of best-selling computer books in the United States. We are proud to have received eight awards from the Computer Press Association in recognition of editorial excellence and three from Computer Currents' First Annual Readers' Choice Awards. Our best-selling ...For Dummies® series has more than 50 million copies in print with translations in 31 languages. IDG Books Worldwide, through a joint venture with IDG's Hi-Tech Beijing, became the first U.S. publisher to publish a computer book in the People's Republic of China. In record time, IDG Books Worldwide has become the first choice for millions of readers around the world who want to learn how to better manage their businesses.

Our mission is simple: Every one of our books is designed to bring extra value and skill-building instructions to the reader. Our books are written by experts who understand and care about our readers. The knowledge base of our editorial staff comes from years of experience in publishing, education, and journalism — experience we use to produce books to carry us into the new millennium. In short, we care about books, so we attract the best people. We devote special attention to details such as audience, interior design, use of icons, and illustrations. And because we use an efficient process of authoring, editing, and desktop publishing our books electronically, we can spend more time ensuring superior content and less time on the technicalities of making books.

You can count on our commitment to deliver high-quality books at competitive prices on topics you want to read about. At IDG Books Worldwide, we continue in the IDG tradition of delivering quality for more than 30 years. You'll find no better book on a subject than one from IDG Books Worldwide.

John Kilcullen
Chairman and CEO
IDG Books Worldwide, Inc.

Eighth Annual
Computer Press
Awards ≥1992

Ninth Annual
Computer Press
Awards ≥1993

Tenth Annual
Computer Press
Awards ≥1994

Eleventh Annual
Computer Press
Awards ≥1995

IDG is the world's leading IT media, research and exposition company. Founded in 1964, IDG had 1997 revenues of $2.05 billion and has more than 9,000 employees worldwide. IDG offers the widest range of media options that reach IT buyers in 75 countries representing 95% of worldwide IT spending. IDG's diverse product and services portfolio spans six key areas including print publishing, online publishing, expositions and conferences, market research, education and training, and global marketing services. More than 90 million people read one or more of IDG's 290 magazines and newspapers, including IDG's leading global brands — Computerworld, PC World, Network World, Macworld and the Channel World family of publications. IDG Books Worldwide is one of the fastest-growing computer book publishers in the world, with more than 700 titles in 36 languages. The "...For Dummies®" series alone has more than 50 million copies in print. IDG offers online users the largest network of technology-specific Web sites around the world through IDG.net (http://www.idg.net), which comprises more than 225 targeted Web sites in 55 countries worldwide. International Data Corporation (IDC) is the world's largest provider of information technology data, analysis and consulting, with research centers in over 41 countries and more than 400 research analysts worldwide. IDG World Expo is a leading producer of more than 168 globally branded conferences and expositions in 35 countries including E3 (Electronic Entertainment Expo), Macworld Expo, ComNet, Windows World Expo, ICE (Internet Commerce Expo), Agenda, DEMO, and Spotlight. IDG's training subsidiary, ExecuTrain, is the world's largest computer training company, with more than 230 locations worldwide and 785 training courses. IDG Marketing Services helps industry-leading IT companies build international brand recognition by developing global integrated marketing programs via IDG's print, online and exposition products worldwide. Further information about the company can be found at www.idg.com.
1/26/00

Credits

Acquisitions Editor
Michael Roney

Project Editor
Chandani Thapa

Technical Editor
David Baldeschwieler

Copy Editors
KC Hogue
Lane Barnholtz
Cindy Lai
Jessica Montgomery
Julie Campbell Moss
Nancy Rapoport
Laura Stone

Proof Editor
Patsy Owens

Permissions Editor
Carmen Krikorian

Project Coordinators
Louigene A. Santos
Danette Nurse

Graphics and Production Specialists
Robert Bihlmayer
Rolly DelRosario
Jude Levinson
Michael Lewis
Ramses Ramirez
Victor Pérez-Varela

Quality Control Technician
Dina F Quan

Media Development Specialist
Brock Bigard

Media Development Coordinator
Marisa Pearman

Illustrator
Gabriele McCann

Proofreading and Indexing
York Production Services

Cover Design
Clark Creative Group

About the Author

R. Shamms Mortier has written and illustrated more than 15 books on computer graphics and animation, all available internationally. He has also written more than 800 articles and reviews for more than a dozen trade magazines since 1985. He owns and operates the Bristol, Vermont design studio, Eyeful Tower Communications, which serves broadcast, education, and entertainment industries.

For Diane, my beloved mate of many years

Preface

Flash 5 Weekend Crash Course teaches the reader how to achieve a basic mastery of Macromedia Flash 5's art and animation capabilities. Please note that this is not a book about the Flash programming language. Although this book is best used when the reader has some degree of familiarity with computer graphics and animation, and has attained a level of comfort, if not proficiency with drawing, the novice artist can also make use of the learning involved. This is because the CD-ROM that accompanies the book contains all of the tutorial images involved. The novice computer artist can simply load these images and proceed with the lessons. The important thing is to learn how Flash works; this book leaves the topic of drawing skills to the reader to explore on her or his own. Many Flash users are not artists themselves. Instead, they gather Flash art and animation elements from prepublished material or other sources and then shape the content into a Flash production. So, you can use this book as would either a computer artist or animator, or as someone who compiles the component resources for a production together without actually creating the basic components.

Bitmaps and Vectors

If you are new to computer graphics and animation, it is important that you understand some basic terminology. Flash is a vector application, but what does this mean? Most computer art and animation software is based upon bitmaps. Software that deals with bitmaps can be used to create 2-D or 3-D art and animation. A 2-D bitmap program is what is called a *painting* program. A painting program enables you to alter the color of each of the smallest units, called *pixels,* of your screen.

Just how many pixels there are on a screen depends upon the resolution of your computer screen. A common resolution of 640×480 pixels contains 640 pixels horizontally and 480 pixels vertically. That means that a 640×480 screen contains 640 pixels multiplied by 480 pixels, for a total of 307,200 separate pixels. A screen set to 800×600 has 480,000 pixels. It takes a lot of disk storage capacity to store bitmap images that contain that many pixels.

The screen's *bit depth* is another important matter to be aware of when considering the amount of storage space required to store bitmap images. Bit depth sets the number of colors that are possible onscreen, and it is computed with powers of 2. See the following chart.

Bit Depth Configurations

Bit Depth	Number of Possible Separate Colors
2^1	2
2^2	4
2^3	8
2^4	16
2^5	32
2^6	64
2^7	128
2^8	256
2^9	512
2^{10}	1,024
2^{11}	2,048
2^{12}	4,096
2^{13}	8,192
2^{14}	16,384
2^{15}	32,768
2^{16}	65,536
2^{17}	131,072

Bit Depth	Number of Possible Separate Colors
2^{18}	262,144
2^{19}	524,288
2^{20}	1,048,576
2^{21}	2,097,152
2^{22}	4,194,304
2^{23}	8,388,608
2^{24}	16,777,216

The most common bitmap depths are 8 and 24. Painting software with a bitmap depth of 8 creates 256 colors, and the associated color palette can be configured to match what most Web browsers expect in the way of online content. The common format for creating photorealistic art and animation displays is 24-bit art and animation. It takes four times more hard disk storage space each time you jump a bitmap-depth level; it takes, for example, thirty-two times more storage space to save a 8-bit graphic as it would a 2-bit graphic (8×4). You can immediately appreciate why it takes so much space to work with photorealistic images.

This is only true, thankfully, for images that are *uncompressed*. Compression enables you to save larger images in a smaller space. Photographic 24-bit images posted to the Web, for example, are usually compressed in either the JPEG or PNG format, while other formats are used to compress other images and animations. This is because file size is important and relates directly to download time (the time it takes an image to display on the browser screen). Web designers who want high-quality imagery and animation must take all of these things into account when designing a site. Enter vectors.

Vector art is best known for its use in desktop publishing applications. These include software packages such as Adobe Illustrator, Macromedia FreeHand, Corel Draw, Deneba Canvas, and others. Vector art is called *resolution independent*, which means that it displays at maximum quality regardless of screen resolution. This is because vector art was not originally targeted to screen imagery at all, but to printed output. Printers, especially professional printers, have resolutions that far exceed what a screen can normally display. Vector art is 8 bit, meaning a maximum of 256 colors. The appearance of additional colors is accomplished by *dithering*, which is blending other colors on the palette together. Unlike bitmap art, vector art is not related to pixels. Instead, what is stored for vector images is the position, direction, strength, and color of a line. This breaks down into mathematical formulae, making vector storage tiny compared to bitmaps. It also makes download time for Web use extremely fast, even when the data stream has to be sent over older phone lines and networks. The problem with all of this is that until recently, there was no way of creating vector art and animation that could be used as the visual components for Web display. Enter Flash.

Flash is vector art and animation creation software, though as you will see, it can also incorporate selected bitmap elements. This means that Flash art and animation displays quickly when used in the design of a Web page, and that means a lot when the viewer is surfing the Web. Nothing is more irritating than waiting forever while a large bitmap graphic slowly comes into view. This loses viewers, and for a business, the loss of viewers is directly associated with the loss of potential business. With Flash, you can design Web sites that contain the level of graphics and animation components that excite viewers and invite people in, and everything happens as quickly as possible — you might even say, in a flash.

Who Is This Book For?

This book is targeted toward beginning to intermediate Flash users. It is meant for users who work with visual components, art, and animation, and not for users who are interested in learning how to write scripts for Flash. The following types of readers should benefit most from this book:

- Individuals with prior experience in other vector drawing applications who want to apply their vector skills to the design of art and animation for the Web.
- Individuals who have some experience with art and animation in traditional or computer-related formats, or both, who need to upgrade their skills for personal use and/or job requirements.
- Web designers who want either new graphics and animation options, or who need to redesign current Web bitmap data into a format that downloads faster for viewing.
- Beginning to intermediate computer graphics and animation users who want to quickly get up to speed with Flash.

Preface

How to Use This Book

What you hold in your hands is more than a book. It is an invitation to engage in an interactive learning experience guaranteed to get you up and running with Flash in the shortest possible time. If you follow the timed lessons carefully, going through each step of the process, you are assured of learning how Flash can be used to design graphics and animation components of a Web site — and all after just one dedicated weekend of study. The book and the files contained on the accompanying CD-ROM are designed to make this learning experience as painless and enjoyable as possible.

Readers engaging in the Flash 5 weekend course come from many different levels of experience and expertise. It is important, however, that you complete each lesson in its prescribed order, regardless of your prior experience with computer graphics and animation, Web design, or even previous versions of Flash. Users of every level find new terms to become familiarized with and new capabilities present in Flash 5. Once you get through the course, the book is always there for future reference, and you can always extrapolate and improvise later. So be diligent in going through the course from start to finish.

Overview

Flash 5 Weekend Crash Course is presented as thirty timed chapters grouped in six parts, and one additional chapter, as follows:

Friday Evening

This part contains four lessons designed to teach or reinforce user knowledge concerning basic Flash operations, terminology, and customizing settings at the start of a project.

Saturday Morning

This part contains six lessons that describe planning and storyboarding considerations, followed by an initial Flash animation project with environmental imagery (air, land, water), flying birds and leaping fish, and a bobbing diver.

Saturday Afternoon

Six lessons that center on the development of a text animation project. These lessons enable you to explore using text components as main animation elements, which is a major animation concept.

Saturday Evening

These four lessons allow you to experience the integration of both bitmap and audio content for Flash animations.

Sunday Morning

These six lessons teach you how to use some of Flash 5's more complex features, including the following: buttons and switches, mask layers, reveals, strobes, and nested animations.

Sunday Afternoon

This part contains four lessons that cover inspectors, painting with bitmaps, setting actions, and usage hints.

Content Options and Post-Production Editing

As an extra, a chapter is included that can be read on your own time that deals with the preparation of content in external applications such as Adobe Photoshop, Illustrator, After Effects, and more.

Appendices

This section consists of appendices that discuss the CD-ROM contents, vendor contact data, and information about Macromedia Generator.

Preface

**20 Min.
To Go**

Layout and Features

When you see this symbol in the margin, you'll get an idea of how far along you are in a lesson. Relax, and don't feel pressured to meet the exact time clock represented. A few minutes more or less will not be held against you. Scattered throughout the lessons are also hints, tips, and relevant information about addendum topics and concerns. You'll also find a number of other margin symbols used to indicate additional information. This is a cross-platform book. Instructions for Windows users appear in the text and instructions for Mac users, when different, appear in brackets.

This symbol means that the accompanying information is important for broadening your awareness of Flash applications, procedures, and terms that deepen your appreciation of the software and that also may broaden your perspectives for further use.

This symbol relates to information meant to give you some options that stretch the importance of the lesson you are involved with.

This symbol is a caution to avoid doing something or a warning about an incorrect approach.

This symbol indicates a cross-reference to material covered in another chapter, for the reader's easy reference.

When you see this symbol, it means that the related file or data is contained on the book's CD-ROM.

The symbol ➪ indicates a menu path. For instance, if you see File ➪ Save, it means go to the File menu and activate the Save option. This is a convention used in most software documentation, as well.

Ready, Set . . .

Now it's time to make sure your workspace is set up for exploration and learning and that you're comfortable. Here we **GO** . . .

Acknowledgments

A number of people have contributed their time and energy to the development and realization of this book:

Thanks to all of the people at IDG Books who helped to shape the book into its final form, especially Mike Roney, senior acquisitions editor at IDG Books Worldwide, and Chandani Thapa, project editor.

Thanks to Macromedia for creating quality products and for the support given during the book's production cycle. A special acknowledgment goes to Leona Lapez for keeping me up to date.

Thanks to my agent at Waterside Productions, David Fugate.

Thanks to all of the folks on the Flash 5 beta team, who provided interesting questions and comments along the way.

Contents at a Glance

Preface ix
Acknowledgments xvii

FRIDAY 2

Part I—Friday Evening 4
Session 1–Menu Options and Preferences...5
Session 2–Basic Shape Explorations..17
Session 3–Using the Pencil, Brush, and Pen Tools 31
Session 4–Working with a Library..51
Part I–Friday Evening Part Review 61

SATURDAY 64

Part II—Saturday Morning 66
Session 5–Working with Layers 67
Session 6–Creating Background Content...81
Session 7–Creating Animated Foreground Content 93
Session 8–Creating a Complex Animated Figure 105
Session 9–Creating Interactive Buttons...119
Session 10–Introducing Button Actions..129
Part II–Saturday Morning Part Review 138

Part III—Saturday Afternoon 140
Session 11–Creating a Title 141
Session 12–Designing a Logo...153
Session 13–Creating Credits..163
Session 14–Creating Text Effects..173
Session 15–Exploring Text Animation Options 183
Session 16–Publishing and Exporting 193
Part III–Saturday Afternoon Part Review..202

Part IV—Saturday Evening..204
Session 17–Exploring Bitmaps...205
Session 18–Understanding Flash Audio 213
Session 19–Working with Audio..221
Session 20–Applying Sound to Animations 229
Part IV–Saturday Evening Part Review 237

SUNDAY 238

Part V—Sunday Morning 240

Session 21–Designing Animations and Buttons 241
Session 22–Wipe F/X 251
Session 23–It's About Time 259
Session 24–Using Onion Skins 267
Session 25–Creating Strobes and Advanced Reveals 275
Session 26–Developing Nested Animations 283
Part V–Sunday Morning Part Review 292

Part VI—Sunday Afternoon 294

Session 27–Exploring Gradients 295
Session 28–Advanced Bitmap Techniques 305
Session 29–Understanding Instance Effects 315
Session 30–Exploring Flash 3-D 323
Session 31–Handshaking 333
Part VI–Sunday Afternoon Part Review 340

Appendix A: What's on the CD-ROM 343
Appendix B: Vendor Contacts 347
Appendix C: Exploring Macromedia Generator 349
Appendix D: Answers to Part Reviews 351
Index 359
End-User License Agreement 378
CD-ROM Installation Instructions 382

Contents

Preface ix
Acknowledgments xvii

FRIDAY 2

Part I—Friday Evening 4

Session 1–Menu Options and Preferences 5
- Preferences Settings 6
- Customizing your Work Environment 11
  - Highlight Color Preference 11
  - View Options 11
  - Window Menu Options 13

Session 2–Basic Shape Explorations 17
- The Line 18
- The Oval 23
- The Rectangle 26

Session 3–Using the Pencil, Brush, and Pen Tools 31
- The Pencil 32
- The Brush 35
- The Pen 46

Session 4–Working with a Library 51
- What Is a Flash Library? 51
  - Creating a new Flash library 51
  - Editing instances 55
- Navigating the Library 58
- Common Libraries 59

Part I–Friday Evening Part Review 61

SATURDAY 64

Part II—Saturday Morning 66

Session 5–Working with Layers 67
- Navigating the Layers Window 67
- Layer Properties and Tools 71
- Managing Layer Content 72

Session 6–Creating Background Content 81
   Creating Stable Background Content 81
      Sky 82
   Creating Animated Background Content 85
      The timeline 86
      Creating an animated cloud 87
Session 7–Creating Animated Foreground Content 93
   Animation on a Path 93
      Developing an animated bird 94
      Developing the fish 100
Session 8–Creating a Complex Animated Figure 105
   Creating an Animated Head 105
      Animating the face 112
   Adding the Diver's Suit 112
Session 9–Creating Interactive Buttons 119
   Creating Buttons 120
   Using Mask Layers 122
   The Four Button States 124
      Up state 124
      Over state 124
      Down state 125
      Hit state 126
   Previewing the Button 126
Session 10–Introducing Button Actions 129
   Designing a Button Project 129
      An Interactive Button Design 130
      The oval animation 131
   Your First Button Actions 132
   Basic Actions 136
Part II–Saturday Morning Part Review 138

Part III—Saturday Afternoon **140**
Session 11–Creating a Title 141
   Creating a Basic Title 141
      Text tools and options 142
   Modifying Text 145
   Animating the Text 146
      Working with a Guide layer 148
Session 12–Designing a Logo 153
   Designing the Logo Text 153
   Designing the Logo Graphic 157
   Incorporating the Logo in the Title Animation 159

Session 13–Creating Credits 163
Listing the Credits 163
Creating Text for Credits 165
Font selection and size 165
Copyright and trademark symbols...166
Text alignment 167
Deep text controls...168
Session 14–Creating Text Effects 173
Using Text Masks..173
Creating Text Drop Shadows 176
Creating Transparent Text 177
Session 15–Exploring Text Animation Options 183
Creating Progressive Reveals 183
Creating Scrolls 187
Generating Pops 188
Developing Fades..188
Understanding DVEs 188
Session 16–Publishing and Exporting 193
Loading a Flash Project..194
Publishing Flash Content 196
Exporting Flash Movies..198
Part III–Saturday Afternoon Part Review 202

Part IV—Saturday Evening 204
Session 17–Exploring Bitmaps 205
Transforming Bitmaps 205
Translating an Image From Bitmap to Vector 208
Cutting Apart Bitmaps...209
Session 18–Understanding Flash Audio 213
Creating Event Sounds...213
Creating Streaming Sounds 216
Publish Settings for Audio 217
Session 19–Working with Audio 221
Creating Multiple Sound Layers..221
Duplicating Sounds on the Timeline 223
Editing the Sound Envelope 224
Creating a warble effect 227
Session20–Applying Sound to Animations...229
Animated Slide Shows 229
Animated titles 230
Placing the slides 233
Adding Sound in a Slide Show 234
Part IV–Saturday Evening Part Review 237

SUNDAY 238
Part V—Sunday Morning 240
Session 21–Designing Animations and Buttons 241
- Creating the Animated Button Character 241
- Creating Button-Driven Animation 244
- Assigning Actions 246

Session 22–Wipe F/X 251
- The Radial Wipe 251
- The Shatter Wipe 252
- Creating an Animated Patterned Background 254

Session 23–It's About Time 259
- Creating the Clock 260
- Creating a Digital Display 263
- Creating an Hour Glass 264

Session 24–Using Onion Skins 267
- Using Rotoscope Editing 268
- Creating Speed Lines 271
- Creating an Onion Skin Background 272

Session 25–Creating Strobes and Advanced Reveals 275
- Creating Strobes 275
- The Animated Pull-On Reveal 277
- The Eyes Have It! 279

Session 26–Developing Nested Animations 283
- The First Symbol 284
- Building a Nest 285
- Creating a Typewriter Effect 288

Part V–Sunday Morning Part Review 292

Part VI—Sunday Afternoon 294
Session 27–Exploring Gradients 295
- Creating Gradients 295
- Animating Gradients 298
- A Gradient Background Project 300

Session 28–Advanced Bitmap Techniques 305
- Using Bitmaps for Painting and Fills 305
- Internal Bitmap Editing 308
  - The Break-Apart method 308
  - The trace-based method 309
- External Bitmap Editing and Tiled Images 310
  - Creating tiled images 312

Contents

Session 29–Understanding Instance Effects 315
    Learning about Instance Fade Effects 315
    Creating Instance Tint Effects 318
    Generating Instance Advanced Effects 320
Session 30–Exploring Flash 3-D 323
    Creating 3-D with Shadows 323
    Building a Magic Box with Layers 327
    Importing 3-D Content 329
Session 31–Handshaking 333
    Macromedia FreeHand 333
    Adobe Illustrator 334
    Corel Painter 335
    Curious Labs Poser 336
    Discreet Logic's 3D Studio Max 336
    Adobe After Effects 338
    Adobe Photoshop 338
Part VI–Sunday Afternoon Part Review 340

Appendix A: What's on the CD-ROM 343
Appendix B: Vendor Contacts 347
Appendix C: Exploring Macromedia Generator 349
Appendix D: Answers to Part Reviews 351
Index 359
End-User License Agreement 378
CD-ROM Installation Instructions 382

Flash™ 5
Weekend Crash Course™

☑ **Friday**

☐ Saturday

☐ Sunday

Part I — Friday Evening

Session 1
Menu Options and Preferences

Session 2
Basic Shape Explorations

Session 3
Using the Pencil, Brush, and Pen Tools

Session 4
Working with a Library

PART I

Friday Evening

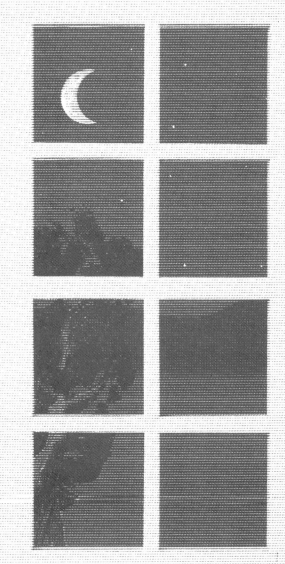

Session 1
Menu Options and Preferences

Session 2
Basic Shape Explorations

Session 3
Using the Pencil, Brush, and Pen Tools

Session 4
Working with a Library

SESSION

Menu Options and Preferences

Session Check List

✔ Learning about Preferences
✔ Loading library content
✔ Using Outline, Fast, and Anti-alias modes
✔ Exploring viewing options
✔ Customizing your work environment

30 Min. To Go

When you hear the word *flash,* what normally comes to mind? The answer may be speed, something that happens quickly, or an instantaneous response. Macromedia's Flash software is all of these, especially when applied to graphics and animation for the Web. With Web sites and Web-based businesses growing by leaps and bounds, and projected to keep doing so for years to come, the speed at which a Web page comes into view continues to rise in importance. When someone is looking for a site that references a category of interest, or even when they are free-browsing and just happen to stumble upon a site that looks interesting, the speed at which the pages are displayed is a dominant factor in whether he or she will remain or move on. With literally millions of diverse sites to choose from, and a limited time to wander on the Web, the speed at which a site displays is barely secondary to site content.

Vector-based graphics and animation content offer both speed and high-quality Web page design possibilities, and Flash rules the roost when it comes to vector-based media creation tools. I spend this first half-hour session exploring some of the parameter settings and options that you will need to keep in mind throughout this book. Flash 5 offers many advancements over previous versions; I point these out as I go along.

Preferences Settings

Do the following to learn how to navigate the Preferences window effectively, so you can design a environment suitable for your needs.

1. Open Flash by clicking its icon with the left mouse button (LMB) [Mac users open Flash by double-clicking the icon]. The Flash interface appears. Go to File ⇨ Close to close whatever is on the screen, and then select New to start a new project screen. See Figure 1-1.

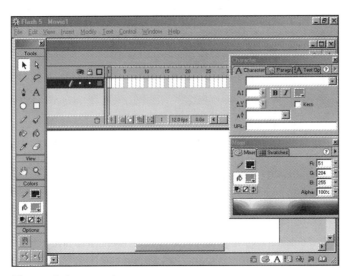

Figure 1-1
A New Flash project. Your screen may look a bit different, depending upon the platform you are using and your window configurations.

Session 1—Menu Options and Preferences

2. Go to Edit ⇨ Preferences. This brings up the Preferences settings window, which has three tabs: General, Editing, and Clipboard. See Figure 1-2.

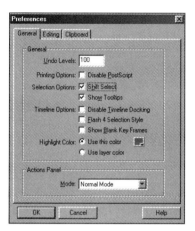

Figure 1-2
The Flash Preferences window includes three tabs at the top.

3. If the system you are using has less than 32MB of available RAM memory, you need to change one of the default settings: Under the General tab click the Undo Levels input area (see Figure 1-3). The input area, which contains the number 100 (the default), changes color, indicating it is ready for your typed input. Type **50**. This Undo levels setting helps prevent system crashes in computers with lower RAM configurations. Click OK to return to the Flash main screen.

If you have 32MB of RAM or less on your system and you plan on doing graphics and animation work, it's time to add more RAM. Graphics and animation work are RAM-intensive. For instance, the systems used in the production of this book included a G3 PowerMac with 375MB of RAM and a Windows 98 system with almost 800MB of RAM. The cost of RAM has dropped radically in the last year, so adding more RAM is less painful than it was previously.

Here's where you learn about loading content to and from a Flash library. To become more familiar with Flash library content, complete the following steps:

1. Go to Windows ➪ Common Libraries ➪ Buttons. The Buttons Library appears on the screen (the *.fla* indicates that this is a Flash file). The Flash Library window allows you instant access to all of the elements in your scene that are based upon symbols. You will see a number of folders on the left-hand side of the lower Library window, as shown in Figure 1-3.

Figure 1-3
The Buttons Library window shows a column of folder icons on the lower left.

2. Double-click the Arrow Buttons icon and a list of its contents opens up beneath it. Click the 1 Left Arrow icon to highlight it, and the corresponding graphic appears in the upper part of the window. See Figure 1-4.

Figure 1-4
Your highlighted selection appears in the upper window area.

Session 1—Menu Options and Preferences

20 Min. To Go

3. Click the Arrow in the Library window with your LMB and while holding the mouse button down, drag the arrow to your work area. Release the LMB. [Mac users simply need to click, drag, and then release their one mouse button.] Congratulations! You have interacted with a Flash library!

4. From the menus listed, go to Modify ⇨ Transform ⇨ Scale to change the size of the image. Notice that the arrow symbol now has circular control points around its border (see Figure 1-5). Grab the bottom-right control point by clicking and holding the LMB; drag to enlarge the arrow to roughly twice its former size. Release the LMB.

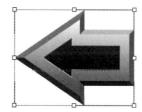

Figure 1-5
The arrow has control points for resizing operations.

5. When the arrow is resized to your liking, click anywhere on the screen, and then click the arrow again. Now the control points have disappeared and the arrow is once again selected.

6. Now I explore the three ways that a graphic can appear on the Flash screen: With the arrow still selected, go to View ⇨ Outlines. The arrow becomes an outlined object. Go to View ⇨ Fast. The arrow appears with shading, but the edges of the lines are a bit ragged. Go to View ⇨ Anti-alias. The arrow now appears with shading and sharp lines (see Figure 1-6).

When working on a large project with a lot of components, it's best to work in Outline or Fast mode to get quicker results, and then change to Anti-alias mode for final previewing and rendering.

With some graphics, such as the arrow, it may be hard to distinguish between Fast and Anti-alias modes. One way to tell is that in Fast mode, the border around a selected graphic is blue. In Anti-alias mode, the corners of the border are black.

Figure 1-6
The arrow in Outline, Fast, and Anti-alias modes.

OK. Now that you understand a bit about Flash library content, the following steps will help you learn about some additional viewing options.

7. With the arrow still selected, go to View ⇨ Hide Edges. Notice that the border disappears altogether. When your work area contains numerous components, it may be easier to see what's going on without borders around selected objects. If you choose Modify ⇨ Transform Scale, the control points still appear, but without the border. Clicking the work area and then the object brings the border back, so you'll have to select Hide Edges again if you want the border to disappear.

8. With the arrow still selected, go to View ⇨ Zoom In, and then to View ⇨ Zoom Out. Notice that the work area is immediately either enlarged or reduced in size. See Figure 1-7.

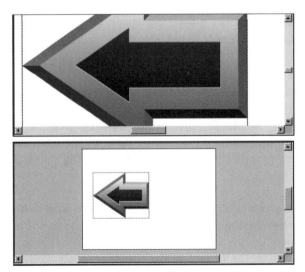

Figure 1-7
Zooming gives you control over the work area view.

9. If you go to View ⇨ Magnification, you'll see that you can also zoom to specific percentages. Selecting View ⇨ Magnification ⇨ Frame zooms in on the stage so that it is as large as possible within the document window; selecting View ⇨ Magnification ⇨ Show All zooms out as far as necessary to include all the objects on your entire work area. Try these options now.

Customizing your Work Environment

10 Min. To Go

If you have a studio for your digital art explorations, or if your physical work space is a special corner of a room with your equipment, you already realize how important it is to arrange your tools in a way that will offer you speedy access and comfort at the same time. The way a work space is arranged is an expression of an individual's personality and can add or detract from their ability to perform their creative tasks. Each person has a prioritized list of requirements when it comes to designing a physical work space.

The same is true for virtual work spaces, including your Flash interface. Flash has options that enable you to design a work space that will enhance your creative endeavors and increase your comfort level and work flow. Obviously, as you become more experienced in Flash, your interface design needs may change. I spend the balance of this session exploring the most important basic ways you can customize the Flash work space. The items I point out are in the View and Windows menus, except for one item in Preferences.

Highlight Color Preference

The Highlight Color is the color of the frame around selected objects. By default it is a light blue, but you can make it any color you like. You already know how to open Preferences, so go to Preferences. On the General tab page is a Highlight Color, and next to that is a color swatch. Clicking and holding the downward-pointing arrow under the color swatch brings up a color palette, where you can select any color for the highlight hue of your choice. See Figure 1-8. If you choose Use layer color, Flash will automatically use a different Highlight Color for the objects on each layer.

View Options

You can View ⇨ Rulers and/or View ⇨ Grid to customize your work space. Adding rulers enables you to make exact placements of project elements, which may be more important on some projects than others. Viewing the grid affords you the same possibility and adds the capacity to make exact placements on any of your project elements. See Figure 1-9.

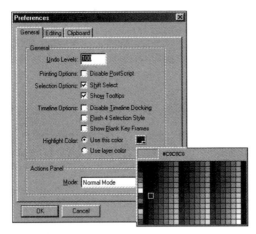

Figure 1-8
Select any color you like for the Highlight Color in the General Preferences window.

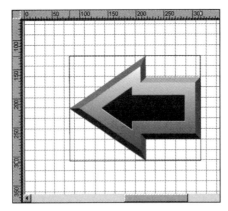

Figure 1-9
The Flash work area, showing both rulers and the grid

When the grid is activated you can *snap* objects to it, enabling a more precise alignment of images. Go to View ➪ Grid ➪ Edit Grid to bring up Grid settings. You can alter the color of the grid and the size (in pixels). You can also set the degree to which Grid Snap works. For the purpose of exercises in this book, select Always

Snap from the Snap Accuracy list. This will be very important when you learn about drawing in Flash, because it snaps all of the drawing elements to the grid. See Figure 1-10.

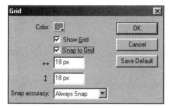

Figure 1-10
The Grid settings window

Window Menu Options

As you design your on-screen work environment, it becomes apparent that a tug-of-war is always going on between tool accessibility and elbow room. The more windows you place on the screen, the more crowded it gets, and the more you have to move things around to see necessary areas of the work space. The only way around this is to design the screen so that it contains only the tools you need at specific points in project development.

Tools

The Tools window is the vertical strip of icons that contains all of your basic drawing and modification tools. If you look in the Windows menu, you will see that Tools is checked. Uncheck it and the Tools window disappears. Most of the time you'll want to leave Tools checked. On Windows platforms the Tools window can be either snapped into place on the left side of the interface or made to be free-floating, so you can move it around as needed. If you are using Flash on Windows, double-click the blue bar at the top of the Tools window to toggle it from one condition to the other.

It you are working on a 640×480 screen size, you'll want to make the Tools window free-floating in order to see all of the options. It's best to set screen size in Flash to a minimum of 800×600 pixels anyway, because a smaller size will truncate the bottom controls. Use the Preferences window to do this.

Toolbars

If you look in Windows ➪ Toolbars, you'll see three options: Main, Controller, and Status. If any of the three options has a check mark next to it, it means the option is activated, and the toolbar is already on the screen. Try checking and unchecking these options to see what they look like and how they influence the work space. See Figure 1-11.

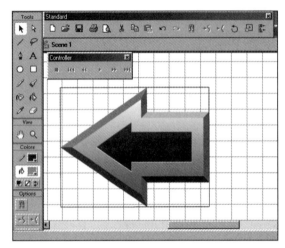

Figure 1-11
The Main (top), Controller (below the Main toolbar) and Status toolbars (bottom) are all placed on the screen.

 Most of the time it's a good idea to keep the Main toolbar on the screen and the others toggled off. Place the Controller toolbar on the screen when you are previewing animations, an activity which is covered later in this book.

Panels

If you go to Windows ➪ Panels, you'll see seventeen panels that can be added to the screen. Don't be frightened; I cover what's involved here in time. Obviously, placing all panels on the screen at once makes the screen too crowded to work. Under the Windows ➪ Panels menu is a Panel Sets ➪ Default Layout option. This brings four of the most common Flash panels to the screen. You can choose this setting and then switch off the panels that are not needed. See Figure 1-12.

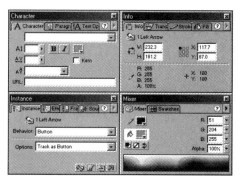

Figure 1-12
The four default panels

Cascade and Tile

Open document windows on your screen can be moved globally by one of two options: Cascade or Tile. You'll find these options in the Windows menu. Selecting either one will initiate the process. With some sample panels on the screen, select Cascade and then select Tile to see what they do.

One final item: Once you have placed panels on the screen that suit your project at a certain point in its development, you can save the panel layout. You can save panel layouts under individual names as many times as you like. Go to Windows ⇨ Save Panel Layout and type in the name that you will use to access your new layout. Explore this now. See Figure 1-13.

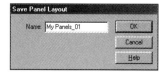

Figure 1-13
The Save Panel Layout window

Done! Select Windows ⇨ Close All Panels to remove all panels from the screen.

REVIEW

This chapter dealt with setting up Flash interface parameters so your work can flow with ease. These included the following:

- Accessing some of the Preferences options
- Accessing the library and placing a symbol on the screen
- Using Outline, Fast, and Anti-alias modes
- Configuring toolbars
- Toggling windows and panels

QUIZ YOURSELF

1. How can I change the color of the frame around a selected symbol?
2. How can I make the Tools window free-floating?
3. How do I save my screen design after I have arranged the panels I want to include?

SESSION 2

Basic Shape Explorations

Session Checklist

✔ Creating and modifying lines

✔ Creating and modifying ovals

✔ Creating and modifying rectangles

30 Min. To Go

Flash handles two general types of content: content that is created within Flash itself and content that is imported. The content that is created in Flash starts with a drawing; the basic drawing elements are the Line tool, the Oval tool, and the Rectangle tool. Learning how to manipulate these drawing tools is vital to understanding how to create more complex content in Flash. This chapter focuses on teaching you how to manipulate these three basic tools. All of these tools can be accessed in the Tools window, found at the left of the Flash interface. Of course, if you have moved it to another position on the interface, as you learned to do in Chapter 1, that's where it will be located. See Figure 2-1.

Figure 2-1
The Tools window

The Line

The Line icon can be found on the left of the Tools window, just below the black selection arrow. (See Figure 2-1.) It's easy to spot because it looks like . . . a line. Clicking on it activates it. Drawing is accomplished by clicking and dragging with the left mouse button (LMB) down, and then releasing the LMB when you've reached the end of the line. Do the following to create a line drawing:

1. Draw a bunch of random lines in the workspace, making sure that View ⇨ Fast is selected. See Figure 2-2.
2. Notice how jagged the lines look? That's because View ⇨ Fast is selected. Select View ⇨ Anti-alias and look at the lines. They are now very clean and straight. Flash uses prioritized technology, which enables you to view vector graphics as if they came from a printer on your monitor.
3. To clear the screen, go to Edit ⇨ Select All, and then Edit ⇨ Clear. Set the Line size by going to Window ⇨ Panels ⇨ Stroke. Move the slider upward to increase the Line size. See Figure 2-3.
4. Draw some lines on the screen. Repeat this action selecting alternate sizes to get a feel for what you are creating. See Figure 2-4.

Session 2—Basic Shape Explorations

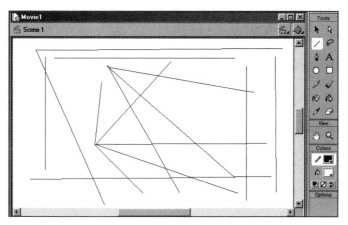

Figure 2-2
Draw a bunch of random lines in the workspace with the Line tool, with View ⇨ Fast selected.

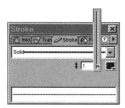

Figure 2-3
The Line size is controlled by the slider.

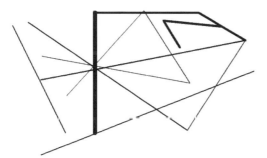

Figure 2-4
Various sized lines

5. Go to Window ⇨ Panels ⇨ Stroke again to select a line style. Select a style from the list that appears when you click the downward triangle next to the word *Solid* and repeat the same process as in step 4, this time selecting from different line styles to create random lines. See Figure 2-5.

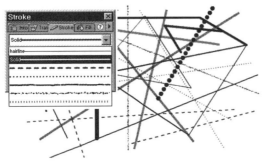

Figure 2-5
On the left are line style selections; on the right are the result of applying those Styles.

By combining different Line sizes with line styles, you have a wide array of possible line components at your disposal.

6. Clear the screen (Edit ⇨ Select All and Edit ⇨ Clear). Go to View ⇨ Snap To Objects. This activates a Snap option, which enables you to draw connected lines that Snap to other lines. Draw the image shown in Figure 2-6. Notice that your lines *snap* to other lines in the drawing, giving you the ability to create enclosed shapes.

It doesn't matter what line style you use when Snap is on. All line styles work with snapping.

7. Two selection arrows are located at the top of the Tools window. One is black and one is white. Click the black arrow (called the Arrow tool) to activate it. Now click a corner point (a point where lines meet) similar to

your drawing in Figure 2-6. Hold down the LMB and drag, releasing the LMB at some other point on the screen. The lines are snapped to common corner points; you have just reshaped the drawing by dragging common corner points. Do this to other nodes, reshaping the drawing further. See Figure 2-7.

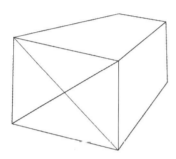

Figure 2-6
Using View ⇨ Snap To Lines gives you the ability to create enclosed shapes.

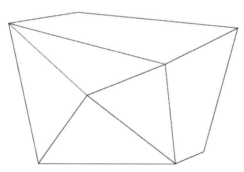

Figure 2-7
Dragging on any snapped node with the Arrow tool enables you to drag the connected lines to a new place and edit the drawing in the process.

8. Now use the same tool, but this time point to a non-nodal point on any line. Click and drag. What happens? The line becomes a curve. Make all of the lines in your drawing curves by using this method. See Figure 2-8.

Figure 2-8
The Lines are transformed into curves by clicking and dragging on any non-nodal point on any line.

9. Click the white Arrow tool (called the Sub-Select tool). Use it to click any node in your curve drawing. What happens? *Bezier handles* appear. By selecting any of the end points of these handles and moving them, you can reshape the curve they represent. By clicking and dragging on the node itself, you can reshape ALL of the connected curves. By clicking on any of the points that appear on any curve, you can reshape the curve at that point. Try these actions on one node in your curve drawing. See Figure 2-9.

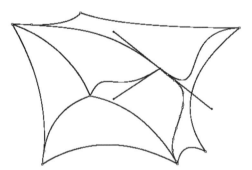

Figure 2-9
Using the Sub-Select tool on any node of a curved-line drawing gives you access to Bezier handles, which enable you to reshape the curve further.

 The addition of Bezier handle editing capabilities is new to Flash 5.

Session 2—Basic Shape Explorations

10. One more experiment with the Sub-Select tool: Activate it and select any non-nodal point on the curve drawing. Click and drag with the LMB held down. The whole drawing is picked up and starts to move. Release the LMB where you want to place your drawing.

The Oval

20 Min. To Go

The Oval tool icon in the Toolbox resembles a circle. Click it and then do the following to create a graphic using the Oval tool:

1. Begin with a blank work area. Hold down the Shift key and the LMB, and then click and drag to create a perfect circle. Next, draw another circle that overlaps it on the right. See Figure 2-10.

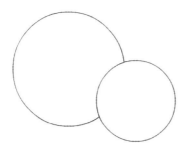

Figure 2-10
Draw two overlapping circles with the Oval tool.

2. Use the Sub-Select tool (white arrow) to move the image so you can see all of it. Notice that the last circle drawn with the oval tool overlaps the first, obscuring part of its boundary, and that selecting and moving the image results in moving both of the now-connected circles at the same time.

Note that holding the Shift key down while drawing an oval, line, or rectangle *constrains* the resulting graphic. The oval is constrained to a circle, the rectangle to a square, and the line is constrained to horizontal, vertical, or an angle of 45 degrees.

Note: Flash always assumes that any two overlapping elements on the same layer (I get to layers later) are joined as one.

3. Notice that by using the Sub-Select tool on this image you reveal a series of *Bezier control points* on all curves. Sub-Select the image again and click on the Bezier control points to reveal the Bezier handles. Edit the curve or curves by manipulating the handles, as you did with the line. See Figure 2-11.

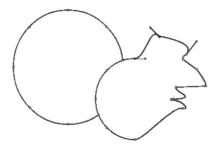

Figure 2-11
By manipulating the Bezier handles attached to any selected control point, you can transform the shape.

4. Now select the Arrow tool (black arrow). Click the common curve between the two joined circles. Notice that it is highlighted. Press the Delete key to remove it. See Figure 2-12.

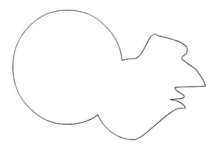

Figure 2-12
Remove the common curve that links the two circles.

Session 2—Basic Shape Explorations

You have just learned that the Arrow tool can be used to select the separate curve elements of an image, so that these separate curves can be removed or otherwise augmented.

5. Activate the Sub-Select tool and then use Bezier handles to reshape the image into one that resembles Figure 2-13. Don't worry about matching it perfectly. Take no more than two minutes to accomplish this task. See Figure 2-13.

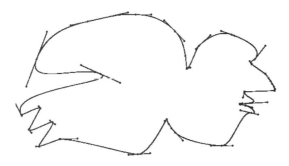

Figure 2-13
Use the Sub-Select tool and Bezier handle editing to create a shape that resembles this one.

6. Use the Sub-Select tool to do the following (though the Arrow tool will also work). Click in an area outside of the boundaries of the image and drag a marquee (a dotted selection border) around the whole image. Make sure all parts are included. Go to Modify ⇨ Group, and then try to select parts of the image with either the Arrow tool or the Sub-Select tool. You can't. The image is now a single whole and is protected from further editing.

7. With the Grouped image still selected, go to Modify ⇨ Ungroup. Now you can edit the separate elements again.

You have just learned that a grouped series of lines and/or curves is protected from further editing. Ungrouping a grouped image enables you to resume editing it.

The completed Grouped drawing displayed in Figure 2-13 is on the book's CD in a Folder called Chapter 1.

10 Min. To Go

The Rectangle

The Rectangle tool appears in the Tools window as the symbol fourth down in the right-hand column, and it resembles a square. To learn more about the rectangle tool, do the following:

1. Clear the screen, and then click the Rectangle tool to activate it. Click and drag the Rectangle tool to create overlapping rectangles in the configuration displayed in Figure 2-14.

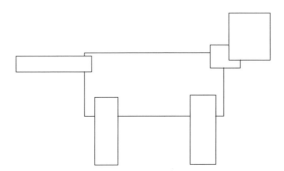

Figure 2-14
Create this shape with overlapping rectangles.

2. Use the Arrow tool to select overlapping elements, as you did in the oval exercise. Use the Delete key to remove them. See Figure 2-15.
3. Select the Sub-Select tool (white arrow) and click any line in the image to show all of the Bezier control points. You need to add more points to edit the image.
4. With the image still selected, use the Arrow tool to transform all of the straight lines into curves. You don't have to pay attention to their shape now, just make them curves by using the same technique you learned in the previous section on lines. See Figure 2-16.

Session 2—Basic Shape Explorations

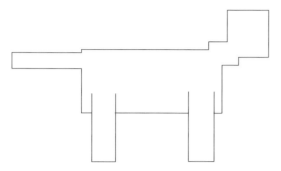

Figure 2-15
Remove selected elements of the overlapping rectangles to create this final shape.

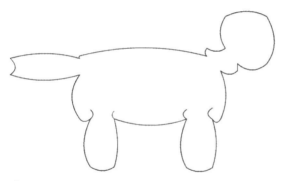

Figure 2-16
All of the straight lines have been translated into curves.

5. Activate the Pen tool in the Tools window (it looks like a pen point). Any curve that you click will now show a new control point at that location. Add more points to the image, using Figure 2-17 as a guide.

6. Use all of the Bezier control points to create an animal form. Each reader will have a unique result, based upon the animal idea they are working with, so just use the author's image as one possible result. The idea is to explore a bit and have fun. Take no more than two minutes to do this. See Figure 2-18.

Figure 2-17
Add control points to the lines of the image with the Pen tool, so it looks like this.

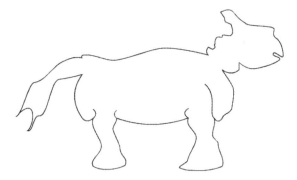

Figure 2-18
By using the Bezier control points and handles, you can transform what started as a series of rectangles into a curved animal form.

 Exactly what the animal form I created represents is at this point unclear, though it does resemble the silhouette of some sheep I saw on Arcturus 7 awhile back.

7. Click the color swatch next to the Paint Bucket icon at the bottom of the Tools window, and select a color for your new animal from the color palette that pops out. See Figure 2-19.

Session 2—Basic Shape Explorations

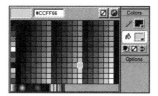

Figure 2-19
Select a color for your animal form.

Done!

8. Select the Paint Bucket tool from the Tools window, and click inside of your animal form. It changes color to match your color palette selection. Group your animal form using the same technique used in step 6 of the Oval exercise. Save your animal form to disk as an .fla file (File ⇨ Save As).

REVIEW

In this chapter, you learned how to use the Line, Oval, and Rectangle tools to create image content. You also learned how to modify and customize that content with the Arrow and Sub-Select tools. This included:

- Drawing with lines and modifying the line's thickness and style.
- Transforming lines into curves.
- Using Bezier control points and handles to modify a line or curve segment.
- Creating imagery with ovals and rectangles.
- Constraining lines, ovals, and rectangles.
- Creating a curved image from rectangular components.

QUIZ YOURSELF

1. How do I change straight lines to curves in an image made entirely of line segments?
2. How do I remove the overlapping curve segments from ovals that overlap?
3. What do I do to get line segments to snap together in a drawing?
4. How do I add control points to curved segments?
5. How is color added to an enclosed shape?

SESSION 3

Using the Pencil, Brush, and Pen Tools

Session Checklist

✔ Creating with the Pencil tool

✔ Creating with the Brush tool

✔ Creating and editing with the Pen tool

30 Min. To Go

Flash offers you three tools to create freehand shapes: the Pencil, the Brush, and the Pen. The Pen is new to Flash 5. These three tools are augmented by the Paint Bucket and Ink Bottle tools. Each of these tools offers you a different range of creative options.

You can use either the mouse or a drawing tablet as input devices in Flash. If you are using a drawing tablet, see the tablet's documentation for installation.

The Pencil

I start exploration of Flash tools with the Pencil tool. The following steps show you how to create a graphic with the Flash Pencil:

1. Select the Pencil tool from the Toolbox by clicking its icon to highlight it, which tells you it's active. See Figure 3-1.

Figure 3-1
The Pencil tool's icon in the Tools window

2. Even though you've selected the Pencil tool, you need to do a few more things before drawing with it. First, go to Edit ⇨ Preferences and click the Editing tab in the Preferences window. See Figure 3-2.

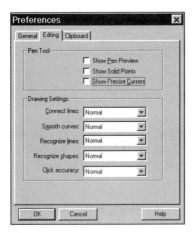

Figure 3-2
Clicking the Editing tab in the Preferences window brings you to the Editing page.

Session 3—Using the Pencil, Brush, and Pen Tools

3. Make sure all of the settings in the Drawing Settings area of the Preferences window read *Normal*. This is the default. I explore changing some of these settings later. By clicking the down arrow next to each setting box, you bring up the options lists. When they all read Normal, click OK.
4. Now go to View ⇨ Grid and make sure Snap To Grid is not checked. If it is checked, selecting it will uncheck it.
5. Go to View ⇨ Guides and make sure Snap To Guides is unchecked. I have inserted these two steps prior to drawing with the Pencil tool in order to give you as much drawing freedom as possible.
6. One more step before drawing: Go to View ⇨ Fast. This turns off anti-aliasing, which in turn speeds system performance.
7. Your Pencil tool should still be highlighted. Go to the bottom of the Tools window; under the Options heading, click the downward pointing arrow to access the Options list. Select the Ink Bottle option. The Options area should now look like Figure 3-3, with the Ink icon displayed.

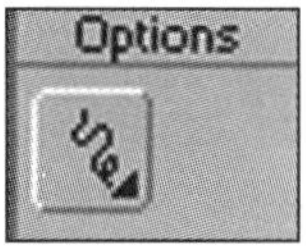

Figure 3-3
Access the Options list for the Pencil tool and select the Ink option.

8. Holding the left mouse button (LMB) down, use the Pencil tool to draw the outline for what will become a cartoon face. Leave a space so that the point at which you stopped does not match the point at which the pencil line started. See Figure 3-4.
9. Activate the Arrow tool. Click and hold at the end of the line you've drawn, and then drag until the end point of the line is on top of the point you first started with. The corner point you are dragging will snap to the first point, closing the shape.
10. Now fill the shape with color. Go to Windows ⇨ Panels ⇨ Fill to bring up the Fill panel. Select Solid from the Fill types list by clicking the downward-pointing arrow. See Figure 3-5.

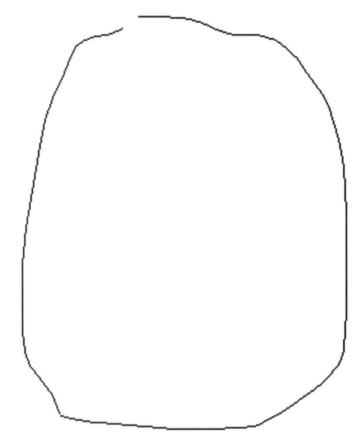

Figure 3-4
Draw a rough outline for the face, but leave a small space at the end so the shape does not close.

11. Click the color swatch arrow to bring up the color picker. Select a light blue color. See Figure 3-6.
12. Click the Paint Bucket tool in the Tools window to activate it. Click inside the shape you drew to fill it with the blue color. See Figure 3-7.
13. Go to File ➪ Save As, and save the file as MyFace_01.fla.

Session 3—Using the Pencil, Brush, and Pen Tools 35

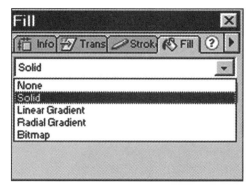

Figure 3-5
The Fill panel, with Solid selected from the list

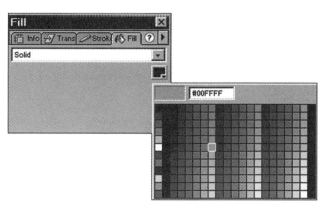

Figure 3-6
Select a light blue color for the fill.

The Brush

**20 Min.
To Go**

The Brush paints with whatever fill color you have selected. If you still have it set to light blue from the last exercise, then it will paint in light blue. Now that you know how to change the fill color from the last exercise, change the fill color to black and then do the following to become familiar with the Brush tool:

1. Select the Brush icon in the Tools window. Notice that the contents of the Options section of the Tools window changes. The Options area contains three selectable items, indicated by the downward pointing arrows.

Click the first arrow to reveal the Paint options. Paint Normal should be selected. Click anywhere outside this area to close it. See Figure 3-8.

2. The second Options pop-up list shows a variety of Brush sizes. Select the third Brush size from the top. See Figure 3-9.

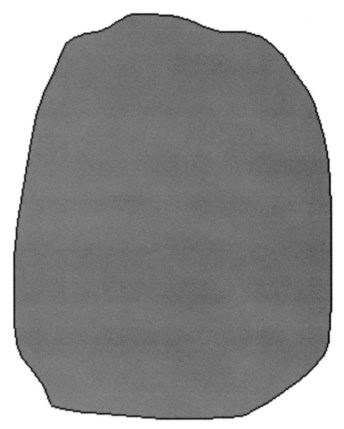

Figure 3-7
Use the Paint Bucket tool to fill the shape with the selected color.

Session 3—Using the Pencil, Brush, and Pen Tools

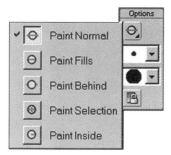

Figure 3-8
Make sure that Paint Normal is the Paint option selected.

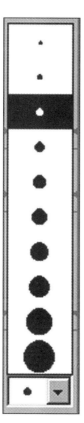

Figure 3-9
Select the third Brush Size from the top.

3. The third Options pop up indicates Brush shapes. The circle is selected by default, which is what you want. Click anywhere outside of this area to close it. See Figure 3-10.

4. Select View ➪ Anti-alias, which will smooth out your strokes. Time to paint! Use the Brush tool to paint the shape that looks like half of a pear. Don't worry about accuracy. See Figure 3-11.

Figure 3-10
Select the circle shape if it is not already selected.

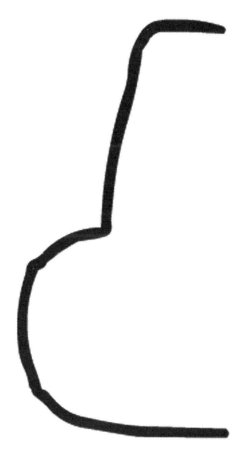

Figure 3-11
Paint a shape that roughly resembles this one.

5. Use the Arrow tool and click on the brush stroke. Do not click and drag, because that alters the shape. With the brush stroke selected, go to Edit ⇨ Copy, and then Edit ⇨ Paste In Place. This creates a cloned image of your brush stroke located directly over the first one. The cloned brush stroke is selected. (Be sure not to deselect it before moving it away from the original.) Hold down the Shift key and drag the cloned brush stroke horizontally. Holding down the Shift key constrains the movement to the horizontal. Move the cloned brush stroke away from the original one. See Figure 3-12.

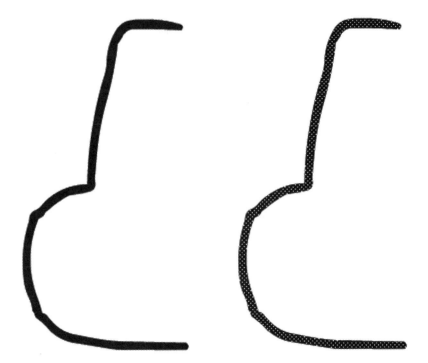

Figure 3-12
Move the cloned stroke away from the original by holding down the Shift key.

6. Now go to Modify ⇨ Transform ⇨ Flip Horizontal; you should now see something that resembles Figure 3-13.

Session 3—Using the Pencil, Brush, and Pen Tools 41

Figure 3-13
After flipping the cloned brush stroke horizontally, you should see something like this.

7. Select the cloned element, and again holding the Shift key down, move the cloned brush stroke to the left until it joins and slightly overlaps the original. With the Arrow tool selected, click anywhere on the screen to deselect everything. Now click on the brush stroke (either half) and move the graphic. As you can see, they are both now joined into one. See Figure 3-14.

Figure 3-14
The connected Brush image

8. Use the Brush tool to paint a curved line that resembles Figure 3-15.

Figure 3-15
Paint another brush stroke that resembles this.

9. Choose a new fill color, and use the Paint Bucket tool to fill the closed areas of the hat so that it resembles Figure 3-16.

Figure 3-16
The hat areas are filled in.

When you use the shape tools or draw and paint shapes in Flash, and lines touch each other, the shapes are immediately joined, as long as they are on the same layer. More on layers later.

10. Use your imagination to paint and fill in the rest of this cartoon character's head. For the purpose of this exercise, make sure that all brush strokes touch some part of an existing stroke. When it's finished, it may or may not resemble the image displayed in Figure 3-17.

Session 3—Using the Pencil, Brush, and Pen Tools

11. After all of the parts are painted and the closed areas of the painting are filled with your selection of colors, use the Arrow tool and marquee to select the entire image (including both the brushed elements and the fills). Go to Modify ⇨ Group, and all the parts will be grouped into one object. See Figure 3-17.

Figure 3-17
Complete the character's head and save to disk.

46   *Friday Evening*

The finished head image is on this book's CD as MyFace_02.fla.

10 Min. To Go

The Pen

You can use the Pen tool, just like you use the Pencil, to draw lines. The difference is that the Pen tool works by the click and drag method, and everywhere you click creates a control point. Bezier handles are connected to these control points, so you can adjust the curve that connects one control point to another. To explore this, do the following:

1. Click the Pen tool to activate it. With the Pen tool selected, go to Window ➪ Panels ➪ Stroke, which brings up the Stroke settings window. Recalling your prior experience with this window from the Pencil exercise, set the color to black and the Stroke type to Solid, with a 6-point weight. See Figure 3-18.

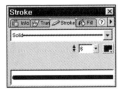

Figure 3-18
Set stroke attributes in the Stroke settings window.

2. Select the Pen tool in the Tools window and click anywhere on the screen. Click again to create another control point and continue drawing with the Pen tool. Curves will be drawn connecting the control points. Note that clicking alone creates straight line segments between control points, while clicking and dragging creates curved segments. Repeat this process several times until you have created a Pen-drawn curve that has several control points. To see the control points, click the curve with the Sub-Select tool (white arrow). See Figure 3-19.

Session 3—Using the Pencil, Brush, and Pen Tools   47

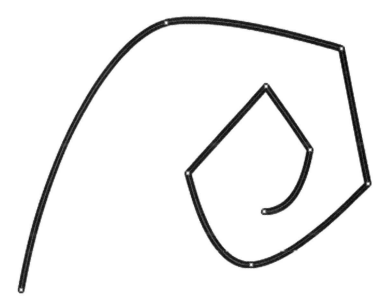

Figure 3-19
Clicking a line drawn with the Pen tool and the Sub-Select tool reveals the line's control points (small white circles).

3. To create control points where none presently exist, simply click the line with the Pen tool at any desired place. Try it.

 Clicking any line with the Pen tool, whether drawn or part of a placed shape (rectangle or oval) creates new control points.

4. To delete a control point, click the control point with the Sub-Select tool and hit the Delete key.
5. Select any control point with the Sub-Select tool and the Bezier handles will be revealed, as long as the control point connects two curved segments. Control points connecting a straight line segment with a curve, or two straight segments, will not display Bezier handles, but you can still move those elements. Move the Bezier handles to reshape the connecting curves. See Figure 3-20.

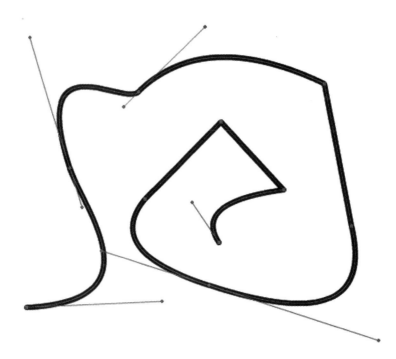

Figure 3-20
Either move the control points or reshape the curved segments by adjusting the respective Bezier handles. Compare this reshaped line to its source, as displayed previously in Figure 3-19.

Delete all of the contents from your workspace by first selecting it by drawing a marquee around it with the Arrow tool and then hitting the Delete key. Now you're ready to explore using the Pen tool to edit brush strokes. Complete the following steps:

1. Set the fill color to a light blue and the stroke color to black. Use the Colors swatches displayed at the bottom of the Tools window. See Figure 3-21.

Figure 3-21
Set the colors by using the Colors swatches at the bottom of the Tools window.

Session 3—Using the Pencil, Brush, and Pen Tools

2. Create the basic profile of a face using the Brush tool. Notice that the Brush tool paints in only the fill color, which in this case is light blue. See Figure 3-22.

Figure 3-22
Paint the profile of a face using the Brush tool and a light blue color.

3. Click the Ink Bottle tool to select it. The Ink Bottle tool references the Foreground Color swatch, which you set to black. Click the edge of your brushed line. You have just added a black stroke around the painted line.

4. Click the Sub-Select tool and draw a marquee around the entire graphic. The control points are displayed. Notice that there are quite a few and that separate control points exist on either side of the painted line. The area in between the stroke boundaries is actually a fill, and the filled area is bordered by a black stroke.

Moving the control points is not the same as moving their handles when the line is drawn with the Pencil or Pen tools. Try it to get a feel for the editing potentials of using this method. Play with this editing method for a few minutes.

Done!

Using the Pen to edit a brushed line is a very complex process because of the number of control points involved. Better to select the Arrow tool to reshape the intervening curves when you need to edit a brushed line.

Review

In this chapter, you learned how to use the Pencil, Brush, and Pen tools to create image content. You also learned how to edit lines using the Pen tool and Bezier handles. This included:

- Drawing a freehand shape with the Pencil tool.
- Setting attribute preferences for line type and thickness.
- Selecting foreground and fill colors.
- Using the Paint Bucket tool to apply color inside of closed shapes.
- Painting freehand image content with the Brush tool.
- Drawing and editing image content with the Pen tool.

Quiz Yourself

1. How do I select the line type and size when using the Pencil tool?
2. How do I select what color to use for the Paint Bucket?
3. How do I set the size and shape of the Brush tool?
4. How do I use the Ink Bottle tool to add elements to a brushed line?
5. Why isn't the Pen tool the best editing option for brushed lines?

OK. Time to stretch. You're doing great and learning a lot. One more session to go for this evening. Then you can catch the late news and get a good rest in preparation for tomorrow's sessions.

SESSION 4

Working with a Library

Session Checklist

✔ Creating a new library and adding symbols
✔ Instances and their modification
✔ Navigation and common libraries

30 Min. To Go

What Is a Flash Library?

A Flash library is a place inside a Flash project where all of the *media* in a project can be saved and used. Most of the elements contained in a Flash library are symbols, which can evidence one of three possible behaviors: *movie clip, button,* or *graphic.* Any Flash library for a specific project is saved with the project when the project is saved and is given the same name as the project. A Flash library may also be saved as a Common Library, which is accessible to any project.

Creating a new Flash library

To create a Flash library for a new project, go to Window ➪ Library. A new empty library window appears on the screen. See Figure 4-1.

Figure 4-1
A new, empty Flash library, ready for content

Creating a new symbol for the empty library

To create a new symbol to place in the library, complete the following steps:

1. With a new Flash library open, go to Insert ⇨ New Symbol. The Symbol Properties window will appear. For Behavior, select Graphic. Name the new symbol MySym_01 and click OK. See Figure 4-2.

Figure 4-2
The Symbol Properties window

2. The stage now becomes the Symbol Edit window, and a small crosshair appears in both the Library preview area and in the Edit window. This crosshair is the center point for the new symbol. When graphics, buttons, and movie clips are resized, rotated, and flipped, the actions reference this center point; therefore, its placement in reference to the symbol is very important. Create a graphic in the Edit window centered upon the center point. Note that as you draw, the same graphic appears in the Library preview window. This is because you are actually creating it within the library. See Figure 4-3.

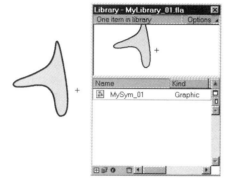

Figure 4-3
As you create the object, it appears in the Library preview window at the same time.

It's impossible to overemphasize the proximity relationship between the symbol and its center point. Note that as you create the symbol on the Edit window, the same proximity between the symbol and its center point exists in the Library preview area as well.

3. As long as you remain in Symbol Edit mode, whatever you do to the on-screen symbol will also be done to the symbol that exists in the library. Try it. Reshape the on-screen symbol any way you like, and watch the Library preview area.

4. When the symbol you have created is exactly what you want, it's time to leave Symbol Edit mode and return to the Flash stage. But how do you do that? Simple. Look at the upper-left corner of the Edit window and you will see the items pictured in Figure 4-4.

Figure 4-4
The upper-left corner of the Edit window looks like this.

5. Click the words that tell you what scene this is — in this case Scene 1. You are immediately taken to the Flash stage. The Library window remains open and displays your new symbol in the preview area.

6. Now you'll explore the usefulness of the library. Click and drag the symbol displayed in the Library preview area to the Flash stage. Do this several times to get the hang of it. The symbol in the library acts as a parent to the cloned examples placed on the stage. These cloned symbols are also known as *instances*. See Figure 4-5.

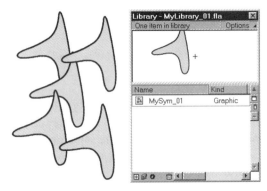

Figure 4-5
Instanced symbols can be placed anywhere on the stage.

7. Use the Arrow tool to select one of the instances, and go to Modify ⇨ Transform ⇨ Rotate. You see eight control points placed around the boundary of the instance. The control points at the corners allow you to click and drag to rotate the instance; the control points at the centers of the boundary lines allow you to click and drag to skew the instances. Try this on all of the instances to create different appearances for each. See Figure 4-6.

8. Select one of the instances and go to Modify ⇨ Transform ⇨ Scale. Eight control points appear on the boundary of the selected Instance. Click and drag on a corner point and the instance scales uniformly. Click and drag on the other points, and the instance can be resized either horizontally or vertically. Rescale all of the instances on the screen to explore this capability. See Figure 4-7.

Session 4—Working with a Library 55

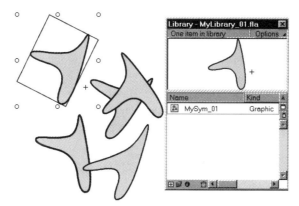

Figure 4-6
All of the instanced symbols can be rotated and skewed individually.

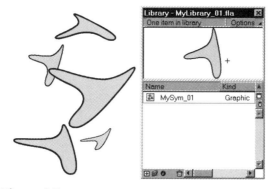

Figure 4-7
All of the symbol instances can be resized separately.

**20 Min.
To Go**

Editing instances

If you try to alter the color or shape of an instance on the stage, nothing will happen. Try it. Why can't you do this? Because the instance is not in itself editable artwork. It is the reference data of a parent symbol in the library. So is instance editing possible in any way? Yes. There are two ways to edit an instance that appears on the stage.

Break-Apart editing

One way to alter the appearance of an instance is to use Flash's *Break Apart* feature. I'll talk more about this later in the book, but for now, do the following to learn more about Break-Apart editing:

Select an instance that appears on the stage. Go to Modify ⇨ Break Apart. Now you can select to alter the shape and/or color of the selected item, because it is no longer an instance. It is now a new object or collection of objects (shapes, text, bitmaps, and so on) on the movie stage. See Figure 4-8.

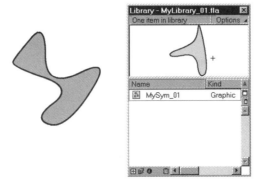

Figure 4-8
Once an instance has been broken apart it is no longer an instance, but a new object or collection of objects on the stage. The symbol displayed in the Library preview area will not show any changes.

Placing the new edited symbol in the library

Here is how to place any new object in a library.

1. Select the object by dragging a marquee around it with the Arrow tool.
2. Go to Insert ⇨ Convert to Symbol. You are asked to name the symbol and select its behavior. You are then jumped to the Edit window, and the new symbol appears in the library.

Session 4—Working with a Library

This works with any selected screen content, not only edited contents. Use this operation to place selected items in a library.

Another way to edit instances

This method for editing instances is based upon the capability to edit the symbol itself. Be warned, however, that editing the symbol will result in a similar transformation of all of the instances of that symbol presently on the stage. Here's what to do:

1. Select a symbol in your library and then place a number of instances of it on the stage. See Figure 4-9.

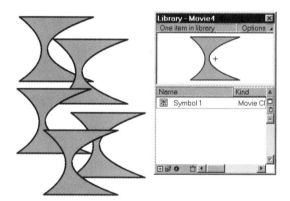

Figure 4-9
Place a number of instances of a symbol on the stage.

2. Make sure the symbol you want to edit is selected on the stage. Open the Library Options list by clicking the triangle next to Options on the upper-right corner of the Library window. Select Edit. You are taken to the Edit window, where you may alter the symbol as you like. Do this.

3. Return to the stage. All of the symbol instances will be transformed in the same way as the parent symbol. See Figure 4-10.

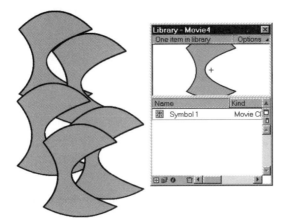

Figure 4-10
After a symbol already in the library is edited, any instances of that symbol on the stage are also transformed.

Navigating the Library

Here is where you learn about library organization. Make sure you have a library on screen that has a few of your symbols in it, and do the following:

1. Take a look at the icons at the bottom-left corner of the Library window. See Figure 4-11.

Figure 4-11
The icons at the bottom-left corner of a Library window

2. The icons stand for *New Symbol, New Folder, Properties,* and *Delete,* respectively. Click a symbol name in the Library window, and then click the Properties icon. The Symbol Properties window opens, allowing you to rename the symbol or alter its selected behavior. See Figure 4-2, shown previously.

3. Click the Edit button in the Properties window and you jump to the Symbol Edit window. This gives you an alternate way to get there. Try it.

4. Back to the Library window again. Click the Folder icon in the Library window. A new folder is placed in the Library window list. Double-click

the Folder's name (which is Untitled Folder by default) and rename it as you like. Now click and drag one or more symbol names over the folder name to place the selected symbols in the folder. See Figure 4-12.

Figure 4-12
It's a snap to create folders in your library and place symbols in it.

Why would you want to have separate folders in your libraries? For housekeeping reasons. Perhaps your project would benefit if all media for the various sections were separated into folders. Your work habits and need to optimize the location of project elements will determine your use of library folders.

5. Click the New Symbol icon, and the Symbol Properties window appears again, waiting for you to name and select a behavior for a new symbol. Once you've done this you are jumped to a new Edit window where you can create the new symbol. Try it. After you create a new symbol, return to your main movie stage by selecting Edit ⇨ Edit Movie. Your new symbol has already been saved in the library.

6. The Delete icon is here for obvious reasons. If you select a symbol or a folder and hit Delete, it will be removed from the library list. But take care! This operation cannot be undone.

Common Libraries

What is a *Common Library?* A Common Library is a library that you can access for any project, old or new. Flash ships with several common libraries included. What if you want your present Project Library to become a Common Library, so that its symbols can be used in any project you are doing? If that's the case, just save your project (your .fla file) to the Flash Libraries directory. From then on, no matter what Flash project you are working on, that library can be selected for use by going to Window ⇨ Common Libraries, where you will see it listed. Try it.

You might want to store your logo and other items that you use repeatedly in a Common Library. In Flash, you always have the option to do so.

Done!

Editing symbols in a Common Library is different than editing symbols in a Project Library. In a Project Library, you can edit the symbol itself. In a Common Library, you can't. If you're using a symbol from a Common Library, you can edit an instance of it in your current movie. The library of your current movie automatically updates to include the newly added symbol. Note that any changes you make to the new master symbol in this library will not be saved to the Common Library from which it originally came. Common libraries are closed to any edits or new symbol additions.

REVIEW

In this chapter, you learned about Flash library use. This included:

- How to create a new Flash library.
- How to create symbolic elements for a Flash library.
- How to edit symbols and instances.
- How to save a Project Library as a Common Library.

QUIZ YOURSELF

1. How many types of symbol behaviors are there in a Flash library, and what are they?
2. What is an instance?
3. What are the two ways that an instance can be edited?
4. How do I place a new symbol in a library?
5. How do I edit a symbol?
6. What is a Common Library?

PART I

Friday Evening Part Review

1. After I have arranged the panels I want to include in my screen design, how do I save it?
2. In an image made entirely of line segments, how do I change straight lines to curves?
3. How do I add more control points to curved segments?
4. How can I add fill color to an enclosed shape?
5. When ovals overlap, how do I remove the overlapping curved segments?
6. How can I change the color of the frame around a selected symbol?
7. How can the Tools window be made free-floating?
8. How can I snap line segments together?
9. How do I select the line type and size using the Pencil tool?
10. How is color selected for the Paint Bucket tool?
11. How many types of symbol behaviors are there in a Flash library, and what are they?
12. What is an instance?
13. What are the two ways that an instance can be edited?
14. How do I set the size and shape of the Brush tool?
15. How can the Ink Bottle tool be used to add color to a line created with the Brush tool?
16. How is a symbol edited?

17. How is a new symbol placed in a library?
18. What is a Common Library?
19. What is the best way to edit Brush-created lines?

☑ Friday

☑ Saturday

☐ Sunday

Part II — Saturday Morning

Session 5
Working with Layers

Session 6
Creating Background Content

Session 7
Creating Animated Foreground Content

Session 8
Creating a Complex Animated Figure

Session 9
Creating Interactive Buttons

Session 10
Introducing Button Actions

Part III — Saturday Afternoon

Session 11
Creating a Title

Session 12
Designing a Logo

Session 13
Creating Credits

Session 14
Creating Text Effects

Session 15
Exploring Text Animation Options

Session 16
Publishing and Exporting

Part IV — Saturday Evening

Session 17
Exploring Bitmaps

Session 18
Understanding Flash Audio

Session 19
Working with Audio

Session 20
Applying Sound to Animations

PART II

Saturday Morning

Session 5
Working with Layers

Session 6
Creating Background Content

Session 7
Creating Animated Foreground Content

Session 8
Creating a Complex Animated Figure

Session 9
Creating Interactive Buttons

Session 10
Introducing Button Actions

SESSION 5

Working with Layers

Session Checklist

✔ Navigating the Layers window
✔ Learning about Layer properties and tools
✔ Dealing with Layer content

30 Min. To Go

Navigating the Layers Window

When Flash first boots up, the Timeline window appears by default. If for some reason you do not see this window on the screen, go to View ➪ Timeline. On the left of the Timeline window is the Layers window. See Figure 5-1.

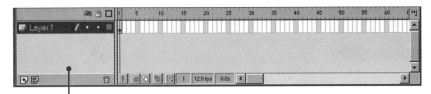

The Layers window

Figure 5-1
The Layers window is on the left part of the Timeline window.

Part of the fun of Flash is that your project can have more than one layer. To learn more about working with multiple layers, complete the following steps:

1. Go to Insert ➪ Layer twice. This adds two new layers to the project, which can be seen in the Layers window. This allows us to navigate the layer controls more clearly. See Figure 5-2.

 New layers are always inserted *above* the current layer.

Figure 5-2
In the Layers window, you can see that two new layers have been added above the initial layer.

2. Select Layer 1 in the Layers window by clicking it. It will turn black with white lettering. On the Layer 1 stage, create an oval with a black stroke and a yellow fill.

3. Select Layer 2 in the Layers window. On the stage, create a rectangle with a black stroke and a blue fill that overlaps the oval on Layer 1.

4. Use the Pencil tool to create a smooth curve with a stroke width of 8.75 on Layer 3 that overlaps both the rectangle on Layer 2 and the oval on Layer 1. See Figure 5-3.

Session 5—Working with Layers

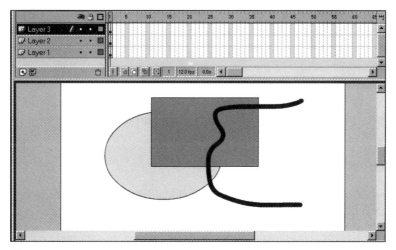

Figure 5-3
Your three layers should look something like this when finished.

5. Go to the Layers window. Select Layer 3 and click the dot in the column under the icon that looks like an eye. This is the visibility control. The layer becomes invisible and a red X appears next to the dot. Do the same to Layer 2. Now all that is visible is Layer 1. See Figure 5-4.

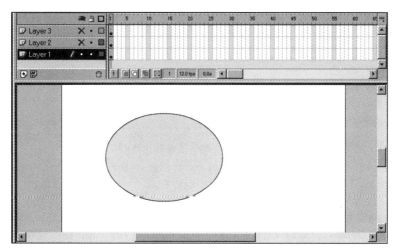

Figure 5-4
Layers 2 and 3 are invisible; all you see is the content on Layer 1.

6. With Layer 1 still selected, click the dot in the column under the Lock icon. The dot becomes a lock. The layer is now locked. Try reshaping the oval's stroke or changing the fill color. Nothing happens. Click the lock on the selected layer to open it, which makes the content on the selected layer modifiable again.

 When a layer is locked, *all* of the content on that layer is locked as well.

7. Make Layers 2 and 3 visible again by clicking the red X in the visibility column. Select Layer 3 and click the Trash Can icon in the bottom-right corner of the Layers window. The layer is deleted. Go to Edit ⇨ Undo to bring it back.
8. Click the color square in each of the layers in the Layer window. Flash displays all of the content on each layer as an outline. See Figure 5-5.

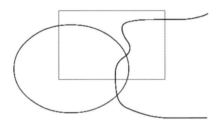

Figure 5-5
Clicking the Square icon on any layer will present that layer's content as an outline.

9. Click the Square icon in each layer again to remove Outline mode.
10. Two controls I haven't discussed yet are at the bottom-left of the Layers window. The controls represent Insert Layer (an option for inserting a new layer) and Insert Guide Layer. I look at what a guide layer is and does a little later. Click each of them once to add new layers, and then delete these layers by selecting them and clicking the Trash Can icon. See Figure 5-6.

Figure 5-6
The Insert Layer and Insert Guide Layer buttons

Layer Properties and Tools

20 Min. To Go

Each layer in your project has its own Properties window. The following steps will help you become more familiar with the elements in the Properties window.

1. Select Layer 1. At the extreme left of the layer name is an icon that looks like a page with a folded corner. Double-clicking it brings up the selected layer's Layer Properties window. See Figure 5-7.

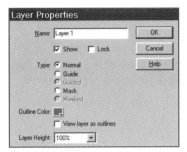

Figure 5-7
The Properties window for a selected layer

2. At the top is the Name box, where you can rename the layer to anything you like. Change the layer name to Oval.

3. Below that are two checkboxes, one for Show (visibility) and one for Lock. Make sure Show is checked and Lock is not; these are the default settings.

4. Next come the Type buttons. By default, Normal is selected, so select it if it isn't already. I get to the other options later. They are: Guide, Guided, Mask, and Masked.

5. Under that is the Outline Color swatch and a View layer as outlines checkbox. Click the color swatch and select another Outline Color, but do not check the box.

6. Last, there is a Layer Height list, with selections for 100%, 200%, and 300%. Select 300% and click OK. This sets the layer height in the Layer Stack to three times the default height. The extra space is really for animation operations in the rest of the Timeline window, which will be covered later. See Figure 5-8.

Figure 5-8
By selecting a Layer Height of 300%, the space occupied in the layer stack by the layer set to a 300% height is three times as high as the default height.

7. There is also an alternate way to change a layer's name, other than opening its Properties window. Double-click the layer's name in the layer stack. You can now type in a new name without opening the Properties window. Try it.

Managing Layer Content

Having learned how to modify and control layers, it's now time for you to explore what layers can provide in the way of creative options. Make sure all three layers and their content are visible, and then do the following:

1. First, let's create a Project Library of the content on these three layers. Select each layer in turn, making the others invisible. Use the Arrow tool to click and drag a marquee around the content of a selected layer, and then go to Insert ⇨ Convert to Symbol. Name the content, select Graphic, and then OK. Delete the content from the layer. Go to Window ⇨ Library and observe that all three graphics have been placed in the library. See Figure 5-9.

Session 5—Working with Layers

Figure 5-9
The contents of your three layers now reside as symbols in the library.

2. Make sure that all three layers have visibility on. Select Layer 1. Drag and drop three rectangle symbol instances from your library into Layer 1, but don't allow them to overlap. See Figure 5-10.

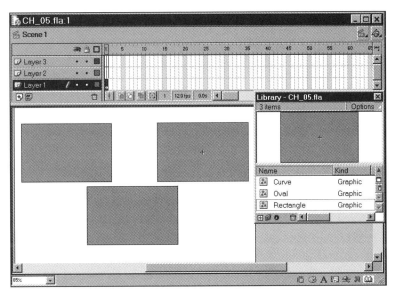

Figure 5-10
Drag and drop three rectangle symbol instances into Layer 1.

3. Select Layer 2, and then drag and drop three instances of the oval symbol so that they overlap the rectangles on Layer 1. See Figure 5-11.

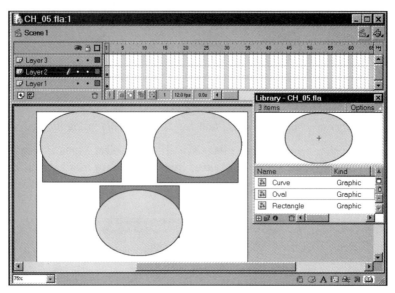

Figure 5-11
Three oval instances are placed on Layer 2 so that they overlap the rectangles.

10 Min. To Go

4. Select Layer 3, and then drag and drop one of the curved lines from the library so that it rests on top of the oval in Layer 2. Go to Modify ⇨ Transform ⇨ Scale and resize the curved line so that it sits entirely inside of the oval on Layer 2. Go to Edit ⇨ Duplicate to create a copy of the curved line. Place the copy over another oval from Layer 2. Do this again, so that you have a collection of symbol instances on three layers that resembles Figure 5-12.

5. You won't need the library anymore, so close it. Click the small icon that looks like an open book on the bottom right below the stage. See Figure 5-13.

6. All of the layers in the layer stack can be moved up and down, which alters what contents are placed on top or beneath other contents. Select Layer 1 and drag it over Layer 2. The stage now looks like Figure 5-14.

Session 5—Working with Layers

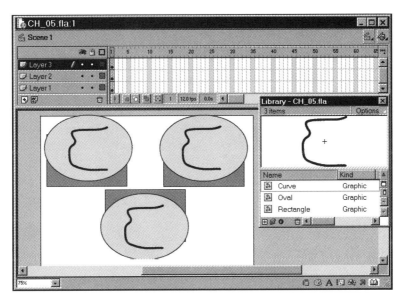

Figure 5-12
The layers now look like this.

Figure 5-13
You can always use the icon on the right to quickly open and close a Project Library.

7. Place Layer 2, the oval, on top of Layer 3, the curved line. Layer 3 is completely hidden from view because the other layer content is above it. You can always use one layer to hide the contents of another. See Figure 5-15.

8. Select Layer 2 and click its Outline icon to make the contents of Layer 2 outlined. Now you can see Layer 3 clearly. Use Outlines to reveal the content of layers beneath them. See Figure 5-16.

9. Move the layers back into their original stacking order, so that Layer 3 is on top, Layer 2 is next, and Layer 1 is at the bottom.

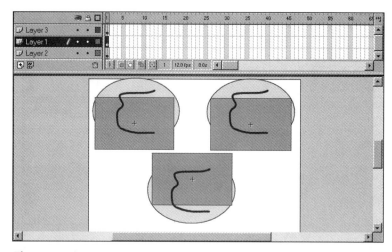

Figure 5-14
Layer 1 and 2, and their contents, have switched places.

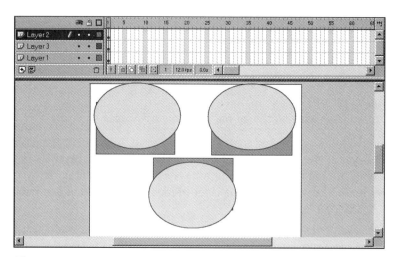

Figure 5-15
Layer 3 has content that is no longer displayed, because it is hidden by the layer on top of it.

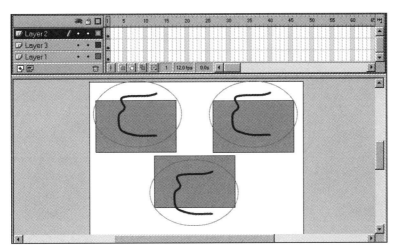

Figure 5-16
By making the contents of the topmost layer an outline, you reveal the layers beneath it.

10. Delete two of the three instances from each layer, so all that remains is one overlapping set of instances. Hold down the Shift key (with any layer selected) and click each instance until you've selected all of them.

11. With all of the content selected, drag the remaining stack of three instances to the center of the stage. Select the oval and then select Modify ⇨ Break Apart, and then do the same thing to the rectangle.

12. Now these two elements are no longer instances. Modify each one's stroke and fill color as you like, to prove it. Use Modify ⇨ Break Apart on the curved line to edit that too, though the original symbols remain in the Project Library. See Figure 5-17.

13. Select the contents of Layer 2 and make the other layers invisible (or lock them). Use the Arrow tool to drag a marquee around what was the oval to select both its stroke and fill, and then go to Edit ⇨ Copy. Select Layer 1 (the edited rectangle) and go to Edit ⇨ Paste in Place. A copy of the edited oval is placed on the rectangle. Because these are not instances any more, this creation is now one flat collection of shapes. See Figure 5-18.

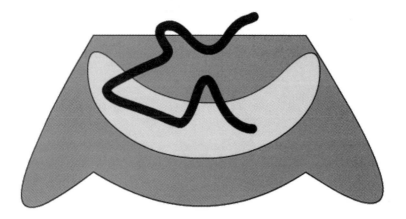

Figure 5-17
Because the content of each layer is no longer an instance, it can be edited with any of the shape and color tools.

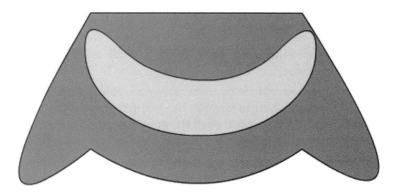

Figure 5-18
The edited oval and rectangle are now blended into one.

14. You no longer need Layer 2. Select it and click the Trash Can icon.

15. Select Layer 3, the edited line, and copy the object by going to Edit ⇨ Copy. Edit ⇨ Paste in Place on Layer 1. Delete Layer 3. Only Layer 1, with all of the shapes, remains. Because these shapes are all on the same layer, the overlaps have punched out the artwork behind them to create one flat illustration. You can now edit it as you like. Do that. See Figure 5-19.

Session 5—Working with Layers 79

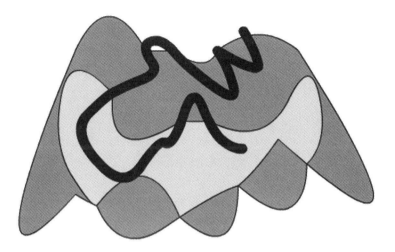

Figure 5-19
One flat collection of shapes remains and can be edited with any of the tools and processes available.

Done!

When finished, save the illustration to the library (Insert ➪ Convert to Symbol). That's it! Stretch, get a cool or warm drink, and get ready to move on.

REVIEW

In this chapter, you learned a lot about layers and how to use them creatively in the following ways:

- How to generate and modify layers with the Layer window's tools.
- How to place content on separate layers.
- How to move the layers in the Layer window stack.
- How to use layers to create new creative alternatives.

QUIZ YOURSELF

1. How do I create a new layer?
2. How do I name a layer?
3. What happens to the content of a layer if I delete the layer?

4. How are layers moved in the stack?
5. When I copy content from one layer, what command do I use to paste it in the same position on another layer?
6. How can I blend layer content so that it is transformed into one editable whole?

SESSION

Creating Background Content

Session Checklist

✔ Creating non-animated background content

✔ Creating animated content for a background

30 Min. To Go

Creating Stable Background Content

Your Flash project can be set against a stable, nonmoving background or against a background that displays selected elements in motion. If you desire a nonmoving background, you can select from the following: a background created with the Paint Bucket tool, a background composed of drawn or painted elements that have all been grouped and locked, or a background that is an imported bitmap (whether the bitmap is displayed as it was imported or has been translated to vector elements). More on bitmaps and bitmap to vector translation later.

The most basic background you can have in Flash is a single color background. Create a single color background now by doing the following:

1. Select a color from the fill color swatch at the bottom of the Tools window. See Figure 6-1.

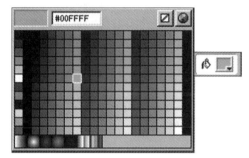

Figure 6-1
The fill color swatch at the bottom of the Tools window

2. With your fill color chosen, click the Rectangle tool to select it. Click and drag a rectangle that covers the entire layer (or that part of the layer you to which you want to apply a solid color).

3. Lock the layer to prevent any alterations to it. Go to Insert ⇨ Layer to create another layer for foreground content.

You can create as many layers as you like for a composite background. Each one should be locked to prevent accidental alterations.

In this part of the chapter, you are going to create a nonanimated background that consists of three layers: Sky, Land, and Water. This should take you about 10 minutes.

Sky

The Sky layer will be one solid color. Do the following:

1. Open a new Flash project (File ⇨ New).
2. Name Layer 1 Sky, and make it a Normal layer. Select a light blue fill color and select the Rectangle tool. Create a rectangle that covers the entire stage area and color it the same light blue that you selected for a fill color. Lock the layer in the Layer window.
3. Go to Insert ⇨ Layer. Name this layer Land. Use the Brush tool to paint a section of Land with a brown color, as displayed in Figure 6-2. Lock the layer. See Figure 6-2.

Session 6—Creating Background Content 83

Figure 6-2
Paint the Land section using the Brush tool and a brown color.

4. Go to Insert ⇨ Layer. Name this layer Water_01, and select a blue that is somewhat darker than the sky background's blue. Select the Rectangle tool and create a rectangle of blue on the Water_01 layer that reaches from the bottom of the stage to where the Land layer content is located. Allow it to overlap the Land by about 10 pixels or so. See Figure 6-3.

5. Notice that the Water segment has a black stroke outline. You could get rid of it by changing the stroke color to the same color as the fill color, but here's another way to do it: At the bottom of the Tools window, below the fill color area at the bottom-right, you will see an icon that looks like a half-circle with arrows at both ends. This icon is a switch that trades the fill and stroke colors with each other. See Figure 6-4.

6. Click the icon, and the fill and stroke colors change places. Now select the Ink Bottle tool and click the black stroke around the blue Water rectangle. The black outline becomes the same blue as the water and blends into the fill color.

Figure 6-3
Add a Water segment to the background.

Figure 6-4
Look for this icon.

7. Click the icon again to set the fill and stroke colors back to their original selections.

8. Now you want to roughen up the top water line a bit to give it some wavy character. There are two ways to do this: You can take the techniques that you acquired previously for editing a stroke by adding new control points with the Pen tool and moving them to get a curved line. The other option is to add some new curved elements with the Brush tool, drawing directly over the rectangle shape to modify it with your new brushwork.

Session 6—Creating Background Content

Decide which of these methods to use and add some wavy personality to the top of the Water rectangle. You might want to make all other layers invisible first in order to see what you are doing more clearly. Lock the layer when you are finished. See Figure 6-5.

Figure 6-5
Give the top part of the Water layer some waviness.

**20 Min.
to Go**

Creating Animated Background Content

In a sense, animated content is animated content, whether relegated to the background or the foreground of a Flash animation. The difference is in the priorities you set for telling a story. Your main actors are considered to be the foreground, while support players (those elements of a project that set a tone or environment) are considered to be background.

The timeline

You've already had some experience with the Timeline window, because the left part of it is where the layers window is located. Now it's time to delve into the rest of it. You will approach it through the tutorials, rather than laying out all of its features at once. The first thing you will use the timeline for is to set a specific number of frames for the background content you have created so far, so you have an environment to target for what will be an animated cloud. Do the following:

1. With your three locked background layers (Sky, Land, and Water) on the stage, open the Timeline window if it is not already open. You will see the Frames area next to the layer names. Select one of the three layer names at a time. Highlight the vertical strip in the timeline that indicates Frame 1, and click it with your right mouse button (RMB) [Mac users Control+Click]. A list of options appears. Select Add Frame. Do this for each of the layers. When finished, you will see an empty vertical rectangle to the right of each selected frame, indicating that you have added a frame with the same content as Frame 2 of the animation. See Figure 6-6.

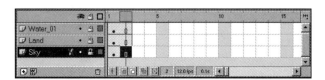

Figure 6-6
When you select Add Frame, another frame with the same contents as Frame 1 is added to each layer's timeline, indicated by an empty vertical rectangle.

2. Click and hold each of these empty rectangles on each layer in turn, and drag them to Frame 120 before releasing the mouse button. Use the slider at the bottom of the timeline if you need to see where the 120 frame mark is located. You will see that a gray area now fills in the timeline for each layer, from Frame 1 to Frame 120. This indicates that you have created static artwork that lasts 120 frames. If you place the cursor over any of these empty rectangles, it will read Static. See Figure 6-7.

3. Go to Window ➪ Toolbars ➪ Controller. This brings up the Controller, which operates much like a VCR Controller. From left to right, the controls indicate Stop, Return to First Frame, Go to Previous Frame, Play, Go to Next Frame, and Go to Last Frame. See Figure 6-8.

Session 6—Creating Background Content

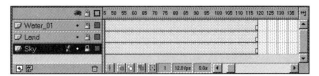

Figure 6-7
By dragging each of the empty Static frame indicators to the Frame 120 position on the timeline from each layer, you create an animation that lasts for 120 Frames.

Figure 6-8
The Controller window

4. Click the Play button on the Controller and watch the animation play. It's not very exciting at this point, because all that you will see moving is the playhead in the timeline. That's because none of the background layers are set to do anything but to remain static for 120 Frames. Make sure all layers are locked, and hide them all using the Hide Layer control on the left of the time line for each layer.

Creating an animated cloud

10 Min. To Go

With all three background layers locked and invisible, you should have a white stage in front of you. This is where you'll create an animated cloud symbol. Do the following:

1. Select the Water layer (the top layer in the Layers window) and insert another layer above it by choosing Insert ⇨ Layer. Name the layer Cloud.

2. Return to Frame 1 by clicking the rewind button in the Controller window. Set the fill and stroke colors at the bottom of the Tools window. Set fill to a light pink, and set the stroke color to the box with a red line through it. This indicates that there will be no stroke color for whatever is created. See Figure 6-9.

Figure 6-9
Set fill to a light pink and stroke to No Color.

3. Use the Oval tool to create a series of overlapping ovals on the stage, until you get what looks like a cloud. See Figure 6-10.

Figure 6-10
Create a cloud shape using the Oval tool.

4. The cloud is automatically set to last 120 Frames because the 120 Frame animation was configured previously. Playing the animation now, with all of the other layers invisible, would merely show the cloud as a static object. You are going to change that.

5. Move the last frame of the Cloud layer Frame Indicator back to Frame 30 by clicking it and dragging it to the Frame 30 position on the timeline. Do not double-click it. Now if you play the animation, the cloud will be visible for only 30 of the 120 Frames and then disappears. See Figure 6-11.

 This immediately alerts you to the fact that layers on the timeline appear and disappear in accordance with the presence of the indicated frames.

Session 6—Creating Background Content

Figure 6-11
Move the Static frame of the Cloud layer back to the Frame 30 position on the timeline.

6. On the Cloud layer, move the playhead (the red box and red vertical line which cross over all the layers at the current frame) to Frame 15. Right-click [Mac Control ⇨ Click] on the Cloud layer of the timeline for that frame, and select Insert Keyframe from the list that pops up.

7. Select the Static frame indicator for Frame 30 and right-click [Control+Click] it. Select Insert Keyframe from the list that pops up.

8. Go to Frame 15, which is now a keyframe, and use any tools you like to alter the shape of the cloud on the stage at that frame.

9. Go to Frame 2 and right-click [Mac Control+Click] the dot that represents that keyframe in the timeline. Select Panels ⇨ Frame from the list that pops up, and the Frame window appears. Select Shape from the Tweening list, and then click the X in the upper right (upper left for Mac users) to close the Panel and accept the setting. See Figure 6-12.

Figure 6-12
Set Shape Tweening on Frame 2 in the Frames window.

10. Repeat the previous step for Frame 15.

11. Select Frame 29 and right-click [Control+Click] and select Insert Frame from the list. You should now have a timeline for the Cloud layer that matches Figure 6-13.

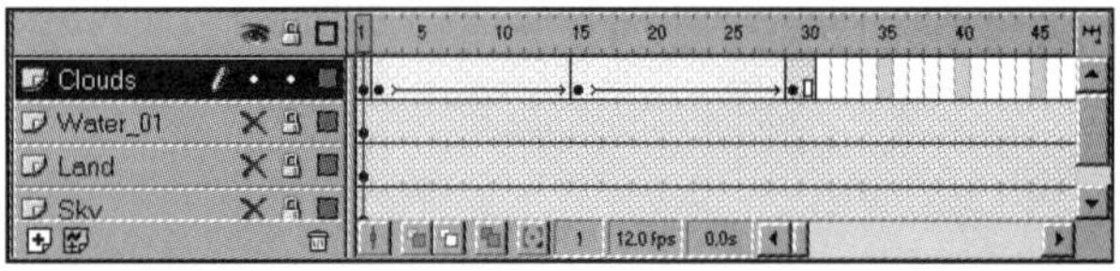

Figure 6-13
The timeline for the Cloud layer should now look like this.

12. Select the animated Cloud clip. Go to Insert ➪ Convert to Symbol. Note that you can not select multiple frames in the timeline and convert them to a symbol in one step. You must copy the frames from the timeline, create a new symbol, and paste the entire sequence on a layer in that new symbol. You will now have a Symbol of the Cloud clip in your library. You can test playback by pressing the Play button in the Library preview window. See Figure 6-14.

Figure 6-14
The Cloud clip is now a symbol in your Project Library.

13. Because the clip is now a symbol in your Project Library, you can delete the cloud from the Cloud layer. After that, move the Cloud layer so that it is between the Sky and Land layers. This places any content targeted to the Cloud layer over the sky but behind the land.

Session 6—Creating Background Content

14. Select the Cloud layer and make sure the other layers are locked. Place an instance of the Cloud clip from your library on the Cloud layer. Move it behind the land so that just the top of the clip is visible. Now place another Cloud clip on top of that one. Go to Modify ⇨ Transform ⇨ Scale and choose 175% to make the second clip larger, and move it up a bit. Go to Modify ⇨ Transform ⇨ Flip Vertical for the second clip. Now you have two animated Cloud clips blended together as a large cloud.

15. Press the Play button on the Controller. Nothing happens to the cloud as the animation runs. Why? Because this is not the way to see an animated instance. Instead, go to Control ⇨ Test Scene. Now the clouds move in front of your eyes! Click the Close button for the Scene Preview to get back to the stage. See Figure 6-15.

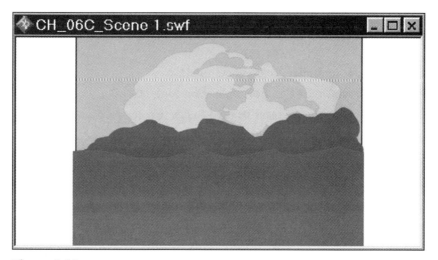

Figure 6-15
Preview the scene by going to Control ⇨ Test Scene.

Done!

Save your project to disk. You might even want to save it twice so you have a backup . . . just in case. You have completed the background elements for an animation that you will continue to work on during the next sessions, adding more content as you go.

REVIEW

In this chapter, you covered a lot of new ground, including:

- Developing content for overlapping layers.
- Becoming familiar with the timeline.
- Developing an animated clip.
- Using instances to develop an animation.

QUIZ YOURSELF

1. Can multiple layers be used to create a background for a project? How?
2. How do I create a specific number of frames for my project using the timeline?
3. How is the Controller accessed and used?
4. How is a symbol created from animation content?
5. How can multiple instances be used to create a complex animation?
6. How do I preview a scene for playback?

SESSION

Creating Animated Foreground Content

Session Checklist

✔ Creating a path-based animation
✔ Creating other animation types

*30 Min.
To Go*

I n this session you expand your knowledge of Flash animation techniques further, by exploring path animation and other animation techniques.

Animation on a Path

Path animation is common in 3-D software, but less so in 2-D. Path animation enables you to develop a path or track that selected objects follow as they proceed along the Timeline.

Developing an animated bird

In this exercise, you're going to develop an animated bird and place it in the library as a symbol that can be instanced. This is to prepare for animating the bird on a path. Follow these steps to create the animated-bird symbol and test its wings:

1. Go to Insert ⇨ New Symbol to create a new symbol for your Project Library. In the Symbol Properties window, call your new symbol Animated Bird and leave the Behavior option set to Movie Clip. This drops you into Symbol Edit mode for your new symbol. Use the Pencil tool and the Oval tool to create a stylized bird shape without wings. Set the Pencil tool's drawing mode to Smooth (under the options section of the toolbox), and set your view mode to Anti-alias. Refer to Figure 7-1, or use your own design.

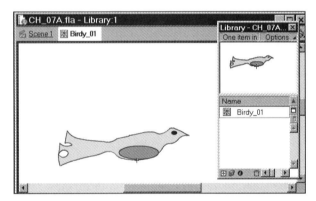

Figure 7-1
Create a stylized bird shape, without the wings.

Note
In Edit Symbol mode, draw the shape so that the place where the wing attaches to the body is at the center point of the symbol's stage.

2. While still in the Symbol Edit mode, name the present layer Bird_Body. Create a new layer, and name it Bird_Wing.

Session 7—Creating Animated Foreground Content

Note

You have just learned that Flash allows layers in symbols and that they are separate from the layers associated with a Scene. This is a very important capability that facilitates animation.

3. Lock the Bird_Body layer. On the Bird_Wing layer in the Symbol Edit window, create a wing for the bird shape. Use your imagination, or refer to Figure 7-2.

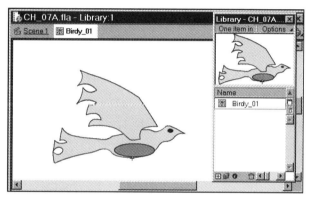

Figure 7-2
Create the Wing and move it into place.

4. Unlock the Bird_Body layer in Symbol Edit mode. Now you'll create some movement for the wing. Go to the timeline while still in Symbol Edit mode. Select the Bird_Body layer. In the symbol's timeline, click the right mouse button (RMB) [Control+Click] on the gray box under Frame 25 to select it and bring up the contextual menu. Select Insert Keyframe. This inserts a new keyframe at Frame 25. Right-click the keyframe at Frame 1 to bring up the contextual menu, and select Panels ⇨ Frame. Select the Shape option from the Tweening list when the Frame window appears, and close the window. Repeat all of these actions for the Bird_Wing layer. The result will be a timeline display in Symbol Edit mode that matches Figure 7-3.

5. Place additional keyframes at Frames 5, 10, 15, and 20 on the Bird_Wing Timeline. See Figure 7-4.

Figure 7-3
Your Timeline in Symbol Edit mode now resembles this one exactly.

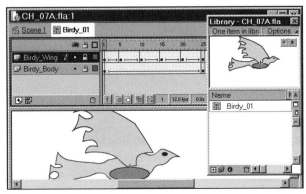

Figure 7-4
The Bird_Wing timeline in Symbol Edit mode, with keyframes at positions 5, 10, 15, and 20

6. Now to animate the wing in Symbol Edit mode. Click the keyframe at Frame 5 on the Bird_Wing layer. This moves the playhead to Frame 5 and selects all the contents of that frame. Now go to Modify ⇨ Transform ⇨ Flip Vertical to flip the wing to the downward position. Select the keyframes on Frames 15 and 25 on the same layer, and repeat the Flip Vertical command sequence to flip the wing downward at all three keyframes. Frames 1, 10, and 20 will be left alone, showing the wing in an upright orientation. After you flip the wing on Frames 5, 15, and 25, you have to move it in relation to the position of the center point (pivot point). When you have completed all of the preceding steps, you can play the animated symbol in the Symbol Preview window of the Library. See Figure 7-5.

Session 7—Creating Animated Foreground Content

Figure 7-5
Preview the animation by clicking on the Play button in the Symbol Preview window while in Symbol Edit mode. Remember that you can always edit the keyframe movements further until you achieve the look you want.

Setting the bird on a flight path

Now you'll test placing the animated bird on a flight path. This is only a test, because the actual background you'll finally place the Bird on will be the Sky-Water-Land-Cloud background you created and saved in Chapter 6. Follow these steps to give your bird a flight path:

1. Exit Symbol Edit mode by selecting Edit ⇨ Edit Movie, and save your project to disk. Keep the Symbol Library open so you can see the animated-bird symbol.

2. Name Layer 1 BirdFly, and insert another layer above it called FishJump. You'll get to the Fish later. Activate the BirdFly layer. Place an instance of the animated Bird symbol off the stage to the left. This places a keyframe at Frame 1 of the BirdFly layer. See Figure 7-6. Scale and position the instance using the Tool options under the Arrow tool in the Toolbox.

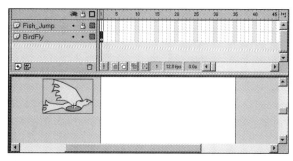

Figure 7-6
The first keyframe shows the animated-bird instance off stage at the left.

3. On the BirdFly layer, click Frame 30. Next, right-click [Control+Click] it, and select Insert Keyframe. Move the animated-bird instance off-stage at the right. See Figure 7-7.

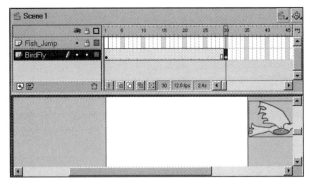

Figure 7-7
Create a keyframe at Frame 30 on the BirdFly layer, and move the animated-bird instance off-stage to the right.

20 Min. To Go

4. Click the Play button in the Controller window. You might expect the bird to move smoothly from left to right. It doesn't. Instead, it flies in place at the left until Frame 30 and then just appears at the right. Why? Because you have left out a step. You have to tell Flash to create *tweens* (in-between frames) to automatically animate the bird from keyframe to keyframe, so let's do that now.

5. Click Keyframe 1 to activate it, and click with the RMB [Control+Click] to bring up the menu. Select Panels ⇨ Frame to bring up the Frame panel. Select Motion from the Tweening pop-up, and leave the other settings at their defaults. See Figure 7-8.

Figure 7-8
Bring up the Frame window and select Motion from the Tweening list.

6. Exit the Frames window, and preview the animation again. The bird now moves smoothly from left to right, but its animated wings are not flapping. Why? The answer is that you cannot preview movie clip instances on the stage of the Flash editing window. Instead you must select Control ⇨ Test Movie. This opens a new testing window where you can preview the exported movie as it will appear on the Web. The bird, now with wings flapping, flies smoothly from left to right. Success! See Figures 7-9 and 7-10.

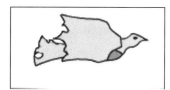

Figure 7-9
Preview the animated bird by going to Control ⇨ Test Movie.

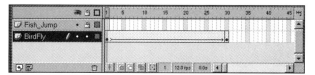

Figure 7-10
The timeline for the BirdFly layer now looks like this.

7. But what if there's an obstacle along the way and the bird has to fly higher to get over it? Simple. Create a keyframe for the highest frame the bird will reach on the timeline for the BirdFly layer, and move the bird instance up at that point. Create a new keyframe at Frame 15. All you have to do is move the timeline indicator to Frame 15. Click and drag the bird instance on the stage to the highest position of its flight. When you move the bird instance, a keyframe is automatically created between the first and last keyframes. Go to Control ⇨ Test Movie to see the results. Now you create the fish.

Developing the fish

You'll use another animation type to create a revolving wheel of jumping fish. Follow these steps to animate the fish:

1. Lock the BirdFly layer and make it invisible. Unlock the Fish layer and go to Insert ➪ New Symbol. This brings up the Symbol Properties window. Type in Fish_01 for this new symbol's name. Make this a graphic symbol by selecting Graphic as the behavior from the Symbol Properties window. You won't need to animate the actual fish.

2. Set the stroke to 2.0 (Window ➪ Panels ➪ Stroke) and select black for the stroke color, with the fill color set to a light blue-green. Draw an oval in the Symbol Edit window. Use the Arrow tool to reshape the oval to match the shape displayed in Figure 7-11.

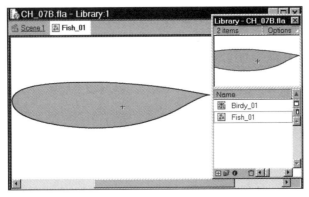

Figure 7-11
Start the fish by drawing an oval and reshaping it.

10 Min. To Go

3. Take three minutes to create your own unique fish design, using the oval shape as a start. Take a look at Figure 7-12 for one possibility.

4. With your fish symbol finished and automatically stored in the Project Library, it's time to create some fish variations. In the library, select the Fish_01 graphic. Go to the Library window and click the downward-pointing arrow next to Options to open the Options menu. Select Duplicate from the list, and name the first duplicate Fish_02. Repeat this procedure to create Fish_03. Edit the new symbols in their own timelines to color each of these fish symbols differently.

Session 7—Creating Animated Foreground Content

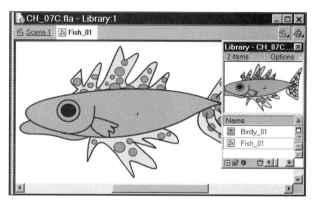

Figure 7-12
Create a fish symbol using the Shape and Pencil tools. Use multiple layers if you like.

5. Exit Symbol Edit mode to continue editing your main movie scene. Place one instance of each fish on the stage, and select Modify ⇨ Transform ⇨ Rotate to create the arrangement shown in Figure 7-13. Make sure you add and edit all three instances on the FishJump layer you previously created.

Figure 7-13
Create this arrangement of three different-colored fish instances on the stage, making sure the FishJump layer is activated.

6. Carefully do the following in order: Hold Shift and then click to select all three fish instances with the Arrow tool. Select Edit ⇨ Copy and then Edit ⇨ Paste in Place. With the newly pasted copies still selected, click and drag so that all three instances are below the originals on the stage. Next, select Modify ⇨ Transform ⇨ Rotate, and use the handles that appear around the three selected fish to rotate them 180 degrees. Finally, move the rotated instances opposite the original three above them to form a circle of instances with the original ones.

7. Select all six fish instances with the Arrow tool, and go to Insert ⇨ Convert to Symbol. Name this new symbol Fish_Group and under Behavior, select Graphic. You see the circle of fish in the Symbol Library preview window when it is selected. See Figure 7-14.

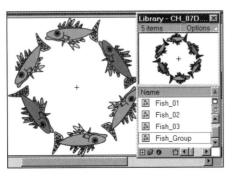

Figure 7-14
When transformed into a symbol, the group of six fish appears in the Symbol Library.

8. You will do a test animation at this point. The real animation will be done later when you composite the bird and fish together with our background. Remember that you already have a 30-frame animation set up from the BirdFly layer, so let's create a 30-frame animation of the circle of Fish.

9. Click Frame 30 of the FishJump layer and select Insert Keyframe.

10. Click Frame 1 in the timeline for the FishJump layer. It's already a keyframe. RMB [Control +Click] to bring up the menu of choices. Select Panels ⇨ Frame, and select Motion from the Tweening list. Under the Rotate pop-up, select CCW (counterclockwise), because that's the way the fish are facing. In the Times entry field next to the Rotate pop-up, type **1**. Close the window. Go to Control ⇨ Test Movie to see the bird fly and the circle of fish spin around. See Figure 7-15.

Session 7—Creating Animated Foreground Content 103

Figure 7-15
With the timeline configured for both the bird and the fish, go to Control ⇨ Test Movie to see the bird and fish move.

The last step is to save the project to your Common Libraries folder, so the library is accessible from another project.

Done!

Review

In this chapter, your knowledge of Flash animation possibilities was extended with the following exercises:

- Creating an animated symbol of a bird
- Using an instance of the bird to create a flight path
- Creating a revolving circle of fish
- Previewing a composite of the bird and fish animations

Quiz Yourself

1. Are the layers used in Symbol Edit mode the same as those used for standard stage operations? If not, how do they differ?
2. Why work with layers in Symbol Edit mode?
3. How can I preview an animated symbol instance?
4. How can I create duplicates of a symbol to create variations?
5. Why save a Project Library as a Common Library?

SESSION

Creating a Complex Animated Figure

Session Checklist

✔ Creating facial animations

✔ Creating costumes that can be applied to Flash characters

30 Min. To Go

I n this session, you create an animated diver for your scene, and you dive into some design complexities along the way.

Creating an Animated Head

You can begin by creating the head for the diver. To create the head, follow these steps:

1. Open a new project by choosing File ➪ New.
2. Choose whatever fill color you want the face to have, and set stroke color to none. Place a vertical oval on the stage, and reshape it into a face with the Sub-Select tool. See Figure 8-1 for an example of how the face should look.

Figure 8-1
The general shape of the face is created by using the Sub-Select tool on a vertical oval.

3. Select the face, and then go to Insert ⇨ Convert to Symbol. The face is transformed into a symbol, and you are transported to Symbol Edit mode. Open the timeline in Symbol Edit mode. Create four new layers, and name them Brows, Eyes_01, Eyes_02, and Mouth.

4. Select the original layer and name it Face. This should be the bottom layer. Lock the other layers. Use the Brush tool with no stroke and a fill color a bit darker than your base color to add some shading to the face for the nose and other non-animated parts. See Figure 8-2 for an example of what the features look like after adding some shading.

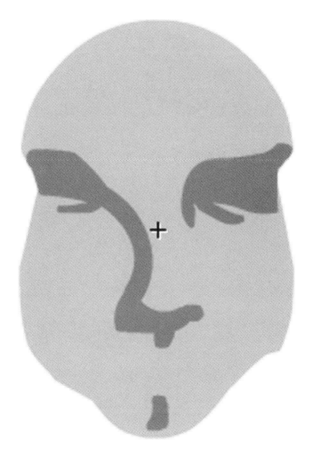

Figure 8-2
Add a little shading to define the eye sockets, nose, and maybe a small cleft in the chin.

5. Lock the Face layer. Unlock the Brows layer and select it.
6. Add some darker eyebrows on this layer. Also, add ears in the same color as the face, and add a patch of hair if you like. See Figure 8-3 for an example of the Brows layer once eyebrows, ears, and hair have been added.

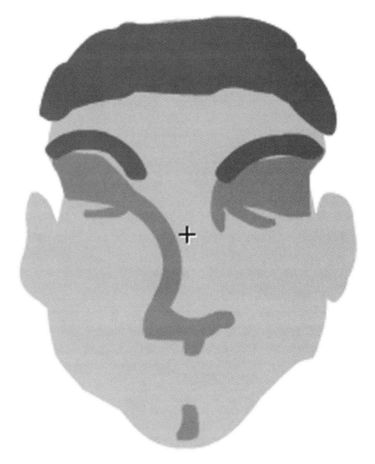

Figure 8-3
Eyebrows, ears, and hair are added on the Brows layer.

Session 8—Creating a Complex Animated Figure

20 Min. To Go

7. Lock the Brows layer. Unlock the Eyes_01 layer and select it. This layer will hold the whites of the eyes. Set a black stroke color and a white fill color. Set a stroke size at 0.75 (Window ➪ Panels ➪ Stroke). Use the Oval tool to create the eye shapes, and the Arrow tool to flatten them out at the top. You can see an example of the whites of the eyes in Figure 8-4.

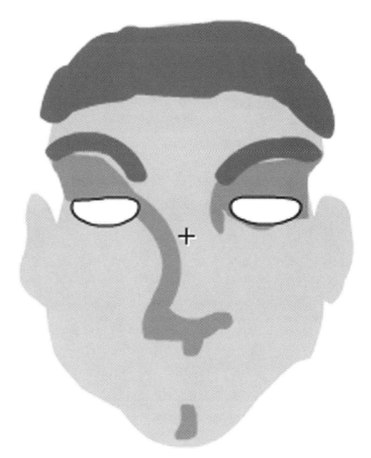

Figure 8-4
Add the whites of the eyes.

8. Lock the Eyes_01 layer, and open and select Eyes_02. Add the pupils of the eyes on this layer. Select a dark color and the Oval tool. Set stroke color to none and fill to a suitable dark color. Create the pupils. Add a small highlight over each pupil to soften the look. See Figure 8-5 for an example of Eyes_02 with the pupils added.

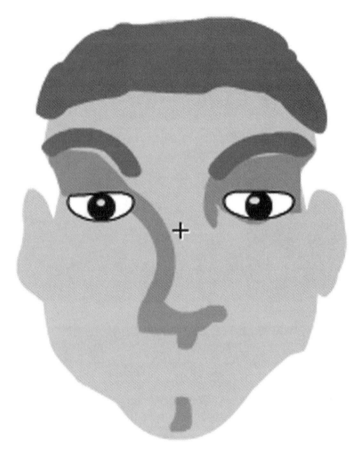

Figure 8-5
The pupils are added on the Eyes_02 layer.

9. Lock the Eyes_02 layer, and select and unlock the Mouth layer. Add a mouth with the Oval tool. Use a dark outline stroke and a white fill color. Use the Arrow tool to shape it. The basic head is finished; you can see an example in Figure 8-6.

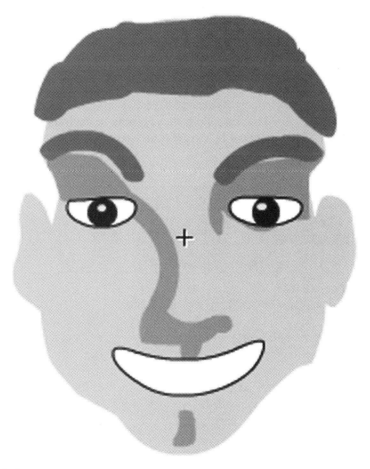

Figure 8-6
The basic head is done.

Animating the face

Using the following steps, spend no more than five minutes to animate the face:

1. Select each layer while in Symbol Edit mode and unlock it. Insert a keyframe on each layer at Frame 30.
2. Use Shape Tweening (select Panels ⇨ Frame) on all of the layers at Frame 1. Your timeline should now look exactly like Figure 8-7.

Shape Tweening can be distinguished from Motion Tweening in the timeline. Both tween types have a long, solid arrow between keyframes. However, Shape Tweening is indicated by a light-green background from keyframe to keyframe. Motion Tweening is indicated by a light-blue background from keyframe to keyframe.

Figure 8-7
The timeline with keyframe indicators added

3. At various points on the timeline, add keyframes and alter the shapes on select layers. Try opening and closing the eyes or moving the pupils. Alter the shape of the mouth and raise/lower the eyebrows. This creates an animated face, as you can see in Figure 8-8. Use the Arrow and Sub-Select tools as needed. See Figure 8-9 for an example of what your timeline might look like.

10 Min.
To Go

Adding the Diver's Suit

With the animated head completed, you're ready to move on to the suit. I'll keep the steps fairly basic because the primary goal here is to learn the process and not necessarily to select a final image. To add the diver's suit, follow these steps:

1. Exit Edit Symbol mode, which brings you back to the movie scene's stage. Place an instance of the completed head on the stage, if one isn't already there. Make sure the layer is named Face.

Session 8—Creating a Complex Animated Figure

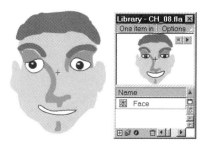

Figure 8-8
Altering the shapes on a layer at specific keyframes causes the facial features to move.

Figure 8-9
Your keyframe alterations will be unique, but here is an example of what the timeline may look like along the way.

2. Create a new layer, and name it Suit. Create another new layer above that, and name it Face Mask.

3. Select the Suit layer and lock the other two. Use the Oval tool with no fill and a black stroke set to a thickness of 5 to draw the oval pictured in Figure 8-10.

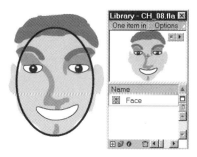

Figure 8-10
On the Suit layer, draw an oval over the face.

4. Draw another larger oval with the same attributes outside of the first Oval, making sure to cover the face perimeter. See Figure 8-11 for an example of the second oval.

Figure 8-11
Draw a second oval.

5. Use the Paint Bucket tool to fill the space between the ovals with black. Use the Brush tool and Paint Bucket tool to paint part of the upper body of the diver, and fill that with black, too. See Figure 8-12 for what your diver looks like now that you've created a wet suit for him.

Figure 8-12
Now you have a diver in a wet suit. You won't need the rest of the body.

6. Draw the diver's face mask on the face mask layer. Use the Oval tool with a black stroke and a yellow fill. Create a piece of hose over the diver's left shoulder.

7. Create a new layer called Tanks beneath all of the other layers. Use the Oval tool with a dark blue stroke and an orange fill to create oxygen tanks. Now the suit is complete. See Figure 8-13 for an example of what your completed suit might look like.

Figure 8-13
The completed suit

8. The face symbol is in the Project Library, so you don't need it on the stage. Select the Face layer and delete it. Click the keyframe on the mask layer to select all the shapes on that layer, and then go to Copy ➪ Paste in Place to place it on the Suit layer. Delete the mask layer. Copy the shapes from the Suit layer using the same selection technique, and Paste in Place on the Tanks layer. Delete the Suit layer. Now you have one layer with all of the suit components. Select all of the shapes with a marquee created by selecting the Arrow tool and clicking and dragging a rectangle. Go to Insert ➪ Convert to Symbol. Name the symbol Suit and select a graphic behavior. Suit now appears as a symbol in your Project Library. See Figure 8-14 for an example of what your Project Library might look like.

Session 8—Creating a Complex Animated Figure 117

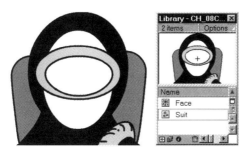

Figure 8-14
Suit is now a symbol in the Project Library.

9. Open the BirdFish Common Library. Click the items one by one, and drag them over to the library with the diver in it. You can always drag items from a Common Library to a Project Library, but not the other way around. Save the Project Library to the Flash Libraries folder so it can be accessed as a Common Library. See Figure 8-15 for an example.

Done!

Figure 8-15
Place all of the symbols in the BirdFish Common Library list into the Diver Project Library to keep everything together.

REVIEW

In this chapter, you learned how to create the components for a complex symbol design. Some of the techniques to remember from this chapter include:

- Using symbol layers to create a face
- Animating facial features
- Using Copy and Paste in Place operations to collapse layer content

QUIZ YOURSELF

1. Why should I use layers in the Symbol Edit window to create the components for an animated face?
2. How can I tell by looking at the timeline if a layer has Shape or Motion Tweening?
3. How can I add symbols from a Common Library into my Project Library?

SESSION

Creating Interactive Buttons

Session Checklist

✔ Creating a button

✔ Designing the four button states

30 Min. To Go

Flash projects are used for graphics and animation displays on the Web and also to provide content for multimedia CDs. In both cases, it is often desirable to involve the audience, to transform passive lookers into more active doers. One way of accomplishing this is to give the audience some control over when Flash events occur, perhaps over when an animation begins or when another page of data or graphics appear. Buttons are a mainstay in this process. In Flash, a button is a graphic device that appears on the stage, either at the start of the Timeline or somewhere further down the line, that can be clicked to start an action.

Creating Buttons

Buttons are symbols. You design them in the same way that you create any other symbol. Buttons have a special type of animated attribute, however, which is covered later in this chapter. Follow these steps to design a button for our large animation project.

1. Open a new project (File ➪ New).
2. Go to Insert ➪ New Symbol, which brings up the Symbol Properties window. Name your new symbol, and choose Button behavior. This jumps you into Symbol Edit mode.
3. In Symbol Edit mode, select View ➪ Timeline if the Timeline is not already visible.
4. Look at the Timeline. You see four named Frames: Up, Over, Down, and Hit. You will learn how to deal with these components later in the chapter.
5. One layer is present; Name the layer Sun. Create three more layers. Name them Eyes, Mask_01, and Mouth. See Figure 9-1.

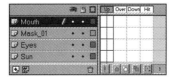

Figure 9-1
In Symbol Edit mode, your four layers read (bottom to top) Sun, Eyes, Mask_01, and Mouth.

6. Select the Sun layer and lock the other layers. Place an oval on the Edit stage. Use a yellow fill and a black stroke. Create rays streaming from the oval by using the Sub-Select and Pen tools. See Figure 9-2.
7. Select the Eyes layer and unlock it. Lock the Sun layer. Create two eyes for the Sun symbol on the Eyes layer, using the Oval tool. For each eye, create a large, white, filled oval and a smaller, dark oval inside of it.
8. Select the Mouth layer and unlock it. Lock the Eyes layer. Create a mouth with the Oval tool and a white fill on the Mouth layer. See Figure 9-3.

Session 9—Creating Interactive Buttons

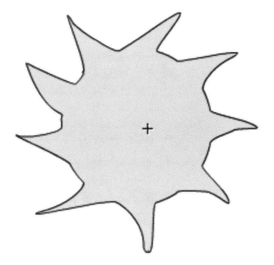

Figure 9-2
Create a sun shape from the oval that looks something like this.

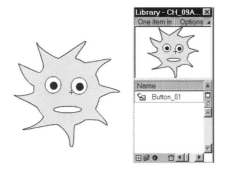

Figure 9-3
Create a mouth for the Sun symbol.

Using Mask Layers

Now let's learn about a new layer type — actually, two integrated layer types. You are going to design content for a mask layer. The mask layer is special. Any fill content on the mask layer will show the content of a masked layer only where the filled area on the mask layer exists. Please read this again, before continuing with an example, because using a mask and masked layer pair provides you with a whole new range of creative possibilities. Do the following:

1. Lock the Mouth layer, and select and unlock the Mask_01 layer. Bring up the Properties window for the Mask_01 layer, and select Mask as the layer type. Close the window by clicking on OK. See Figure 9-4.

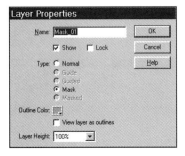

Figure 9-4
Select the Mask layer type in the Mask_01 Layer Properties window.

20 Min. To Go

2. Now select the Eyes layer and unlock it. Bring up this layer's Properties window. Select Masked as its layer type, and close the window by clicking on OK. See Figure 9-5.

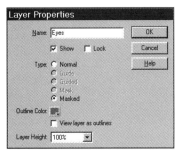

Figure 9-5
Select Masked in the Eyes Layer Properties window.

3. Look at the Layers window in the Timeline. The mask layer (Mask_01) displays a square, down-arrow icon that tells you at a glance it is a mask layer. Below it is the Eyes layer, which is indented and displays a different icon that tells you it is a masked layer. The mask layer is a source of a mask operation, and the masked layer is the target of that mask. The masked layer is always below the mask layer. Several layers below a mask layer can be the target of any mask layer above them. See Figure 9-6.

Figure 9-6
You can see mask and masked layers by looking for their icons in the Layers window on the Timeline.

4. Remember, all fill content (not stroke content) placed on a mask layer will become a transparent area, revealing all content on the masked layer beneath. The mask layer will hide anything not underneath a filled area of the mask layer. Select the Mask_01 mask layer, and create two oval areas above the eyes on the masked layer beneath. Deform these oval masks with the Arrow tool. Look at the left-hand illustration in Figure 9-7. This is what the symbol looks like in Edit mode, showing the squashed ovals on the Mask_01 layer. Now compare that with the right-hand illustration in Figure 9-7, which displays what the symbol looks like when an instance of it is placed on the stage. Masking can create wondrous effects. See Figure 9-7.

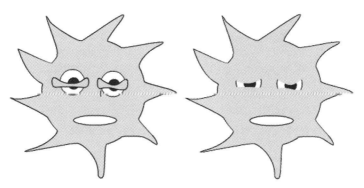

Figure 9-7
Using mask layers, you can create some diverse effects.

The Four Button States

As you can see by viewing the Timeline in Symbol Edit mode, the way the Timeline is segmented for a button symbol presents you with some new parameters to attend to. These parameters center around four possible conditions for a button: Up, Over, Down, and Hit. Insert a keyframe in all of the four areas of each of your four Sun symbol layers while in Symbol Edit mode. See Figure 9-8.

Figure 9-8
After inserting the keyframes, your Timeline looks like this.

Up state

The *Up state* of a button is how the button appears when the mouse pointer is not over the button's active area. The first frame of your button symbol's Timeline indicates the Up state of the button. You can create new artwork at this keyframe, as in other symbols you have created, or you can place any graphic or Movie Clip Symbol instance from your Libraries at this frame. In the case of your Sun button design, leave it as it has been designed on all four of its layers.

Over state

The *Over state* of a button is how the button appears when the mouse pointer enters the button's active area. You see this effect all the time when you surf the Web. As the mouse pointer glides over a graphic, the graphic lets you know it is special by changing color or becoming animated. For your Sun symbol, do the following:

1. Click the Over frame in the Timeline to edit the Over state of the button.
2. On the Mask_01 layer, reshape the eye masks to expose a bit more of the eyes on the masked layer below. Use the Arrow tool.
3. On the Sun layer of the Over state, use a new fill color on the Sun shape.
4. On the Mouth layer of the Over state, make the mouth smaller. Use the scale option of the Arrow tool in the Toolbox. See Figure 9-9.

Session 9—Creating Interactive Buttons

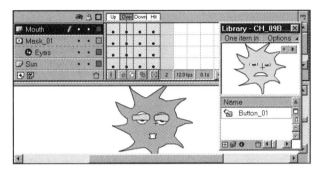

Figure 9-9
By making these changes to the Over state for the button, the eyes open a bit, the mouth shrinks, and the shape changes color when the pointer passes over the Hit area.

**10 Min.
To Go**

Down state

The *Down state* of a button is how the button appears when it is clicked. Select the Down heading in the Timeline to activate the Down state of your Sun button, and then do the following:

1. On the Mouth layer, use the Arrow tool to change the mouth to a smile.
2. On the Mask_01 layer, enlarge the masked areas using the Sub-Select tool to allow the entire eye elements to show through the mask from the layer beneath.
3. Use the fill tool on the Sun layer to give the shape another color. See Figure 9-10.

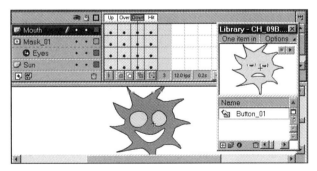

Figure 9-10
When the button is clicked on in the final production, all of the changes you made to the Down state layers will be displayed.

Hit state

The *Hit state* of a button refers to the area of the screen that is set aside for the selected button's active area. Create a Hit state area for the Sun symbol by doing the following:

1. Select the Hit frame on the Timeline to edit it, and click the Sun layer to make it the current layer.
2. Draw an oval in any fill color that covers the entire Sun shape. This area will become the live area that will tell the Button instance when to go from the Up state to the Over state.

Previewing the Button

After saving your button project to disk, let's preview the button in action.

1. Exit Symbol Edit mode by selecting Edit ➪ Edit Movie, and place an instance of the button on the stage.
2. Go to Control ➪ Enable Simple Buttons. The button is now activated. When you pass the mouse pointer over its live area (the Hit state you designed), the button changes from the Up state to the Over state. When you click it, it changes to the Down state. See Figure 9-11.

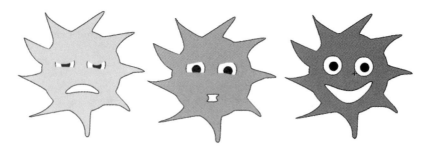

Figure 9-11
The Sun button's Up state, Over state, and Down state (left to right)

Done!

Note

The buttons in Flash not only change their looks based on the user's mouse position, but more importantly, they are assigned actions in order to initiate interactive events. You will look at button actions in the next chapter.

Session 9—Creating Interactive Buttons 127

REVIEW

In this chapter you learned to do the following:

- Create an interactive button
- Design all four button states
- Use mask and masked layers

QUIZ YOURSELF

1. What is the Up state of a button?
2. What is the Over state of a button?
3. What is the Down state of a button?
4. What is the Hit state of a button?
5. What is the difference between mask and masked layers?

SESSION

Introducing Button Actions

Session Checklist

✔ Working on a button project

✔ Exploring button actions

30 Min. To Go

In the previous session, you created an animated button. But what does a button do besides display its set states? Buttons initiate *actions* and act as an interactive bridge between your project content and the audience. In this session, you explore how actions are assigned to buttons.

Designing a Button Project

It's always best to design the interactive portion of a project from the start, when you first begin laying out your ideas. In the older tradition of multimedia interactive design, interactive projects were known as *branching* projects because the audience was given a choice at certain junctures to make a selection from among several options and to take an action that fostered how and where the program would *branch* from there. With button actions, you have a number of other branching options as well.

An Interactive Button Design

You are going to develop a simple animation that will be controlled, in part, by an interactive button. To develop a shape to work with, follow these steps:

1. Open the button project you finished and saved from the last session, or load the CH_09.fla file from the CD-ROM that accompanies this book. The finished button, with all four states determined, should now be in your Project Library.
2. Rename the default layer in the timeline to OvalAnim_01. Create a new layer above it called Button.
3. Go to Window ⇨ Panels ⇨ Stroke, set the stroke size to 6.25, and close the window. Figure 10-1 shows the Stroke window with the stroke size set to 6.25.

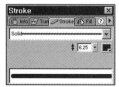

Figure 10-1
Set the stroke size to 6.25.

4. Select a light-blue fill color and a black stroke color, and select the Oval tool. Create an oval on the stage. See Figure 10-2 for an example of what your oval should look like.

Figure 10-2
Create an oval on the stage.

Session 10—Introducing Button Actions

5. Select the Arrow tool and click once on the stroke (the black outline around the oval). Click Modify ➪ Shape ➪ Convert Lines to Fills. The stroke around the oval has been converted to a fill. Reshaping it now presents different possibilities. Strokes maintain their set size when reshaped, but once converted to a fill, the new shape can be modified to whatever look you like. Select the Arrow tool and reshape the black fill as displayed in Figure 10-3.

Figure 10-3
Reshape the new black fill around the oval with the Arrow tool.

You can see how transforming strokes (sometimes called *lines* in Flash) provides more ways to design your projects.

The oval animation

**20 Min.
To Go**

Now that you have a shape to work with, you can create an animation that your button can initiate. To create an animation, follow these steps:

1. Go to the OvalAnim_01 layer on the timeline. Move the time indicator to Frame 30, and choose Insert Keyframe.

2. RMB-click [Control+Click] on the Frame 1 keyframe at Frame 1 of the OvalAnim_01 layer on the Timeline. Select Panels ➪ Frame and set the Tweening pop-up to Shape. Your timeline for the OvalAnim_01 layer should look like Figure 10-4.

   If you used the Controller to play the animation at this point, nothing would happen because the shape remains the same for all frames. Time to change that.

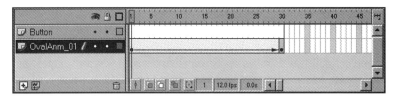

Figure 10-4
The Timeline now looks like this.

3. Move the Timeline playhead to Frame 15, and click Insert ⇨ Keyframe. Use the Arrow tool to reshape the graphic so it looks something like Figure 10-5.

Figure 10-5
Use the Arrow tool to modify the shape to look like this.

4. Running the animation now will display the original shape at Frame 1, changing to the new shape at Frame 15, and back to the original shape at Frame 30. And that's it for the animation aspect of this example.

Your First Button Actions

Time to explore button actions. The following steps show you how to create a button and assign basic actions to it.

1. Select the Button layer. Drag an instance of the Sun symbol from your Project Library to the stage and resize it (click Modify ⇨ Transform ⇨ Scale) as displayed in Figure 10-6 for Frame 1 on the Timeline.

Session 10—Introducing Button Actions

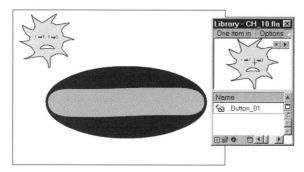

Figure 10-6
Place and resize an instance of the sun symbol on the stage.

> You could have used only one layer and placed the instance on the same layer as the animated graphic, but I prefer using different layers and keeping elements separated.

2. Go to Control ➪ Enable Simple Buttons if buttons are not already enabled. This activates the button on the stage so you can see its various active states (Up, Over, and Down).
3. RMB-click [Control+Click] the button to bring up the contextual menu of options. Select Actions.
4. The Object Actions window appears. In this window, you decide what actions the button is to initiate and when these actions will be triggered. Figure 10-7 shows the Object Actions window.

Figure 10-7
The initial appearance of the Object Actions window

5. In the Object Actions window, you create and modify Flash action scripts that allow for interactive control of the animation. This can be accomplished by assigning actions to a button, as you will do here. The process of assigning actions to buttons begins with the Object Actions list at the left side of the Object Actions window. This list is broken into six categories: Basic Actions, Actions, Operators, Functions, Properties, and Objects (see Figure 10-7).

This book covers only those actions available in the Basic Actions category. The rest of the actions are specific scripting actions, which are outside the focus of this book.

6. Click the Basic Actions button in the Object Actions window to display the following actions: Go To, Play, Stop, Toggle High Quality, Stop All Sounds, Get URL, ESC Command, Load Movie, Unload Movie, Tell Target, If Frame is Loaded, and On Mouse Event. You can see these options in Figure 10-8.

Figure 10-8
The Basic Actions list in the Object Actions window

A list of definitions of all of these actions is included at the end of this chapter for your reference. I do not cover all of them in a tutorial fashion in the book because all do not apply to the project you're doing. Once you know what a Basic Action does, however, and how to apply an action to a button, the rest will come easily.

7. Double-click the Go To action to assign it to the button. Flash automatically writes the appropriate action script in the right side of the Object Actions window. Highlight the line in the new script that reads "on (release)" (see Figure 10-9).

Figure 10-9
The mouse event parameter options open when the first line of the script is selected.

8. The bottom half of the Object Actions window is now devoted to your input for Line 1 parameters for the Go To script. This first line tells the button when it will activate. You can select what mouse event will be used to initiate the button action. Place a check mark in the box next to Release. The action will begin as soon as you release the mouse after clicking a button.

9. Now it's time to determine what Go To actions will be accomplished. At the right of this window, select the second line of the Go To script, which says "GoToAndPlay." In the input area below, type the number **15** into the Frame text entry field (see Figure 10-10).

10. Close the Object Actions window, and then click and release your button on the stage. Watch the Timeline indicator and the animation on the stage. What happens? Instead of playing from Frame 1 to Frame 30, the animation plays from Frame 15 to Frame 30, in accordance with the action you just assigned to the button.

Figure 10-10
Type the number 15 in the Frame text entry field for the second line of the Go To script.

Done! You've now completed your first button action assignment!

Basic Actions

For your reference, the following is a list of the Basic Actions and what each one does when assigned to a button:

- **Go To:** Enables you to play an animation from any frame on the timeline
- **Play/Stop:** Plays and stops a movie
- **Toggle High Quality:** Adjusts the movie's display quality
- **Stop All Sounds:** Instantly shuts off the audio track
- **Get URL:** Instantly jumps to a selected Uniform Resource Locator (*URL*) — a Web site address
- **Load Movie, Unload Movie:** Loads and unloads additional selected Macromedia Flash .swf movie files
- **On Mouse Event:** Enables you to select when the button will trigger actions based on the user's mouse interaction with the button
- **FSCommend, Tell Target, If Frame is Loaded:** Using these actions demands a more thorough knowledge of Flash scripting commands.

Session 10—Introducing Button Actions 137

REVIEW

In this chapter you learned how to do the following:

- Use the Convert Lines to Fills command
- Assign a basic action to an animated button

QUIZ YOURSELF

1. How do I convert lines (strokes) to fills?
2. Why should I convert lines (strokes) to fills?
3. How do I get the Object Actions window to appear?
4. What is the basic process for applying an action to a button?

PART II

Saturday Morning Part Review

1. How do I create a new layer?
2. How can I blend layer content so that it is transformed into one editable whole?
3. How can multiple layers be used to create a background for a project?
4. How is a layer named?
5. When a layer is deleted, what happens to its contents?
6. How are layers moved in the stack?
7. How do the layers used in Symbol Edit mode differ from those in standard stage operations?
8. Why work with layers in Symbol Edit mode?
9. When I copy content from one layer, what command do I use to paste it in the same position on another layer?
10. Using the timeline, how do I create a specific number of frames for my project?
11. How do I access and use the Controller?
12. How is a symbol created from animation content?
13. How can multiple instances be used to create a complex animation?
14. How do I preview a scene for playback?
15. How can I preview an animated symbol instance?
16. How can I duplicate a symbol to create variations?

Part II–Saturday Morning Part Review

17. Why save a Project Library as a Common Library?
18. How can I add symbols from a Common Library into my Project Library?
19. What is the difference between mask and masked layers?
20. Why should I convert lines (strokes) to fills?
21. How do I convert lines (strokes) to fills?
22. What is the Up state of a button?
23. What is the Over state of a button?
24. What is the Down state of a button?
25. What is the Hit state of a button?
26. How do I get the Object Actions window to appear?
27. What is the basic process for applying an action to a button?
28. Why should I use layers in the Symbol Edit window to create the components for an animated face?
29. How can I tell by looking at the Timeline if a layer has shape or motion tweening?

PART III

Saturday Afternoon

Session 11
Creating a Title

Session 12
Designing a Logo

Session 13
Creating Credits

Session 14
Creating Text Effects

Session 15
Exploring Text Animation Options

Session 16
Publishing and Exporting

SESSION

Creating a Title

Session Checklist

✔ Designing a basic title

✔ Modifying text

✔ Animating the title

30 Min. To Go

The sessions you will engage in this afternoon are targeted toward text-based projects. When creating Flash movies, it is often necessary to blend in titles, credits and, perhaps, text-based graphic logo elements. All of these elements incorporate text, and you can be as creative with text in Flash as you can with any other graphic component. You'll start by developing a title animation for your project.

Creating a Basic Title

To create a title for a project, you must keep two things in mind: what your creative instincts are telling you and which tools or processes in Flash can be used to bring your ideas to life.

Text tools and options

The title is often the first thing the audience sees, so it sets the overall tone for what is to follow. Because I want you to see how Text tools and options work, the title of your project is Deep See. In this chapter, you will focus your attention on three text attributes for this title: font, size, and style.

Font

Font is the name given to the general look of a typeface, or the look of its "family." *Alphanumeric fonts* (those with letter and number characters) can be grouped into two global categories: *serif* and *sans serif* (no-serifs). A *serif* is the embellishment you see on a letter or number, while sans-serif fonts lack that embellishment. The font you select for a title should reflect the content and the name of the production. See Figure 11-1 for an example of both a serif and a sans-serif font.

Figure 11-1
On top is an example of Times New Roman, a common serif font; below is an example of Verdana, a sans-serif font.

Session 11—Creating a Title

Note: Designers are more likely to use serif fonts in titles with classic or elegant themes because that's reflected in the font appearance. Sans-serif fonts are bolder and more affirmative, and are thus used when a designer wants to reflect a certain boldness in a title. In the end, however, it is the eye and intent of the designer that rules; such guidelines are certainly not cast in stone.

You are going to use two different fonts to create our title, one for "Deep" and another for "See." To begin creating the title, follow these steps:

1. Click the Text tool on the Tools menu to activate it. You can see the Text tool, along with all of the other tools, in Figure 11-2.

Figure 11-2
The Text tool in the Tools menu

2. Go to the Text menu, and select Font. A contextual submenu appears in which you can select a specific font. Select Helvetica, Verdana, or Sans.
3. Click on the screen and drag out a text insertion box. Type the word DEEP (in all capital letters). The text will be fairly small at this point.

Size

Now it's time to alter the size of the text block. Follow these steps:

1. With the original text block still selected on the screen, use your mouse (with the pointer now changed to a text cursor) to highlight the entire line of text by clicking and dragging over the letters.

2. Go to Text ⇨ Size, and select 120 from the submenu of size options. Now the text is sized correctly for our title. See Figure 11-3 for an example of resized text.

Figure 11-3
Enlarge the text by selecting Text ⇨ Size.

3. Name the layer that this text is on Deep. Create a Motion Tweening sequence of frames from 1 to 90 for this layer, for use in later animation procedures.

4. Create a new layer on top of the Deep layer, and name it See.

Style

The following styles are selectable by going to Text ⇨ Style and selecting them from the submenu of options: Plain, Bold, Italic, Subscript, and Superscript. To add a style to the text "Deep," follow these steps:

1. You should have two keyframes on your timeline for the Deep layer: one at Frame 1 and the other at Frame 90. Insert another keyframe at Frame 60.

2. Select the Text tool, and highlight the word "Deep." With the playhead at Frame 60, and the word Deep selected, go to Text ⇨ Styles, and select Italic. Play the animation. The Deep text remains the same from Frames 1 to 59, but then changes to Italic text at Frame 60 and remains italic until the end of the sequence at Frame 90.

Session 11—Creating a Title | 145

You have learned how to use font families, font sizes, and font styles.

Modifying Text

**20 Min.
To Go**

You are going to modify the text for the word "See" by breaking the letters apart and repositioning them. First, create the text:

1. Select the Text tool. Open the Fonts submenu under the Text menu, and select a font for "See." Use a serif font (Times, Times New Roman, and Century Schoolbook are good choices). Size it to 120 by selecting Text ⇨ Size ⇨ 120, and apply both Bold and Italic styles under the Text ⇨ Style submenu.

2. Move the playhead to Frame 60 of the timeline and click the See layer to make it active. With the Text tool active, select a light-blue fill color. Next, click and drag a text box on the stage, and type the word "See" below the word DEEP, overlapping it a bit. Your title should look like the example in Figure 11-4.

Figure 11-4
Place the word See below the word DEEP on Frame 60 of the See layer's timeline, as shown here.

3. Lock the Deep layer. Using the Arrow tool, select the See text block on the See layer. Text objects are all fill and no stroke. If you want a stroke on the text, you will need to turn the text block into shapes first. With the See text block selected, go to Modify ⇨ Break Apart. This breaks the text block object into separate shapes for each letter, much like Create Outlines does in other illustration tools, such as FreeHand and Illustrator.

4. Select just the letter "S" with the Arrow tool, and then choose Modify ➪ Transform ➪ Scale, and scale it to about 50 percent larger. Select each of the lowercase "e's" and offset them from their present position, as shown in Figure 11-5.

Figure 11-5
Your text for See should now look something like this.

Now that your text has been designed and modified, it's time to create the animation.

10 Min. To Go

Animating the Text

You are going to animate the text so that each layer's contents does something different. Variety in an animation creates audience interest. Variety breaks expectation, even in a small text animation. Do the following.

1. Lock the See layer, and make it invisible. This allows you to see what you are doing more clearly. Go to Frame 1 of the Deep layer, and move the text on that layer off the stage at the top. Figure 11-6 shows the distance you're looking for.

2. Because all of the keyframes are already set, the position of the word Deep is set from Keyframe 1 to Frame 59. Play the animation. The text remains offstage until Frame 60, and then pops onstage. You want the text to move smoothly from its position at Frame 1 to its position at Frame 60. Right-click [Control+Click] the Frame 1 keyframe on the timeline for the Deep layer. Select Panels ➪ Frame, and select Motion as the Tweening type in the Frames panel. See Figure 11-7 for an example of what your window should look like.

Session 11—Creating a Title

Figure 11-6
Move the text on the Deep layer off of the stage at the top, similar to the distance shown here.

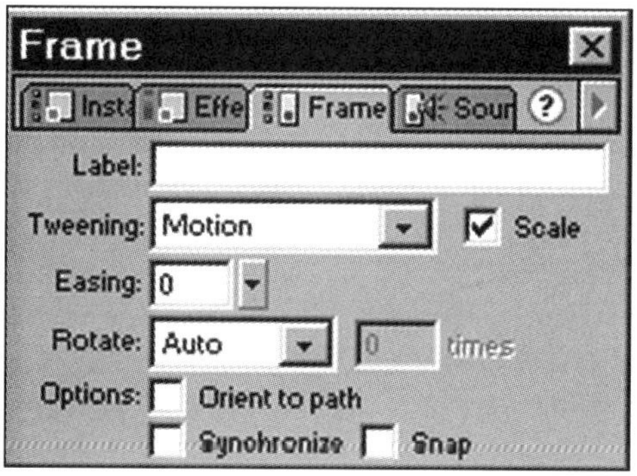

Figure 11-7
Remember to set Motion Tweening if you want the selected item to move smoothly from one keyframe to the next.

3. Set Motion Tweening using the same technique at Keyframe 60 on the same layer.

4. Play the animation now. The DEEP text starts offstage at Frame 1, moves smoothly into position at Frame 60, and transforms into italic text at the same time. Magic!
5. Now, unlock the See layer. Lock the Deep layer and hide it.
6. You know where you want the text on this layer to wind up because you placed it there at Frame 60. You do not know, however, where it is supposed to be at the start. It's now time to introduce a new feature: the guide layer.

Working with a Guide layer

A guide layer displays content for reference only. Nothing on a guide layer is rendered in the final animation. A layer is transformed into a guide layer by opening the layer's Properties window and selecting guide for the layer type. When a layer has been transformed or created as a guide layer, it displays the guide layer symbol. See the new guide layer in the Layers window in Figure 11-8.

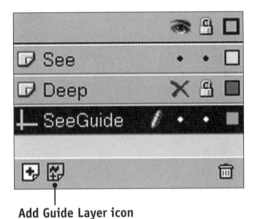

Add Guide Layer icon

Figure 11-8
The Layers window is displayed with a new guide layer placed at the bottom of the layer stack.

To position the letters, follow these steps:

1. Insert a new layer in the timeline, and then right-click [Control+Click] the new layer and select Guide from the contextual menu. A new guide layer is created. Move it to the bottom of the layer stack. Name the layer SeeGuide.

Session 11—Creating a Title

2. Select the See layer, and go to Frame 60. Select the ink bottle, and then select black for the stroke color. Use the ink bottle to place a black stroke with a thickness of 2 around each of the letters in the word "See." Don't forget to add strokes to the inside of each letter *e*.
3. Using the Arrow tool, double-click the fill of each letter separately to select both its fill and stroke. Select Modify ➪ Group to group each letter.
4. Use the Arrow tool to select all of the letters on the See layer, and then select Edit ➪ Copy.
5. Click the SeeGuide layer to make it current, and select Edit ➪ Paste in Place on Frame 1. Delete the See layer, and create a new layer on the top of the stack called the See layer.
6. On Frame 1 of this new See layer, select Edit ➪ Paste in Place. The three grouped letters are pasted, and Frame 1 of this new See layer becomes a keyframe. Add another keyframe at Frame 60 of the See layer, and another at Frame 90.
7. Select Frame 1 of the See layer, and move the letters offstage to the positions shown in Figure 11-9.

Figure 11-9
On Frame 1 of the See layer, move the letters off the stage as shown here.

8. Select each letter in turn on Frame 1 of the See layer, and choose Modify ⇨ Transform ⇨ Rotate to bring up the rotation editing handles. Rotate each letter as displayed in Figure 11-10.

Figure 11-10
Rotate each of the letters as shown here.

9. Go to Frame 1 of the See layer and bring up the Frame panel. Select Motion Tweening, and close the panel. You used the guide layer to create the original text for the See layer, and by using Paste in Place, you guaranteed that it would be in the correct position and orientation at Frame 60. The SeeGuide layer is no longer useful. You may delete it or make it invisible, although even if left as is, it won't appear in the final movie so nobody will ever see it, and it won't affect file size.

 You can place each of the three "See" letters on a separate layer. I like having control over their separate movements as much as possible, and placing each element on a separate layer gives me that control.

Done!

10. Go to Control ⇨ Test Movie to preview your creation and to see if anything needs tweaking. Save your scene.

Review

In this chapter you learned a lot about creating and manipulating text, including:

- Selecting fonts, text sizes, and styles
- Placing text elements on layers
- Using a guide layer to place text
- Animating text

Quiz Yourself

1. What menu options work in conjunction with the Text tool?
2. How do I resize text once it is placed on the stage?
3. How can I change a font for selected text?
4. Why use a guide layer?
5. How do I change a layer into a guide layer?

SESSION

Designing a Logo

Session Checklist

✔ Text for a logo

✔ Logo graphics

✔ Incorporating a logo in a title animation

30 Min. To Go

Logos, whether they are personal or corporate, can be an important part of your Flash title. You may already have a logo stored on disk, in which case you can incorporate it into a title animation. Bitmap-to-vector translation is a method for taking stored bitmap content and folding it into a Flash vector artwork. In this chapter, you will look at logo creation and placement in a title animation.

Designing the Logo Text

There may be a time when you need to create a Logo inside the Flash program. This chapter contains methods for handling the challenge. Here you learn how to develop a logo with and from text components.

Always develop a logo as a symbol. Chances are, you'll want to use it at different stages and for different purposes in a production. Logos can serve as graphic and animation elements, and also as interactive button designs.

The logo you are going to develop is for a production company: Sea Snake Productions. The following steps show you how.

1. Open the finished project that you saved from the tutorial in Chapter 11. If you didn't save it, don't worry. You can find it on the book's CD (CH_11.fla) in the Projects directory.
2. Create a new layer on top of the stack, and name it Logo. Lock all of the other layers and then make them invisible.
3. Insert ➪ New Symbol on the Logo layer. In the Symbol Properties window, name the new Symbol LogoText, and give it a graphic behavior. Click OK. You are then jumped into Symbol Edit mode. See Figure 12-1.

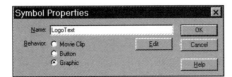

Figure 12-1
Create a New graphics Symbol named LogoText.

4. In Symbol Edit mode, create another layer on top of the default layer. Name the bottom layer TextGuide, and make it a guide layer either using the contextual menu or by accessing Modify ➪ Layer to edit that layer's Layer Properties window. Name the top layer CircleText, and make sure it is a Normal layer. Lock the CircleText layer and select the TextGuide layer.
5. Place a circle (constrained oval) on the Symbol Edit stage on the TextGuide layer at Frame 1. Give it a thin, red stroke and no fill. Draw it so that it takes up about 60 percent of the screen height. See Figure 12-2.

 Don't expect to see the circle appear in the Library Preview window, because it is on a guide layer.

6. Lock the TextGuide layer. Select and unlock the CircleText layer.

Session 12—Designing a Logo

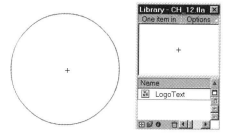

Figure 12-2
Draw a constrained oval on the guide layer.

7. Select a yellow fill. Place a text box on the screen and type in the words Sea Snake. Select the words with the Text cursor, and then set the size to 72. Use any font that appeals to you. Place the Text cursor between each letter and hit the Space bar. This gives you more room for each letter. Stretch the box to make sure the text appears on one line without word wrapping.

8. With the text block selected, go to Modify ⇨ Break Apart. Select the Ink Bottle tool and add a black stroke with a thickness set to 2 for each letter, inside and out.

9. Select each letter with the Arrow tool by dragging a marquee around it, and go to Modify ⇨ Group. Now you have a string of separate letters ready for further transformation. See Figure 12-3.

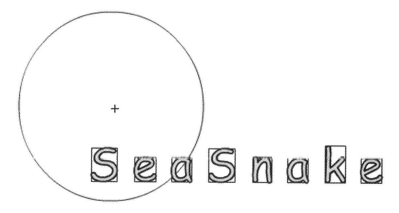

Figure 12-3
Now you have a series of letters that you can manipulate individually.

10. Using the CircleGuide layer as a template, move the letters so they loosely follow the circle shape.
11. Rotate and move the letters into a neater arrangement around the circle. See Figure 12-4.

Figure 12-4
The final arrangement of the letters after rotation and repositioning

20 Min. To Go

12. Select all of the individual letters with the Arrow tool by dragging a marquee around all of them. Go to Modify ➪ Transform ➪ Rotate and reposition to balance the letters over the vertical center of the CircleGuide layer. See Figure 12-5.
13. Use this same process as Steps 7 through 12 for the word Productions, but select a different font. However, when placing the letters around the circle, don't rotate them. You should wind up with a text layer that resembles Figure 12-6.

Session 12—Designing a Logo

Figure 12-5
Rotate the entire group of letters so they look evenly balanced on top of the circle.

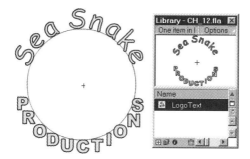

Figure 12-6
The finished Text layer for the logo

Designing the Logo Graphic

Let's add some graphic elements to the logo design by doing the following:

1. Select the circle you drew on the CircleGuide layer and then go to Edit ➪ Copy. Exit Symbol Edit mode to return to Edit Movie mode. Select Insert ➪ New Symbol. Name the Symbol LogoBkgrd, and give it a graphic behavior.

Select OK. This jumps you to a new Symbol Edit mode for your new symbol. Go to Edit ⇨ Paste in Place. You now have a circle placed for the LogoBkgrd Symbol. Go to Modify ⇨ Transform ⇨ Scale, and manually reduce its size by about 10 percent using the scaling handles that appear.

2. Select Radial Gradient from the pop-up on the Fill panel, and select the black and white radial fill option from the Fill color palette in the Toolbox. Use the Paint Bucket tool to fill the circle. Use the Arrow tool to drag a marquee around the fill and the stroke, and then go to Modify ⇨ Group. See Figure 12-7.

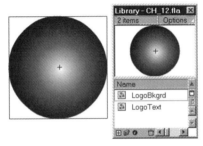

Figure 12-7
The LogoBkgrd symbol contains this circle filled with a black and white radial fill.

3. Exit Symbol Edit mode. Go to Insert ⇨ New Symbol again. Give this new symbol a graphic behavior, and name it SeaSnake.

4. Give the SeaSnake symbol two layers — a lower guide layer (name it Guide) and a top Normal layer called Graphic. Insert and rename these layers now.

5. Select the LogoBkgrd Symbol from your library and select Edit from the Options list. Select Edit ⇨ Copy in the LogoBkgrd Edit mode, and then exit that mode. Enter the SeaSnake Symbol Edit mode again and select the guide layer. Go to Edit ⇨ Paste in Place. Now you can use the radial-filled circle as a guide.

6. On the graphic layer, create a capital letter S with a light blue fill that's sized at 120 using a sans serif font. Place it inside the circle visible from the guide layer. Use the Arrow tool to select the letter by clicking on it, and then go to Modify ⇨ Break Apart. Create a black stroke around the letter with the Ink Bottle tool. Go to Modify ⇨ Transform ⇨ Scale to make it larger, so that it just about fills the circle on the guide layer. See Figure 12-8.

10 Min. To Go

Session 12—Designing a Logo

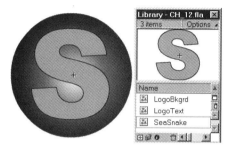

Figure 12-8
The letter S now fills the radial-filled circle on the guide layer, with some room to spare.

7. Use the Arrow tool to reshape the S into a snake symbol. Add an eye using the Oval tool and the same technique as in previous chapters. When complete, go to Modify ⇨ Group. See Figure 12-9.

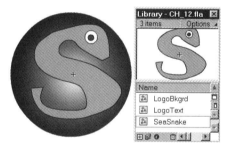

Figure 12-9
Reshape the letter into a snake symbol.

Incorporating the Logo in the Title Animation

Now let's place the logo in the title animation by completing the following steps:

1. Return to the stage and select the Logo layer. Insert a keyframe at Frame 90. Select the LogoBkgrd, LogoText, and SeaSnake elements from the library, and then place instances on the stage. Arrange them to form the finished logo. Select them all and go to Modify ⇨ Group. From here, choose Insert ⇨ Convert to Symbol. Name the new symbol LogoFinal and give it a graphic behavior. When done, delete the logo from the stage. See Figure 12-10.

Figure 12-10
The finished logo is complete.

 Having the separated elements of the logo in the library as well as the finished composite logo gives you a lot of creative freedom to use everything involved as needed.

2. With Frame 90 still selected on the Logo layer, drag an instance of the LogoFinal symbol to the stage. Move the Logo layer just above the guide layer in the layer stack. Make all of the other layers visible and place the logo relative to the text as displayed in Figure 12-11. You'll have to go to Modify ⇨ Transform ⇨ Scale and resize the logo to fit.

Figure 12-11
Frame 90 should look like this.

Session 12—Designing a Logo

Done!

3. There is one thing left to do. You want the entire title animation to last a while longer, so the logo remains in view for a few more seconds. Drag the Keyframe placed at 90 on the timeline for each layer to frame 120. Play the animation to preview it. Save to disk.

REVIEW

In this chapter you explored the design of a composite logo, including:

- Designing a logo in parts, placing each part in the symbol library.
- Using text elements in a logo.
- Translating text into a graphic.
- Placing a finished logo in a title animation.

QUIZ YOURSELF

1. How can I place text around a shape?
2. How can text be used as a shape resource?
3. Why should I create logo elements on separate layers?

SESSION 13

Creating Credits

Session Checklist

✔ Creating credits text
✔ Modifying credits text
✔ Using the Text Options panel

30 Min. To Go

Listing the Credits

Credits appear at the end of a movie, listing all of the people and organizations that contributed to the project. This is done as a matter of courtesy and also to satisfy laws and policies related to posting credit for creative work. The general list of credits includes the following:

- **Producer:** The producer is a person or organization who obtains the necessary funds to get a project off the ground. In the case of your Flash movie, you are probably the producer.
- **Director:** The director is responsible for shaping a movie — making the choices as to who does what and where. In your Flash movie, you will probably assume the role of producer/director.

- **Story:** The story for a movie may be an original script written for the production or it may be adapted from a different medium. For example, many films are adapted from published novels. Credits give the details of the process and the people involved.
- **Animator(s):** In traditional hand-drawn animation, a long list of animators may have worked on the film. Some are given credit as animation directors; others are listed for specific tasks, such as effects, storyboarding, or coloring.
- **Actors, Character Voices, and Narration:** If you are folding live actor sequences into your movie, the actors should be listed in the credits. If the movie incorporates any voices for animated characters, you should give credit to the actors providing those voices. Many productions, especially documentaries, include narration at various points in the presentation. The narrator(s) should be given credit.
- **Music & Sound Effects:** The audio you incorporate in your movie may come from copyright-free sound libraries or it may have been created specially for the production. If any musicians' works were used in the production (especially if they are members of the American Federation of Musicians), you should give them credit. Even when a copyright-free source is used for music and/or sound effects, it's considered courteous to list it. Many copyright-free sound libraries come with a stipulation that you must list them in the credits for a production.
- **Other:** If you folded real-world sequences into your Flash movie and included scenes that required artificial lighting, the lighting person or organization should be credited for their work. If you have included any copyrighted elements, the listing must appear in your credits. There may be special *Thanks to* lines that you'd like to add, such as "Thanks to the city of Denver for feeding me during the creation of this Flash movie."
- **Dedication:** The dedication is a special thank you that appears last in the list of credits, for example, "This movie is dedicated to my family, who suffered the long hours of my insane work schedule so this movie could be created."

 Even if you are the person who did all of the work to bring your Flash movie into reality, you still should consider listing the credits. At a minimum, the credits should read "Created, Produced, and Directed by" and perhaps "Music by." If your name is the only one to be listed, don't stretch the credits too far beyond this, unless ego gratification is an overwhelming necessity.

Session 13—Creating Credits

Creating Text for Credits

Now that you have a basic list of what your credits will be, it's time to explore the text to be used in credits design. You should be aware of several specific considerations, including: font selection and size, alignment, color, and background. For this project, you will create just two credit elements: Produced and Directed by, and a Thanks to listing that gives credit to Macromedia and the Flash software.

Font selection and size

When creating credits, keep in mind that a sans-serif text is easier to read. The only exception is large-sized text, which can be created with a wider variety of typefaces. Because you are using a limited amount of text data for your credits, you are free to select serif or sans serif typefaces. Do the following to create the credits for your Flash movie:

1. Click the Text tool to activate it, and then click and drag a text marquee on the stage. Make it almost as wide as your stage area for now.
2. Input the following text: **Produced and Directed by (your name)**.
3. Place the Text cursor behind your name, and hit the Enter [Return] key. This places your name on a second line. See Figure 13-1.

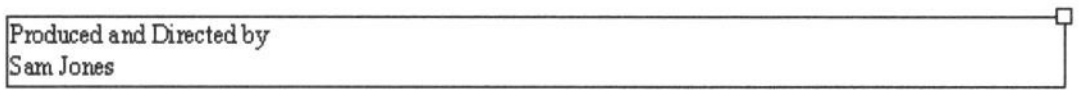

> Produced and Directed by
> Sam Jones

Figure 13-1
Create a credit that resembles this.

4. With the Text tool still selected, drag the text cursor over your text to highlight it. Go to Text ⇨ Fonts and select any font you like (sans serif or serif, because the text will be large) from your Font list. The text is now redrawn in that font. If you prefer, you can select your name and set it to a different font. Remember, however, that every font you use adds to the file size of your final movie on the Web.
5. With the text still selected, go to Text ⇨ Size and select a size for this credit line that enlarges the font as large as possible without exceeding the width of the stage. Use separate sizes for your name and the other elements if you like. See Figure 13-2.

Figure 13-2
When you select text, its color reverses on the stage. You can set different fonts and sizes for various credit components.

20 Min. To Go

6. Set this text block aside for a moment by hiding the layer it is on (click the dot under the Eye column on that layer). Create a new layer, and name it Credits_02.
7. Create a text block on the Credits_02 layer that reads as follows: **this animation was created with FLASH from Macromedia**. Select fonts, sizes, and styles to your liking.

Copyright and trademark symbols

Macromedia and *Flash* are registered trademarks. You must include the trademark symbol when mentioning Macromedia or Flash in the credits. The symbol for a registered name (the capital letter "R" in a small circle, placed to the upper-right of the name) is best created in Flash and saved as a symbol in the Project Library, and if you choose, to a Common Library.

Do the following to create a trademark:

1. With the Credits_02 layer active, go to Insert ⇨ New Symbol. In the Symbol Properties dialog box, name it Register, and select Graphic Behavior.
2. In Symbol Edit mode, create an italic sans-serif capital letter R using the Text tool. Size doesn't matter, because you can always resize an instance of a symbol.
3. Create a circle with a black stroke around the R and fill set to none. Center the R within the circle. Exit Symbol Edit mode. The symbol is now in your Project Library. Do not place the instanced symbol in the movie scene yet. See Figure 13-3.

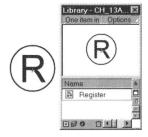

Figure 13-3
The completed registration symbol

Text alignment

Flash offers you special controls for aligning a text block with other on-stage elements and also for aligning the contents inside the selected text block.

Internal text alignment

Do the following to align the text in the text block:

1. Select all of the text on the Credits_02 layer with the Text cursor by clicking and dragging the mouse over it.
2. Go to Text ⇨ Align ⇨ Align Center. The three text lines are automatically vertically centered on each other. You also have the options for aligning selected components left, right, or justifying them to fill out the line width as much as possible. See Figure 13-4.

Figure 13-4
Align Center is a quick way to align multiple text lines.

Global alignment

Text blocks themselves (separate from the text within them) can be aligned with any other object on the Flash stage. The following steps show you how to do this.

1. Go to View ⇨ Grid ⇨ Show Grid. Using the grid enables you to align selected elements on the stage precisely. You can access the Grid size and color settings window from the same submenu.
2. Select View ⇨ Grid ⇨ Snap to Grid to snap any selected stage element to a grid line. See Figure 13-5.

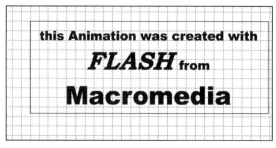

Figure 13-5
You can align any selected object on the stage with another object by using the grid.

10 Min. To Go

Deep text controls

When it comes to fine-tuning a text block, Flash supplies another option. Do the following to learn more about the Text Options panel:

1. Lock the Credits_02 layer and hide it. Select the Credits_01 layer and unlock it. Select the Text tool, and right-click [Control+Click] on the text. When the menu appears, go to Panels ⇨ Text Options.
2. The Text Options panel has three tabbed pages: Character, Paragraph, and Text Options. See Figure 13-6.
3. Click the Character Tab. Use the Text tool to highlight the first letter of your first name. On the Character panel, open the Font Size slider by clicking the arrow next to it. Move the slider up 10 points to 82 points in size. See Figure 13-7.

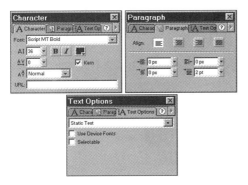

Figure 13-6
The three tabbed pages of the Text Options panel: Character, Paragraph, and Text Options.

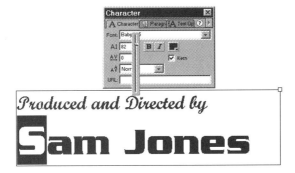

Figure 13-7
Each selected letter can be scaled in point size using the Font Size slider control.

4. Select the Produced and Directed by line of text by dragging over it with the Text tool. Below that on the Character panel, change the number in the Tracking text field (the "A V" with the horizontal arrow below it) to 5. This widens your line of text. See Figure 13-8.

5. As you can see by looking at the Character page in the Text Options panel, you can also alter any selected text's font, color, and style. The Kern option spaces adjoining characters in a more visually pleasing way. Leave it on as a default. You can also see a text input area named URL.

By selecting a text character or string of characters and then typing in a Web address here, the text becomes *hot*, so that when the text is used as a Web page, clicking these specified characters will transport the user to the URL address (if you are exporting the movie to the Macromedia Flash 5 Player).

Figure 13-8
You can widen or narrow the tracking of any line of text, or even just the kerning of a few selected characters.

6. Use the Text tool to select all of the text in the text block. Open the Paragraph panel. Highlight the second option for the text alignment to center your text. The four settings below that on the Paragraph panel are for adjusting paragraph settings. You are not working with paragraphs, so altering them has no visible effect in this exercise.

7. A Zoom indicator is located at the lower-left corner of your document window. This indicator displays a percentage number that indicates the zoom level you are using. You can either type in a zoom percentage or select one from the pop-up list of zoom presets, which is activated by clicking the arrow next to the percentage area. See Figure 13-9.

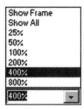

Figure 13-9
The Zoom indicator at the bottom-left of the stage area.

Session 13—Creating Credits 171

8. Select the 800% zoom preset, which is an extreme close-up. Make sure that View ⇨ Anti-alias_Text is checked. If you scroll the view to the edge of a letter and it looks smooth, the font will be embedded in the Flash movie file. Flash also contains three device fonts, which in some ways act as a placeholder for similar fonts on the viewer's system. These are *sans*, *serif*, and *typewriter*. Choosing to replace your font selection with any of these, and then checking Device Font in the Text Options panel, enables Flash to replace the font with whatever font on the viewer's system is closest to it.

9. If you click the downward pointing arrow in the Text Options panel, next to the words *Static Text*, you will see two other options — Dynamic Text and Input Text. These selections are beyond the scope of this book.

10. As a last step, place instances of the trademark symbol from your library on the upper-right of the Macromedia and Flash text on the Credits_02 layer and resize as needed.

Done!

REVIEW

In this chapter, you expanded your knowledge of text, including:

- Adjusting font selection and size
- Creating trademark symbols
- Exploring Global and Internal text alignment
- Using the Text Options panel

QUIZ YOURSELF

1. If I need to expand the width of a line of text, how can I do it?
2. Can each letter of a line of text display a different font? If so, how is it done?
3. Name the three Flash device fonts?

SESSION

Creating Text Effects

Session Checklist

✔ Using text masks for great effects
✔ Creating text shadows
✔ Using transparent text

30 Min. To Go

Using Text Masks

You have already learned how mask layers work in Flash. Now it's time to see how masks can create text effects that will wow your audience. Do the following to create a full-color text graphic:

1. Create a new scene. Give the scene two layers. Name the top layer Text; make it a mask layer by selecting it to make it current. Next, select Modify ➪ Layer and choose Mask from the list of options. Lock it.

2. Name the bottom layer Color, and make it a mask layer by selecting it and choosing Modify ➪ Layer again as before.
3. With the bottom layer selected, draw a series of random, multicolored rectangles with no stroke. See Figure 14-1.

Figure 14-1
Create a series of random, multicolored rectangles.

4. Use the Arrow tool to add curves to the rectangle borders. See Figure 14-2.
5. Lock the Colors layer. Select the Text layer and unlock it.
6. On the Text layer, type the word **COLOR** with the Text tool and appropriate Text menu selections. Use the Character panel to make the letters black and as large as possible, and use the Sans typeface.

Session 14—Creating Text Effects

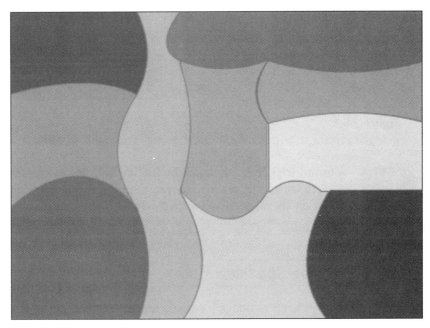

Figure 14-2
Add curves with the Arrow Tool.

 Remember that text is created with fill only and no stroke. Also note that any fill content placed on a mask layer will show through to the masked layer underneath.

7. With text on the mask layer and swatches of color on the masked layer beneath, you should see the colored areas through the text characters, right? Try it. Go to Control ➪ Test Movie for a preview. What do you see? There is no text on display. Instead all you see is the Color layer. Why?

8. Unfortunately, text blocks set to use the device fonts (Sans, Serif, and Typewriter) cannot be used as masks. They must either be converted to a similar non-device font (like Arial, Times, and so on), or broken apart. With the text block selected, go to Modify ➪ Break Apart. Now preview the scene again. See Figure 14-3.

Figure 14-3
Now you can see color through the text.

> A useful trick to know is that by locking both the mask and masked layers in the timeline, you can preview the masking effect on the stage of the main Movie Editing window.

Creating Text Drop Shadows

20 Min. To Go

Drop shadows give objects on the stage a 3-D appearance. The following process can be used to create drop shadows for text, or any other object on the stage:

1. Create a new scene. Type the word **Shadow** using the Text tool and Character panel. Give it a very light gray color. Use any typeface you like and make it large enough to fill the stage. See Figure 14-4.

Figure 14-4
*Create a text block and type **Shadow**.*

2. Select the text block, go to Edit ⇨ Copy, and then Edit ⇨ Paste in Place.
3. Use the Character panel to color the copied text solid black.
4. Move the black text block using the arrow keys on the keyboard so that it is slightly above and to the right of the light gray text version of the word "Shadow." Select both of them, and then go to Modify ⇨ Group. See Figure 14-5.

Session 14—Creating Text Effects

Shadow

Figure 14-5
The shadowed text is complete.

Creating Transparent Text

Transparency effects are often needed to mute the objects and to add more visual interest in a Flash movie. Do the following.

1. Open a new Flash scene.
2. Using the Text tool, type the word **GLASS** in all caps. Color doesn't matter, because you are going to alter it.
3. With the word selected, open the Character panel. Set the font size to 150, and the tracking to 18. Use the Helvetica typeface. See Figure 14-6.

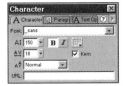

Figure 14-6
Use the Text Options panel to set font size and tracking.

4. Your letters may be too large to fit on one line. In this case, that's OK. See Figure 14-7.
5. Select the text block and go to Modify ⇨ Break Apart to separate the letters.
6. Go to Window ⇨ Panels ⇨ Stroke, and set the stroke size to 4. Make the color black.
7. Using the Ink Bottle tool on the separated letters, add a black stroke to all of the letters. Don't forget the internal triangle of the letter "A". See Figure 14-8.

GLA
SS
SS

Figure 14-7
The letters may appear on two lines.

8. Deselect all of the letters by clicking anywhere on the stage, except over a letter, with the Arrow tool.
9. Go to Window ⇨ Panels ⇨ Mixer. The Mixer panel appears. See Figure 14-9.
10. Look at the components of the Mixer panel. At the top is the Mixer icon, which is shaped like a color palette. You will find this same icon at the bottom-right of the stage. By clicking the icon at the bottom-right of the stage, you have an alternate way of bringing up the Mixer panel. On the left of the Mixer panel, you see the same arrangement of color options visible at the bottom of the Tools window. On the right side, however, are some components you haven't seen before. These are the R, G, B, and Alpha channel settings for a selected color. Click any color in the color area below to see the numbers in the R, G, and B boxes change. That's because every color is composed of RGB (Red-Blue-Green) components. By altering the values in the R,G, and B boxes, you can change colors. The values range from 0 to 255. Try it.

**10 Min.
To Go**

Session 14—Creating Text Effects

But what about the Alpha box? What does Alpha mean? An Alpha channel holds the opacity/transparency data for a color. Standard Alpha values range from 0 to 255, but Flash uses percentages from 0 to 100%. You can set R, G, B, and Alpha values for either or both the stroke or fill, depending on which is selected at the left side of the Mixer panel. You are going to set a range of fill R, G, B, and Alpha values for each letter, so make sure the Fill control on the left is selected.

Figure 14-8
Add a stroke around all of the letters.

Figure 14-9
The Mixer panel

11. Use the Arrow tool to select each letter, including its stroke. In the Mixer panel, with each letter in turn selected, alter the fill color. Next, set the Alpha value somewhere between 25% and 40%. Do this for each letter in turn, one by one.
12. Next, use the Arrow tool to select each letter's stroke and fill, and then go to Modify ➪ Group. Now you have a series of letters that have different R, G, B, and Alpha fill values.
13. You can't tell if an object is transparent unless you place something behind it. Arrange the letters so that they each overlap a bit, enabling you to appreciate their transparency. See Figure 14-10.

Figure 14-10
The finished text shows its transparent attributes.

Done!

You can use these techniques to make transparent any Flash-drawn or -edited graphic.

REVIEW

In this chapter you learned about applying some effects to text, including:

- Working with text masks
- Developing drop shadows for text
- Creating transparent text

Quiz Yourself

1. What must be done to text on a mask layer before it acts as a mask?
2. How is a drop shadow created for text?
3. What is the name of the channel that controls transparency?
4. How do I access the Mixer panel?

SESSION 15

Exploring Text Animation Options

Session Checklist

✔ Understanding progressive reveal animations
✔ Creating scrolling animations
✔ Using pops
✔ Using fades
✔ Developing DVEs

**30 Min.
To Go**

In this chapter we'll explore five different methods used to animate text objects on the Stage: progressive reveals, scrolls, pops, and DVEs.

Creating Progressive Reveals

The term *progressive reveal* comes from the use of overhead transparencies to display data. The presenter simply reveals the text a bit at a time, using an opaque piece of cardboard to block out the light. In the video age, the term is *wipe*, and the creative options broaden immensely with digital technology options. To create a scene with a progressive reveal, complete the following steps:

1. Create a new scene with two standard layers. Name the bottom layer Text and the top layer Reveal.
2. Select the Text layer and lock the Reveal layer.
3. On the Text layer, create the four text blocks, and in each type the text for a four-step process, such as the one shown in Figure 15-1. Go to View ⇨ Show Grid to align the text.

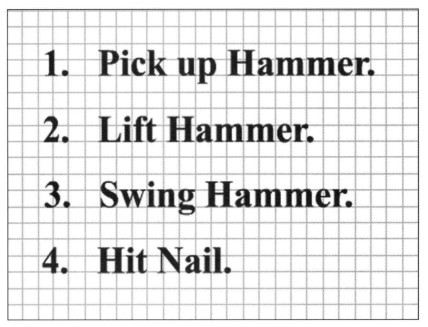

Figure 15-1
Text blocks for a four-step process are placed on the Text layer.

4. Lock the Text layer. Select and unlock the Reveal Layer.
5. Create a solid-color filled rectangle on the Reveal layer that covers the entire stage. Place a stroked circle with no fill at the top that vertically lines up with the left edge of the text blocks on the layer below. When completed, your Reveal layer should look like Figure 15-2.

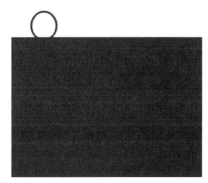

Figure 15-2
Your Reveal layer should look like this.

6. Group the Reveal layer contents. Create a hand that points to the circle with the Pencil tool's Smooth option. The layer will not accept the drawing? That is correct. You have just learned that you cannot draw on a grouped element.
7. Create another layer on top and name it Hand. Now draw the hand. Fill it with a lighter color, as shown in Figure 15-3. It is best to draw new artwork on a new layer above previous artwork in many cases, because Flash always floats groups and other objects on a layer (text, bitmaps, symbols, and so on) above all shapes on the same layer.

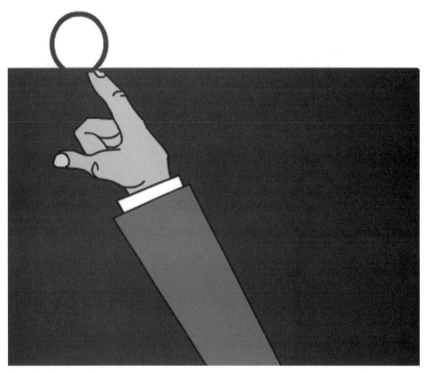

Figure 15-3
Add a pointing hand.

8. Let's return to a two-layer production. Select the Reveal layer and unlock and ungroup it. Select the contents on the Hand layer. Go to Modify ⇨ Group, and then go to Edit ⇨ Cut. Select the Reveal layer again. Go to Edit ⇨ Paste in Place. Delete the Hand layer.

9. Now animate the movie using keyframes. First, estimate the length of the movie. The animation should show the movie beginning with the Reveal layer completely blocking out the Text layer, then moving down to step 1 and holding, then moving to step 2 and holding, then moving to step 3 and holding, and finally moving and holding on step 4. Hold long enough for the audience to read each line of text. Figure 15-4 shows the progression.

 Now that you have the progressive reveal process down, you can see that there are at least a gazillion-and-two variations on this theme. You can explore and invent more next week while the lessons from this book are still buzzing in your memory.

Session 15—Exploring Text Animation Options 187

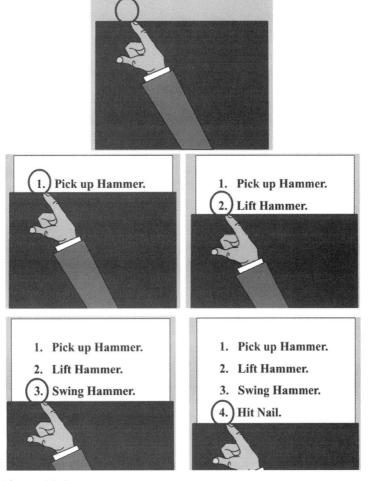

Figure 15-4
As the animation progresses, the step-by-step data is revealed.

**20 Min.
To Go**

Creating Scrolls

A *scroll* is the easiest effect to understand and the quickest to create. Scrolls are used all the time for credits animations. Scrolls usually proceed from bottom to top. To achieve this effect in Flash, simply animate a symbol containing your credits text from the bottom of the stage to the top at a speed slow enough for the audience to read. You are not going to spend time creating a scroll here; instead, let's move on to the other text animation types.

Generating Pops

Pop is not shorthand for the Boston Orchestra of the same name, nor does it refer to your dad. Pop is a video animation term that refers to the way that data appears onscreen. It can appear smoothly, or suddenly "pop" onto your screen. Flash makes pop animations extremely easy, once you get the hang of navigating on the timeline. To create text that pops, do the following:

1. Create multiple lines of text.
2. Create an animation in which each line starts at a different keyframe on the timeline. You might want to make all of the lines last until the same end point, or you may want to pop them off one at a time. The choice is up to you.

Developing Fades

Like the last two items (scrolls and pops), this information on *fades* is meant as a reference, rather than something you should do now. That's because we want to make sure that the rest of this session is devoted to the DVE material to follow, which is something you'll be asked to work with later in the chapter.

Creating a text fade animation is easy to understand. Just set up an animation with four keyframes, and select your text block. Set the Alpha channel to 0 for the first keyframe (for either or both fill and stroke), 100% at the second keyframe, 99% at the third keyframe, and 0% at the last keyframe. The text block will fade in, remain in view, and then fade out. Fades are standard ways to create animated titles and credits.

Understanding DVEs

DVE (Digital Video Effect) is also known by another term: *spinning logos*. Everyone who works in computer graphics and animation has created at least one (and probably a hundred or more) DVEs at one time or another. Here's how to use Flash to do it:

1. Create a filled rectangle that takes up about ¾ of the stage. Use a light fill color if the text is to be dark, or a dark fill color if the text is to be light.

Tip

Visual research into a range of color combinations that are easy on the eyes in all projected media has shown that light text on a dark backdrop, especially with larger sized typefaces, is easier and quicker to read and causes less eye fatigue after long viewing sessions. Perceptual research has also shown that a dark blue backdrop with light yellow text is best. Light text on a darker backdrop makes the text seem larger than it is; reversing this combination makes the text seem smaller. Sans-serif is the best choice for smaller typefaces in projected media (such as overheads, slides, video, films, and the Web).

2. Create another layer above the Rectangle layer to develop the text. DVE animations work best when the quantity of Text is limited to no more than about ten words. DVEs are also prime real estate for animating logo symbols.

3. After the Text is developed and aligned the way you want it, go to Edit ➪ Copy. Next, go to Edit ➪ Paste in Place on the Rectangle layer. This duplicates the content. Group everything.

10 Min. To Go

4. Now that you have created content at Frame 1, you will see a keyframe placed at position 1 on the timeline. Select the keyframe, and then choose Insert Frame. Drag the new frame to position 90 on the timeline. Select it, and then select Insert Keyframe.

5. Now you have two keyframes — one at Frame 1 and one at Frame 90. Select Frame 1 to bring up the Frame panel (Window ➪ Panels ➪ Frame is another way to do it). In the Frame panel, select Motion Tweening, and then close the Panel.

6. Select Frame 1 and go to Modify ➪ Transform ➪ Scale. Reduce the size of the graphic at Frame 1 to about 10%. Play the animation and watch the graphic smoothly grow in size from tiny to normal.

7. Let's set some additional items in the Frame panel at Frame 1. Bring it into view. Make sure Scale is checked, because you will alter the scale as the animation progresses. In the Easing area, input a value of **-100**. This makes the graphic move slower at the start of the tweened animation and then speed up as it reaches the end of the tween. On Frame 1 of the animation, move the graphic offstage at the upper-right.

8. Click the triangle next to the Rotate area. You will see four options: None, Auto, CW (clockwise), and CCW (counter-clockwise). Select CW. In the times area next to the Rotate area, type **4**. This makes the graphic rotate four times in a clockwise direction from the start of the animation to the end. Use the Controller to play the animation to preview it, and then save the project file to disk. See Figures 15-5 and 15-6.

Figure 15-5
Use the Frame panel to control the direction and number of times a selected object will rotate in an animation.

Done!

Figure 15-6
The DVE starts off-screen at a small size and rotates to a normal size at its target position.

Session 15—Exploring Text Animation Options

REVIEW

In this chapter you learned about a number of different text animation concepts, including:

- progressive reveals
- scrolls
- pops
- fades
- DVEs

QUIZ YOURSELF

1. What is a progressive reveal?
2. How is a pop animation created?
3. How can you access the Frames panel by using the Windows menu?
4. Where is one place that a rotating animation's direction of revolution and number of rotations are set?
5. What is the common name for a DVE?

SESSION

Publishing and Exporting

Session Checklist

✔ Importing and customizing Flash project content

✔ Publishing a Flash file

✔ Exporting a Flash file as an image for modification

*30 Min.
To Go*

The basic difference between publishing and exporting a Flash movie concerns the connection each option has with the Flash file. When you publish a Flash movie, the saved published data maintains a connection with the Flash (.fla) file. This means that you can update the Flash project later and save the connected published formats, which remain as they were set previously. If you export a Flash movie, the exported content no longer maintains any connection to the .fla file. You can edit exported content in an external application.

Saturday Afternoon

Loading a Flash Project

To begin our exploration of the differences between publishing and exporting, do the following:

1. Go to the Flash Projects folder on the book's CD-ROM, and open the CH_16A.fla file. Look at the Animation window to see how the file is set up. You can see that it has two layers: FishJump and BirdFly. See Figure 16-1.

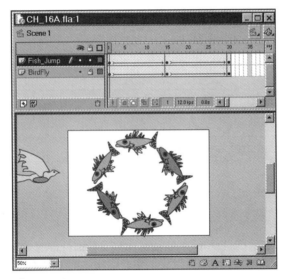

Figure 16-1
The imported file has two layers and looks like this.

2. Play the animation to see what it looks like so far (Control ➪ Play).

3. Go to File ➪ Open As Library. This allows you to import another Project Library. Find the file Bic_Anim_01.fla on the Library folder on this book's CD-ROM and select it. That library appears next to your Project Library on the Flash stage. Select the Face file from the Imported Library, and then click and drag it to your Project Library. The face now appears in your Project Library See Figure 16-2.

Session 16—Publishing and Exporting   195

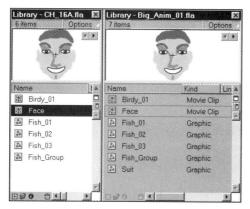

Figure 16-2
Drag the Face file from the Imported Library to your Project Library.

4. Create a new layer by going to Insert ⇨ Layer; name the new layer Face. Move the Face layer under the Fish layer and on top of the Bird layer in the stack. Go to Control ⇨ Test Movie to see what you have created. Save the file as CH_16B.fla. See Figure 16-3.

Figure 16-3
The animated face lies behind the fish and over the flying bird.

 You have just learned how to transfer files from one library to another. This greatly expands your creative resource options.

**20 Min.
To Go**

Publishing Flash Content

Now that you have the Flash movie (CH_16B.fla) saved, you can always call on it to create extra content for any future project. Time to publish. Go to File ⇨ Publish Settings to set the parameters. See Figure 16-4.

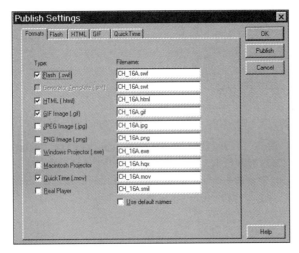

Figure 16-4
The Publish Settings window

Do the following to generate the settings you want for the published document:

1. Under the Formats tab, uncheck the Use Default names setting. This gives you the option to alter the published file's name.

2. Check all of the file types to which you would like to publish. The Flash .swf file format will include all of the selected formats when publishing takes place.

3. Go to the Flash tab. Look at all of the settings here. The two most important ones to configure first are the Joint Photographic Experts Group (JPEG) Quality and Version options. If you are publishing to the JPEG format, consider setting the JPEG Quality slider to 85 or so. There is usually little perceived image degradation at this value, and it saves storage space. Many Flash designers choose to support an audience who may be using older versions of Flash, which is especially true if your audience is

Session 16—Publishing and Exporting

large. In that case, you might even consider selecting to publish to at least two versions of Macromedia Flash Player, the current one and the last one (this has to be done in two separate publishing sessions).

4. If you have selected HTML (Hypertext Markup Language) as one of the published output options, even though this book does not walk you through HTML/Flash operations, there are several options under the HTML tab that you should note. Set these according to your preferences. Leave the template settings at their default positions unless you are an experienced HTML user. This just enables the HTML Flash file output to run as expected in your browser. Under Dimensions, you can select Match Movie for the same dimensions as preset in Flash or you can use customized dimensions calculated by Pixels or Percent.

5. Set Quality, Window Mode, HTML Alignment, and Scale to their defaults until after you have previewed the published results in a browser. Set Flash Alignment to the default (center/center) for the same reasons.

6. If you have selected GIF as one of your publishing output options, you should set any needed GIF options under the GIF tab. Set the output size if it is to be different than the Flash dimensions.

Be aware that GIF animations are commonly very tiny — they appear as small vignettes on a Web page — so size the GIF dimensions accordingly.

7. Playback is static for images and animated for animations. Set either Infinite Looping or a Times-to-Repeat value for animations. As a default, until you see the preview, leave the Optimize Colors and Smooth options selected (checked). If the GIF animation is to appear over a background page, use a Transparent setting. Flash movies usually work well when Dithering is set to None under the GIF tab, but if you are using a lot of gradients, you may have to accommodate them by using a dithered pattern. Start by using the default Palette Type (Web 216) and change this as needed after you preview the results.

8. If you have selected QuickTime as a Flash publishing output option, set the parameters required under the QuickTime tab. Set the dimensions as needed. Use the default Alpha and Layers settings most of the time (Auto), and change only after previewing.

Chapter 18 details the Sound settings.

9. Most of the time, you'll leave the Controller set to None or Standard, selecting QuickTime VR only when you are creating a QuickTime Virtual Reality (QTVR) format movie.
10. Standard Playback is preset to Loop, but if your design calls for it, you can select Play At Start. Play Every Frame is seldom used. Leave Flatten selected.
11. Go to File ➪ Publish Preview and select the output format you want to preview. When everything looks as you want it to, go to File ➪ Publish.
12. Your published files can be selected and viewed in any browser that has the Macromedia Flash Player installed.

10 Min. To Go

Exporting Flash Movies

When you use File ➪ Export on a Flash movie, the exported file, you have the ability to edit the file in an image or video editing environment (FireWorks, Photoshop, After Effects, and others). Do the following:

1. With the CH_16B.fla file still loaded in Flash, go to File ➪ Export Movie or Export Image. Decide what file type you want to export it as, and select it. Type its name in the standard area in the File area. See Figure 16-5.

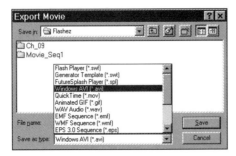

Figure 16-5
The Export Movie window

2. Export the Flash file as an Audio Video Interface (AVI) Movie. Now you can open it in any video-editing software.

3. Select any frame of the file in the Timeline that looks interesting. Go to File ⇨ Export Image. Name the file, select the format, and save it. Open your favorite image-editing software (Photoshop is suggested) and import the saved Flash image file. See Figure 16-6.

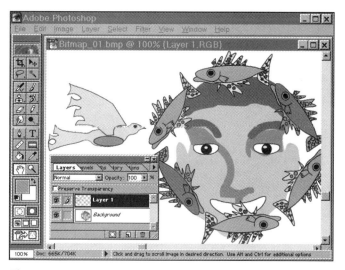

Figure 16-6
The Flash image file is imported into Photoshop. Note that it is imported with a separate Bird layer over the image.

4. If you have some experience with Photoshop, go to Layer ⇨ Duplicate the Background Layer to duplicate the Flash non-Bird content, move the duplicate over the Bird layer, and then delete the original background layer. Now the non-Bird image content is on top in the duplicated Bird layer, and the Bird layer is on the bottom. See Figure 16-7.

Figure 16-7
Create a new layer order like this.

5. Make the Bird layer the active one, and make the other layer invisible. Use the Magic Wand tool to select the non-Bird part of the layer, and add a background gradient.
6. Make the top layer visible and select it. Delete (Edit ➪ Clear) the white area from the layer. Go to Layer ➪ Flatten Image. Save as a BMP file [PICT for Macs]. Name it CH_16_Img (.BMP or .PICT). See Figure 16-8.

 You will find this file on the book's CD in the Resources folder.

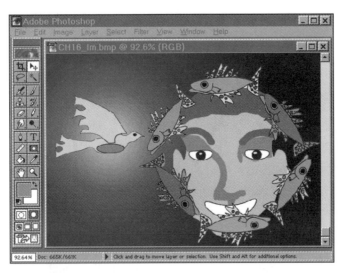

Figure 16-8
Add a background gradient in Photoshop and save as a BMP or PICT image file.

7. Import the image into Flash as an element that can be used as a background or content of an animation. See Figure 16-9.

Session 16—Publishing and Exporting

Figure 16-9
Import the image back into Flash to be used in a movie.

REVIEW

In this session you explored the following:

- Setting the parameters for Publishing operations
- Publishing to a number of file formats
- Exporting Flash files
- Modifying image files in a bitmap painting application

QUIZ YOURSELF

1. Where do I set Publish parameters?
2. When publishing a Flash HTML file, what are the important considerations I should note?
3. What is the main difference between publishing and exporting a Flash project?
4. How are Flash images exported?
5. Once a Flash Image file has been altered in a bitmap application, how can it be used in Flash again?

PART III

Saturday Afternoon Part Review

1. What are the main menu options that work in conjunction with the Text tool?
2. Why use a guide layer?
3. Why bother to create logo elements on separate layers?
4. How is text resized once it is placed on the stage?
5. Where do I set Publish parameters?
6. When publishing a Flash HTML file, what are the important considerations to note?
7. What is the main difference between publishing and exporting a Flash project?
8. How can I change the font for selected text?
9. How is the width of a line of text altered?
10. How can I make each letter of a line of text display a different font?
11. What are the names of the three Flash device fonts?
12. What must be done to text on a mask layer before it acts as a mask?
13. Where do I set a rotating animation's direction of revolution and number of rotations?
14. What is the meaning of the acronym "DVE"?
15. How is a text drop shadow created?
16. What channel controls transparency?

17. How do I change a layer into a guide layer?
18. How can I place text around a shape?
19. How can text be used as a shape resource?
20. How is the Mixer panel accessed?
21. What is a progressive reveal?
22. How is a pop animation created?
23. How can I access the Frames panel by using the Window menu?
24. How are Flash images exported?
25. Once a Flash image file has been altered in a bitmap application, how can it be used in Flash again?

PART IV
Saturday Evening

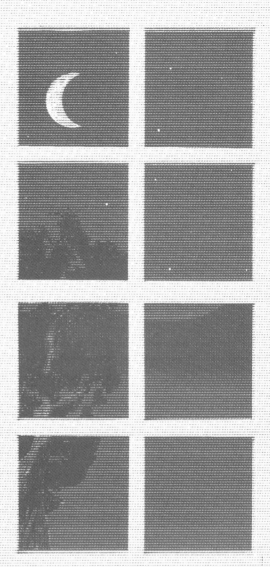

Session 17
Exploring Bitmaps

Session 18
Understanding Flash Audio

Session 19
Working with Audio

Session 20
Applying Sound to Animations

SESSION 17

Exploring Bitmaps

Session Checklist

✔ Scaling and rotating bitmaps
✔ Translating a bitmap into a vector image
✔ Exploring the use of the Break-Apart process

30 Min. To Go

If all Flash did was to provide the capability to create super-sharp vector graphics and animations, it would still dominate the market. But Flash can do much more, such as enabling you to integrate bitmap images and animations. This session focuses on the ways that Flash can be used to enhance and modify image and animation content.

Transforming Bitmaps

Unlike vector-based graphics and animations, bitmaps are based upon pixelated data, which is *resolution dependent*. This means that enlarging a bitmap will reveal the pixels that compose it; at very close magnifications the pixelated image or animations look decidedly ugly, so there are some cautions involved. Do the following:

1. Find the CH16_Im.bmp file on the book's CD (Resource folder), or on the disk to which you saved it if you created it in Chapter 16.

 Note
Windows users: Flash expects to see the proper three letter file extension in the image file's name. If for some reason the file extension is missing, open the folder where the graphic is located and rename the file, adding the proper three letter extension (.bmp, .tif, .jpg, .png, and so on).

2. The bitmap file appears in Flash. See Figure 17-1.

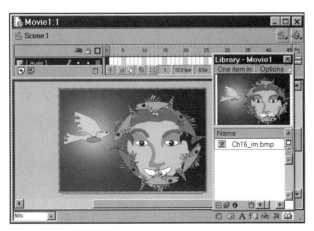

Figure 17-1
The bitmap file appears on the Flash stage.

3. Go to Modify ➪ Transform ➪ Flip Horizontal. This flips the bitmap on its horizontal axis, since you flipped an instance of it on the stage, not the master bitmap itself. Note that the original image remains unaffected in the library. See Figure 17-2.
4. Go to Modify ➪ Transform ➪ Flip vertical to turn the bitmap upside down.
5. Go to Modify ➪ Transform ➪ Scale and Rotate. The Scale and Rotate window opens. See Figure 17-3.
6. With the Scale and Rotate window open, input a value of **75%** for Scale and **-25** degrees for Rotate. The bitmap image adjusts accordingly when you click OK. See Figure 17-4.

Session 17—Exploring Bitmaps

Figure 17-2
The bitmap is flipped horizontally.

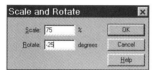

Figure 17-3
The Scale and Rotate window.

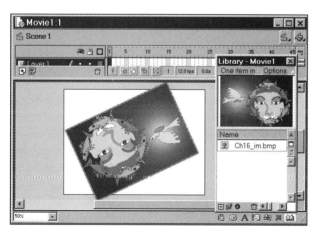

Figure 17-4
The bitmap image reacts to your parameter values.

20 Min. To Go

Translating an Image From Bitmap to Vector

As you can see, there are a number of ways you can modify a bitmap image in Flash with the Transform options. But what if you needed all of the content in a project to be in vector format. Remember that vector art can also be resized in either direction without the pixelization problem present in zoomed bitmaps. Fortunately, there is a way of translating a bitmap to a vector image in Flash. Do the following:

1. Load any bitmap file that Flash can import.
2. Go to Modify ➪ Trace Bitmap. The Trace Bitmap settings window appears. See Figure 17-5.

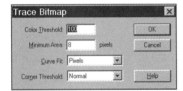

Figure 17-5
The Trace Bitmap settings window.

3. All bitmaps take varying amounts of time to be transformed, and no two bitmaps respond to the same parameter settings, so you will have to experiment here. Parameters to watch out for especially include setting the Minimum Area value too low, although only experimentation can prove what settings are best.

When the process is complete, your bitmap image will be transformed into a vector image.

Tracing a bitmap, especially getting the parameter settings right, is an inexact science to say the least. The Flash bitmap-to-vector conversion process is far too slow for practical use. I recommend that you use the same operation in FreeHand instead. In the Resources folder on the CD are two traced examples in the swf format; these examples are related to an image I took with a digital camera of the famous leaning tower of Pisa (it's included too, as Tower.bmp). They took about 5 seconds in FreeHand and more than 20 minutes in Flash. This was on a Pentium III system running Windows 98 with 750MB of RAM with a processor speed of 733MHz.

Even with FreeHand's exemplary Tracing operation, you can see how the traced image on the right has degraded from the original on the left (Figure 17-6). The settings were modified to create a high-quality trace. Moral? Try to avoid tracing complex images, unless the rather loose, painterly effect is what you want.

Figure 17-6
Avoid tracing overly complex bitmap images.

10 Min.
To Go

Cutting Apart Bitmaps

It is possible to use bitmap parts to create new images in Flash. Do the following:

1. Import the FHandTrace_02.swf file from the Resources folder on this book's CD. You will see two images of the Leaning Tower of Pisa (Figure 17-7). The one on the right is a traced image. Use the Select Arrow tool to place a marquee around it and delete it. All that remains is the one on the left, which is a bitmap. Enlarge it so that it fills more of the stage.

Figure 17-7
The bitmap image is our target for this exercise.

2. Go to Modify ⇨ Transform ⇨ Rotate and straighten out the tower (how about that?!). See Figure 17-8.

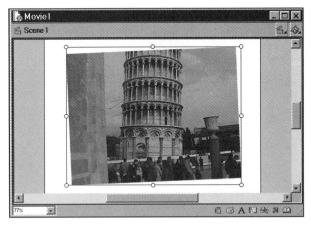

Figure 17-8
Rotate the image so that the tower looks straighter.

3. Select the image with the Arrow tool. Go to Modify ⇨ Break Apart. This converts the floating image object to an editable vector shape with a bitmap fill, making it possible for you to select portions of it and modify it, just as you would any shape you had created with the drawing tools. You will see a pattern of white dots covering the image, telling you it has been broken apart. See Figure 17-9.

4. Click the Lasso tool to activate the image, and select the Polygon mode option at the bottom of the Tools palette. Use the Lasso tool to outline the tower, aiming to get a section that looks like a complete building. When the outline is complete, double-click the mouse to close the lasso path you have drawn. The area you have outlined is now selected. Move it upwards, and completely away from the rest of the bitmap. See Figure 17-10.

5. Use the Arrow tool to select the rest of the image, and then delete it. Use the Arrow tool to drag a marquee around the tower. Go to Modify ⇨ Group and move the tower to the bottom of the stage. Copy and Paste another two towers next to it. You have just built a medieval city. See Figure 17-11.

Session 17—Exploring Bitmaps

Figure 17-9
The image is broken apart, as evidenced by a pattern of white dots.

Figure 17-10
Outline the tower and move it away from the rest of the bitmap.

Figure 17-11
A row of towers now fills a Flash scene.

6. Add a new layer and name it Sky. Move it below the towers layer. Fill in a rectangular shape on the layer with a light blue color. Go to the Align Panel and choose Align To Stage. Then paint some clouds on it. Your scene is complete and waiting for other possible actors. See Figure 17-12.

Figure 17-12
Breaking a bitmap apart gives you more creative options.

Done!

Review

In this chapter, we explored the following:

- Translating bitmaps
- Converting bitmap images into vector images
- Using the Break Apart process

Quiz Yourself

1. Can imported bitmaps be scaled and rotated? If so, how?
2. Will I get a perfect vector translation of a complex image? If not, why?
3. What process is used to cut apart a bitmap in Flash?

SESSION

Understanding Flash Audio

Session Checklist

✔ Configuring event sounds

✔ Creating stream sounds

✔ The Publish audio settings

30 Min. To Go

Just as our perception of the world is based on sound as much as sight, so too does Flash offer you the opportunity to fold audio components into your projects. In this chapter, you'll see exactly how. Flash deals with two types of sounds: event sounds and stream sounds. This chapter looks at both.

Creating Event Sounds

Event sounds are used to accentuate some "event" in the movie. In a sense, you can look at event sounds as sound effects. An event sound file will not start playing until that sound file has completely downloaded. (Remember that a Flash movie (.swf) can start playing immediately, before the whole file has downloaded, but that the sound within that file must be completely streamed down before it will start to play.) Let's explore the creation of an event sound. Do the following:

1. Load the CH_17Tower.fla file from the Projects folder on this book's CD-ROM.

2. When it appears, you will see that it has two layers — Sky below and Towers above. Add another layer on top, and name it My_EventSound_01. Make sure that the layers below the Sound layer have a 45 frame animation set. See Figure 18-1.

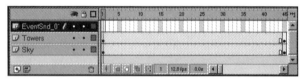

Figure 18-1
Add a layer for the sound file on top of the stack and create a 45-frame animation timeline for the other layers.

3. Go to File ⇨ Import. Find where your sound files are stored on your system, making sure the WAV format is selected for Windows users [AIFF for Mac users]. Either system can also incorporate MP3 sounds. If you have QuickTime 4 or higher on your system, other sound formats can be accessed as well. Select one of the sound files. See Figure 18-2.

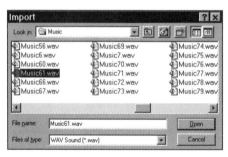

Figure 18-2
Select a sound file.

Session 18—Understanding Flash Audio

4. After the sound file has been imported, it appears in the Library window, along with a Preview/Playback button. See Figure 18-3.

Figure 18-3
The sound file appears in the Library window.

5. With the Sound layer selected, drag the sound file you imported from the library to the stage. Go to Window ➪ Panels ➪ Sound to access the Sound settings panel. See Figure 18-4.

Figure 18-4
The Sound settings panel.

6. Select the imported sound file in the Sound list of the settings panel. Select any effect you might like. Set Sync as Event and decide on a number of Loops. Preview your project to see what it "sounds" like.

7. Event sounds are set to a specific keyframe and last as long as the sound file is specified to. Some event sounds target one frame only, though they may repeat for whatever the value indicated under the Loops setting. See Figure 18-5.

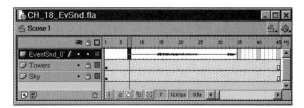

Figure 18-5
Here, the sound begins at frame 7 and lasts until frame 34. Event sounds are completely downloaded at once as a Flash Player file streams over the internet to a web browser, though they may play and repeat for whatever the value indicated under the Loops setting.

Please note that if you load this project from the book's CD instead of creating it on your own, you will have to supply your own sound file.

Creating Streaming Sounds

20 Min. To Go

You can add as many sound layers, each with different content, as you like. Try to keep each individual sound on its own layer. Streaming sound differs from event sound in that sync the playback of the animation is directly related to the playback of the sound, ensuring that the sound lasts as long as the animation does. You might think of streaming sound as a music or narration sound track. When the animation ends, the streamed sound ends as well. Flash usually tries to render every single frame of an animation. But if a streaming sound is playing, Flash locks the playback of animation to the playback of the streaming sound. This ensures that the animation will always remain exactly in sync with the streaming sound, but can result in some frames of the animation being clipped (skipped over during playback if the user's machine is too slow to render them in sync with the streaming sound). Streaming sound starts playing as soon as the animation downloads and is used for adding sound tracks to Web animations for that reason, although any animation can have both streaming and event sounds together on different layers. Looping, however, is not recommended for streaming sounds.

To create a streaming sound, do the following:

1. Go through the exact same process as for event sounds (in terms of importing sound files), but when you come to the use of the Sound settings panel, select Stream from the Sync list. Do this now, selecting an appropriate sound from your sound storage files. See Figure 18-6.

Session 18—Understanding Flash Audio

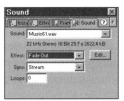

Figure 18-6
Select Stream from the Sync list.

2. To force any sound to stop at a specific frame on the timeline, place a keyframe on the sound layer at that frame number. Then go to the Sound settings panel and select Stop from the Sync list. See Figure 18-7. Make sure that you designate which sound you want to stop at that keyframe by selecting its name from the Sound pop-up.

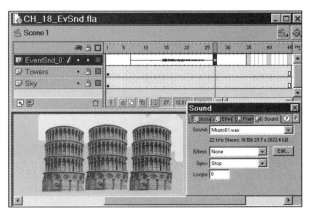

Figure 18-7
To stop the sound at a specific keyframe, select the keyframe and select the Stop function from the Sync list in the Sound settings panel.

You are ready to preview your streaming sound project.

Publish Settings for Audio

10 Min. To Go

Having already explored the Publish settings for graphics and animation data in Chapter 16, you are primed for learning something about configuring these settings for audio.

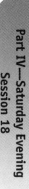

Note: Please remember that this is not a book about digital audio, so there is no guarantee that you will be an audio expert after reading these chapters. In fact, all I'm doing here is pointing you in the right direction to get to the audio configuration tab in the Publish Settings window. If you already know something about how these parameters differ from one another, knowing how to locate them will be a big plus.

Complete the following steps:

1. Go to File ➪ Publish Settings. The Publish Settings window appears. Check all of the Type options except Windows Projector and Mac Projector (these have no associated control pages). For all of the rest, a tab with the corresponding name appears at the top of the Formats page. See Figure 18-8.

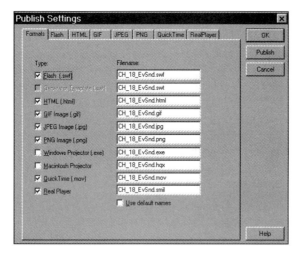

Figure 18-8
Tabs appear at the top of the Formats page, indicating that the selected format has control options.

2. Click on each of the tabs to access the control parameters; see if there are audio-related controls.
3. You will discover that the following formats have audio-related control parameters: Flash, QuickTime, and RealPlayer. That means that any of these three file formats are the ones to select to incorporate audio content for a Web page. See Figure 18-9.

Session 18—Understanding Flash Audio

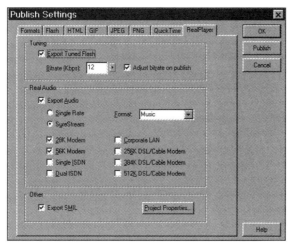

Figure 18-9
The RealAudio parameters can be found by accessing the RealPlayer tab in the Publish Settings window.

If you are planning to develop a Web movie that integrates audio, you will wind up using one of these three formats. You will want to learn as much as possible about the control parameters for the format or formats you are using. Just enter any or each of these terms in your Web search engine, and take note of the recommended sites listed.

REVIEW

In this chapter, you explored the following:

- Adding event and stream sound files to a Flash movie
- Configuring event sounds
- Configuring stream sounds
- Accessing the sound parameter controls in the Publish Settings window

QUIZ YOURSELF

1. What are the differences between event sounds and stream sounds?
2. How can I use event sounds in a Flash movie?

3. How can I use stream sounds in a Flash movie?
4. How can I stop a sound file at a specific point in a movie?
5. Where are the global audio parameter controls located in Flash?

SESSION

Working with Audio

Session Checklist

✔ Exploring multiple sound layers
✔ Duplicating sounds
✔ Using the Edit Envelope window

**30 Min.
To Go**

The last session showed you that adding an audio layer to a Flash movie is simple and straightforward. This chapter extends your awareness of Flash audio processes.

You must use your own sound files in these exercises. This book cannot provide you with copyrighted data.

Creating Multiple Sound Layers

Most movies would be rather boring with just one sound looping over and over again. A soundtrack sets an emotional tone, and that tone probably doesn't remain the same for the entire length of the animation. A narration has to start and stop at specific frames, and a sound effect has to be targeted to a frame in which an event takes place. For all of these reasons, most animations require more than one sound layer. Do the following to create multiple sound layers for your Flash movie:

1. Start a new Flash project (File ➪ New).
2. Create two new layers in the layer stack, giving you a total of three layers. Name them *Sound 1*, *Sound 2*, and *Sound 3*, respectively. Your Layer stack now looks like Figure 19-1.

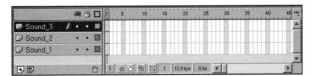

Figure 19-1
Your layer stack now looks like this.

3. Go to File ➪ Import and find the folder that contains your sound files. Import any three of your choice. They will appear in your library window, along with a Play button for previewing. Preview the sound if you like. See Figure 19-2.

Figure 19-2
Your three sound files will appear in your Library window.

4. Select Sound_1 in the stack to make it the current layer. Decide which sound in the library will be placed on Layer 1. Drag and drop it from the Library window to the Flash stage. The Sound appears in the Timeline window of the Sound_1 layer. Repeat this procedure for the other two layers.

Session 19—Working with Audio

5. Select the first frame of Sound_3 and go to Insert ⇨ Add Frame. This adds a frame just after frame 1. Drag this added frame to whatever position on the timeline represents the planned last frame in your animation. As you drag the frame, you see more of that layer's waveform revealed. Do this to each of the other two layers as well. See Figure 19-3.

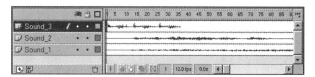

Figure 19-3
As you drag out the new frame, you reveal more of that layer's sound waveform.

Duplicating Sounds on the Timeline

20 Min. To Go

You may need to have the same sound repeated two or more times in a movie. Do as follows:

1. Make active one of your layers with a relatively short sound sample. Open the Sound panel (Window ⇨ Panels ⇨ Sound).

2. Select Event as the Sync option. Look at the way the waveform appears in the timeline for that layer. See Figure 19-4.

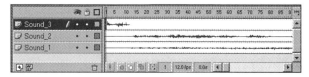

Figure 19-4
Notice the waveform's appearance on the current (top) layer.

3. Change the Loops setting from 1 to 3 in the Sound panel. Close the panel and click in the timeline for the current layer. The waveform is repeated three times in a row. See Figure 19-5.

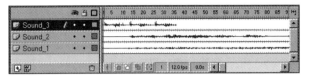

Figure 19-5
The waveform is now repeated three times in a row.

4. Click to select the current layer at the keyframe containing your looping sound, and go to Edit ⇨ Copy Frames. Click the same layer further along in the frame sequence — at an empty frame that has no waveform. After you have selected a blank frame, go to Edit ⇨ Paste Frames. The entire looped sequence is copied to that frame, so once the movie plays back, the sound sequence is heard at each of the exact frames where the sound begins, looping three times on each occasion. See Figure 19-6.

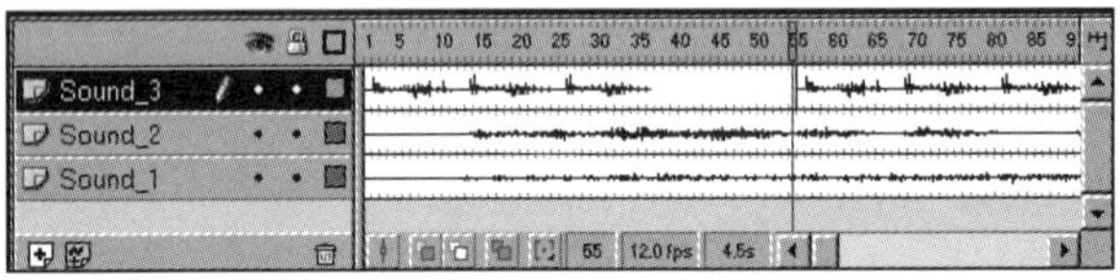

Figure 19-6
Copy a duplicate keyframe to the frame designated by the playhead.

> **Tip:** If you plan to use the same event sound at different points along the timeline, it's usually best to leave looping set to 1, and then copy and paste that single sequence where it's needed on the layer's timeline.

Editing the Sound Envelope

Think of the envelope as a way of picturing the sound amplitude (volume) over time. Do the following to edit the sound envelope:

1. To edit the sound Envelope, you need to first click the Edit button in the Sound panel for the selected sample. See Figures 19-7 and 19-8.

Session 19—Working with Audio 225

Figure 19-7
Click the Edit button in the Sound panel to access the Edit Envelope window.

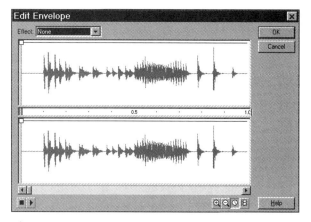

Figure 19-8
The Edit Envelope window appears.

2. As you can see in the Edit Envelope window in Figure 19-8, the sound's waveform is displayed twice. The top display is for the left audio channel; the bottom display represents the right audio channel.

3. Open the Effect list at the top left of the Edit Envelope window and select Fade Left to Right. Look at the envelope. The left audio channel shows the sound amplitude going from full volume to zero, while the right audio channel is doing the opposite. The result? The sound gets progressively quieter in the left channel and increasingly louder in the right channel. See Figure 19-9.

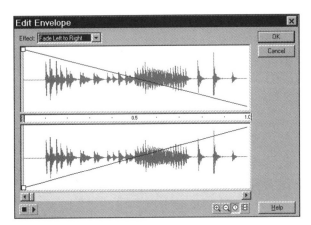

Figure 19-9
The graph tells you what Fade Left to Right looks like.

4. Now select Custom from the Effect list. Click the graph line in either the left or right channel displays. This creates a control point, which you can move up or down to effect the sound's amplitude and left or right to determine what time in the sounds playback time or frame in the timeline the amplitude occurs at. Do this on both channel graphs, moving the amplitude randomly. You can create interesting bi-channel panning effects in this manner when you are working with sounds saved in stereo. See Figure 19-10.

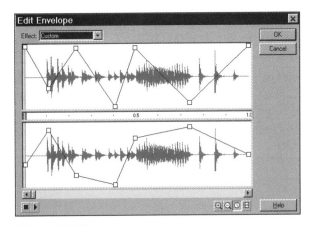

Figure 19-10
You can create interesting effects by moving the control points on the amplitude line for either or both the left and right audio channel.

Creating a warble effect

To create a warble effect for a selected sound, refer to the shape on the Edit Envelope window, as displayed in Figure 19-11.

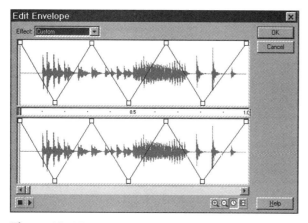

Figure 19-11
This Envelope shape creates a warble effect for the sound.

Done! Save your project to disk.

REVIEW

- Creating sounds on multiple layers
- Configuring sound placement on layers
- Copying and pasting sounds
- Editing sound envelopes

QUIZ YOURSELF

1. How do I get to the Sound panel?
2. What does looping do?
3. Looping is not recommended for what sound Sync type?
4. What is amplitude?
5. How do I create sound effects in the Edit Envelope window?

SESSION

20

Applying Sound to Animations

Session Checklist

✔ Creating an animated title

✔ Configuring slide-show images

✔ Adding integrated sound layers

30 Min. To Go

N ow that you have an understanding of how Flash enables you to manipulate Sound files, it's time to integrate your awareness of sound with the sound of graphics and animation.

Animated Slide Shows

An animated slide show is a series of still images that remain onscreen for a few seconds before another image replaces them. Animated slides are an important option for displaying information. In this example, you'll create a sequence of animated slides, accompanied by a sound effect when each gives way to the next slide.

Animated slide shows commonly display a dozen or more images, but this exercise uses only five images. When you understand the process, you can always plug in more images.

Animated titles

We'll start by creating an animated title, drawing on processes you have learned thus far. Do the following:

1. Make sure you start with a frame in the default layer. Name the default layer Title.
2. Click the Text tool. Click the stage to create a new text box.
3. Go to Text ⇨ Font and select any font you want to use. Go to Text ⇨ Size and select 72. This is just our beginning size, because we will be animating the size of the text. Go to Text ⇨ Style and select Bold.
4. Type **My Images**. The text appears in your new text box on the stage. See Figure 20-1.

Figure 20-1
The text appears onscreen.

5. Time to do a calculation to set the total length of the movie. Set the length of the Title layer animation to two seconds. The five slides will be given one second each. Each second contains a specified number of frames. You can set the frames-per-second (fps) value by selecting Modify ⇨ Movie in the menus or by double clicking the fps box at the bottom of the Timeline window. See Figure 20-2.

Figure 20-2
The fps box at the bottom of the Timeline window.

6. Double-click the fps area to bring up the Movie Properties window, shown in Figure 20-3.

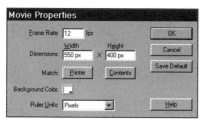

Figure 20-3
The Movie Properties window

7. In the Movie Properties window, keep the Frame Rate value at its default of 12 fps. Set the Width and Height Dimensions to whatever you like. I prefer 320×240 pixels. Set the Background Color to a light blue. Click OK to activate the settings.

8. With the fps set to 12, calculate the length of the animated slide show. The Title layer animation is two seconds long. With the rate of 12 fps, the Title layer animation is 24 frames long (12 fps×2 seconds). The five slides are each one second long. Therefore, with the rate of 12 fps, these five slides are a total of 60 frames long (12 fps×5 seconds). So, the total length of the animation is 84 frames (60 frames plus 24 frames).

9. Add a layer and name it Timing. Draw a small oval far outside of the active stage layer, causing the Timing layer to create a keyframe at frame 1. Select the keyframe and add a frame. Frame 2 is added. Drag the added frame to position 84 on the Timeline window. This sets up the animation length, independent of any other layer. See Figure 20-4.

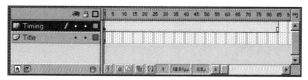

Figure 20-4
The animation length is set up by adding a Timing layer.

10. Select Frame 1 of the Title layer and select Add Frame. Drag the added frame to position 24 on the Timeline window. Create a Motion Tween. Play the animation so far. The text stays onscreen for 24 frames and then disappears. See Figure 20-5.

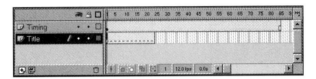

Figure 20-5
The Timeline window now looks like this.

11. Select the first frame of the Title layer. Enlarge the text so that it is huge, extending far beyond the borders of the stage.

12. Move the playhead to Frame 12. Resize the text so that it fits within the borders of the stage. Note that a Motion Tween is automatically created from Frame 1 to Frame 12. The rest of the Title segment remains static, so the Frame 12 size remains until Frame 24, when the Title disappears. Run the animation to test it. The Title animation creates what is called a *zoom out*. See Figures 20-6 and 20-7.

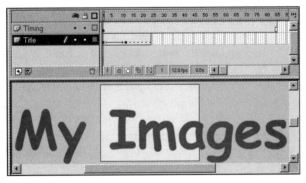

Figure 20-6
At Frame 1, the title is huge.

Session 20—Applying Sound to Animations

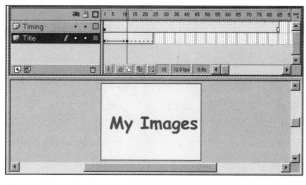

Figure 20-7
At Frame 12, the title fits on the stage.

Placing the slides

**20 Min.
To Go**

Now it's time to import and position five images. You can use your own images or use images provided on the CD-ROM. The images on the CD-ROM are named AA1.jpg, AA2.jpg, AA3.jpg, AA4.jpg, and AA5.jpg. They are in the Resources folder. Proceed as follows:

1. Create five new layers and name them Slide_1, Slide_2, Slide_3, Slide_4, and Slide_5.
2. Import the five images and open the Library window so that you can see the images.
3. Place each image at frame 1 on its appropriate layer (slide 1 on the Slide_1 layer, and so on). Resize and position each to fit within the stage area.
4. Move the starting and ending frames of each layer so that they overlap, first frame to last frame on the Timeline window, with each layer lasting 12 frames (1 second at 12 fps). See what this looks like in Figure 20-8.
5. Control ⇨ Test Movie to see your animation so far.

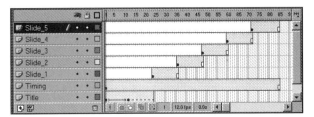

Figure 20-8
The Timeline window should look like this when the slides have been placed and the frames configured.

Adding Sound in a Slide Show

Now comes the final step in a slide show — adding sound. Do the following:

1. Create two new layers. Name the first layer SFX (for sound effects). Name the second layer Score.
2. Use your own sound score for the Score layer or load the Score.wav file from the Resources folder on the CD-ROM (you must be able to use a WAV file if you load the Score.wav file).
3. Make sure the Score layer sound's Sync pop-up is set to stream. Select Edit in the Sound panel and create a graph in the Edit Envelope window that resembles Figure 20-9.

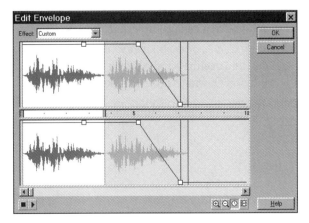

Figure 20-9
This envelope shape causes the score sound to fade out at the end of the animation.

Session 20—Applying Sound to Animations

4. Open the Flash Common Library called Sounds; drag the Camera Shutter 3 file into your own Project Library. See Figure 20-10.

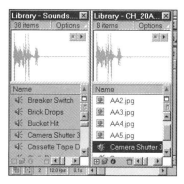

Figure 20-10
Drag the Camera Shutter 3 sound from the Sounds Common Library to your Project Library.

5. Place this sound on the SFX layer and move it to Frame 24, where the first slide comes in. Make sure it is an event sync sound with Loop set to 1. Copy and paste four more of these sounds on the same layer, at the frames where the other slides start. Your Timeline window should now resemble Figure 20-11.

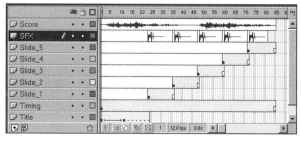

Figure 20-11
The finished project Timeline layers.

Preview the animation using Test Movie. Go back and tweak the timing if necessary and save to disk. Congratulations on completing your first Flash slide show!

Done!

If you like, you can edit the score sound again, decreasing the amplitude (volume) throughout so that the SFX stand out more.

Review

In this exercise, you learned how to create an animated slide show, including the following:

- The animated title
- The slide content
- The addition of sound layers

Quiz Yourself

1. What is a zoom out animation?
2. What is the process for making images appear and disappear as it relates to the Timeline window?
3. What can I use an SFX sound layer for?
4. What can I use a Score sound layer for?
5. What is the process for fading out a sound at the end of a Flash movie?

PART IV

Saturday Evening Part Review

1. What is amplitude?
2. How are sound effects created in the Edit Envelope window?
3. How can imported bitmaps be scaled and rotated?
4. Will I always get a perfect vector translation of a complex image?
5. What is the Timeline process for making images appear and disappear called?
6. What is an SFX sound layer used for?
7. What are event sounds used for in a Flash movie?
8. What are stream sounds used for in a Flash movie?
9. How do I get to the Sound panel?
10. What does looping do?
11. What sound sync type is looping not recommended for?
12. How can a sound file be forced to stop at a specific point in the movie?
13. Where are the global audio parameter controls located in Flash?
14. What is a *zoom out* animation?
15. What is a score sound layer used for?
16. What is the process used to cut apart a bitmap in Flash?
17. What are the differences between event sounds and stream sounds?
18. How can I fade out a sound at the end of a Flash movie?

☑ Friday

☑ Saturday

☑ **Sunday**

Part V — Sunday Morning

Session 21
Designing Animations and Buttons

Session 22
Wipe F/X

Session 23
It's About Time

Session 24
Using Onion Skins

Session 25
Creating Strobes and Advanced Reveals

Session 26
Developing Nested Animations

Part VI — Sunday Afternoon

Session 27
Exploring Gradients

Session 28
Advanced Bitmap Techniques

Session 29
Understanding Instance Effects

Session 30
Exploring Flash 3-D

Session 31
Handshaking

PART V

Sunday Morning

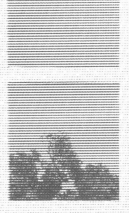

Session 21
Designing Animations and Buttons

Session 22
Wipe F/X

Session 23
It's About Time

Session 24
Using Onion Skins

Session 25
Creating Strobes and Advanced Reveals

Session 26
Developing Nested Animations

SESSION

Designing Animations and Buttons

Session Checklist

✔ Creating an interactive button
✔ Designing an animation
✔ Controlling playback with a button

**30 Min.
To Go**

The main character in this session's animation is also an interactive button that controls his own fate, so he can't blame anyone but himself for his circumstances. He either enjoys the pain, or forgets what has just happened to him the last time he gave the orders. The character is at once an interactive button and the target of the action.

Creating the Animated Button Character

Using a character in an animation opens up all sorts of possibilities. This session lays out some basic ideas, allowing you to explore the topic further. Here's what to do:

1. Select the Pencil tool and open the Stroke panel (Window ➪ Panels ➪ Stroke). Set the Line Thickness to 2.25 with a Solid Stroke. See Figure 21-1.

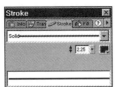

Figure 21-1
Set the pencil line thickness and stroke type in the Stroke panel.

2. Draw a simple profile of a cartoon character's head. Use your imagination. You eventually will make this a symbol, so size is not a concern.

3. Next to the character's head, use the Text tool to create the word *Ready* in any font and size you prefer. Draw a small pointer coming from the character's mouth to the text. See Figure 21-2.

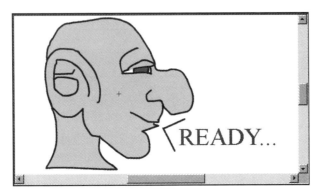

Figure 21-2
A character's head with text next to it.

4. Select the entire figure with the Arrow tool and go to Insert ⇨ Convert to Symbol. When the Symbol Properties window appears, select Button and name the Button *Face*. See Figure 21-3.

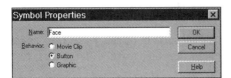

Figure 21-3
Name the symbol Face *and make it a Button.*

Session 21—Designing Animations and Buttons

5. After closing the Symbol Properties window, the Face object appears as a symbol in your Library window. See Figure 21-4.

Figure 21-4
The Face object appears in your Library window.

6. Open the Options list in the Library window and select Edit. Now you are in Symbol Edit mode for the button, and the Timeline window looks slightly different than it does in standard mode. Four button "states" appear in the Timeline window. From left to right, the states are *Up, Over, Down,* and *Hit*. The last state, Hit, enables you to define any shape and size you like as the *hot area*, the area that triggers transformation when a mouse cursor passes over it. Up defines the button's Up position, Over is when the mouse cursor glides over the Hit area that you have defined, and Down is a mouse click over the Hit area. See Figure 21-5.

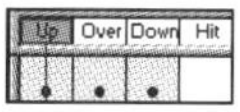

Figure 21-5
The Button Edit Timeline, displaying the Up, Over, and Down states, and the Hit area trigger state.

7. By default, the character you drew is placed in the Up frame of the button. Move the Playhead to the Over frame and use the drawing tools to alter the figure. In this example, lace the word *Set* next to the figure, erasing the word Ready first. See Figure 21-6.

8. Now for the Down state. Move the Playhead to the Down frame in the Timeline window and reshape the figure again. This time, type the word **GO** in somewhat larger letters. See Figure 21-7.

Figure 21-6
Alter the figure any way you like and place the word Set next to him.

Figure 21-7
Reshape the figure for the Down state of the button.

9. As a final editing step, designate the button's active Hit area by selecting the rectangle tool, then dragging to create a new rectangular shape on the stage. Make sure your new rectangle is about the size of your character's face. Your face symbol is complete.

20 Min. To Go

Creating Button-Driven Animation

Now you'll create the animation that the Face button will interact with. Do the following:

1. Add a frame to the layer with the Face button content. Drag out the new frame to Frame 45. This sets the animation length.

Session 21—Designing Animations and Buttons

2. Create three or four new layers. With each new layer selected in turn, create a basic oval and/or rectangle offstage. You will create a total of four. Place the shapes offstage so that they can enter the stage later.

3. Use your accumulated knowledge of keyframe animation to create a movie that enables each object to enter the stage, strike the character, and then bounce offstage again. Give each of the objects a different animation path, enabling each to strike the character a different number of times from a different angle. Your Timeline window might resemble the one displayed in Figure 21-8.

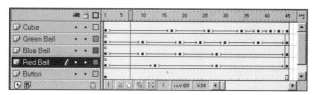

Figure 21-8
Here is a Timeline window that shows random keyframes for all of the objects that are in play.

4. Control ⇨ Test Movie to see what needs to be adjusted. So far, the movie plays with no interference from or with the character Button. See Figure 21-9.

Figure 21-9
Frames from the animation show the objects bouncing off the character.

Make sure that the objects are offstage at the start and at the end of the animation.

**10 Min.
To Go**

Assigning Actions

Now let's assign some actions so that the character not only interacts with the objects, but also controls them. Do the following:

1. Click the Face object on the stage and go to Window ⇨ Actions. Because we are assigning actions to an object, the Object Actions window opens. See Figure 21-10.

Figure 21-10
The Object Actions window.

2. Actions are scripts. Some are simple, and some require a knowledge of programming. You are going to stick to an action script that is very basic. On the left of the Object Actions window is a list of the types of actions that you can assign, all under separate categories. Open the list of Basic Actions.

3. By double clicking any action, the selected action appears in the right-hand column as one element in a script. Script actions can be moved, deleted, copied, and pasted when they reside in the right-hand column. Their order is important, indicating in what order each action is processed. Double-click the following actions in the Basic Actions list for the Face object *GoTo*. That's the only Action you need in this script.

4. The GoTo script has two lines. The top line determines what the mouse must do (or what a keyboard entry should do) to trigger the action. The bottom line determines what the action is. Highlight the first line of the GoTo action, and its parameter settings controls appear below it. Click Release to set the mouse action. Release designates that the button action will be triggered after the user clicks the mouse and releases the mouse button. See Figure 21-11.

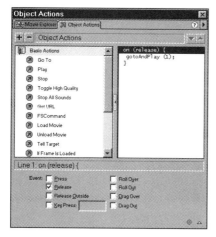

Figure 21-11
Check Release for the first GoTo action parameter.

5. Highlight the second line of the action script. Make sure "Go to and Play" is checked and that the Frame number is set to 1. See Figure 21-12.

6. Close the Object Actions window. Play the movie now. It isn't exactly what you want. The animation runs constantly, although it starts all over again when the Face button is clicked. You have to do one more thing — assign another action.

7. Click any of the other Object layers at Frame 1 to activate it. Go to Window ⇨ Actions. This time the window that appears is called *Frame Actions* (see Figure 21-13). The Frame Actions window targets the frames in a layer, not a specific object. You want to create a script that tells the contents of that layer to stop, so nothing will happen until it is triggered by the Face button's action script. Select the Stop action as the only action script component. Repeat this for the other Object layers (not for the Button layer, however). Preview the movie — it's very funny. Save it to disk.

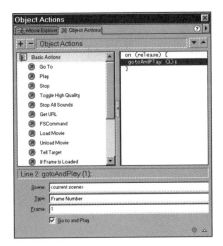

Figure 21-12
Make sure "Go To and Play" is checked and that the Frame is set to 1.

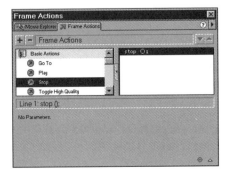

Figure 21-13
Use the Stop action for the only action script component for the layers.

  If you want to explore adding some Sound layers, think about using separate event sounds on each Object layer. Use a *Thunk* or a *Sprong* each time one of the objects interacts with the character. Perhaps you might also use an *Ouch!* soon after that.

Done!

Session 21—Designing Animations and Buttons

REVIEW

In this session, we explored how an element in a Flash movie can be both a main character and an interactive button, allowing you to control animation through interaction. This opens up a wide range of possibilities, from interactive-learning module designs to entertainment presentations. This session covered the following:

- The design of a character or a button
- Assignment of the button states
- The creation of animation controlled by a button
- Assigning Frame and Object actions

QUIZ YOURSELF

1. What are the three animated states of a button?
2. What is the fourth state used for?
3. What is an Object action?
4. How is a Frame action different from an Object action?
5. Name three projects that would benefit from interactive character buttons?

SESSION

Wipe F/X

Session Checklist

✔ Creating a radial wipe

✔ Creating a shatter wipe

✔ Creating a patterned animation array

**30 Min.
To Go**

In video terminology, a *wipe* is an effect that enables one image to move, dissolve, or break apart in order to reveal another image. You can see wipe effects used on television all the time. Wipes are related to reveals, which you learned about in Chapter 14. This chapter extends your learning in that direction by detailing how you can use Flash to create more advanced projects.

The Radial Wipe

The radial wipe moves in a circular manner from the center of the overlaying image to the edges, and vice versa. Radial wipes usually involve two bitmap images. As one image is cleared from the screen, it reveals the presence of another layer's content. In the following exercise you'll work with one bitmap image, although you can apply the same technique later to your own unique animation content.

In the following exercise, you can use your own image or the image labeled CH22_01.jpg, which is located in the Resources folder on the CD-ROM that comes with this book.

1. Create three layers. Name the bottom layer Image. Name the middle layer Wipe. Name the top layer Text.
2. Select the bottom layer and import a bitmap for it. Make it a nature picture.
3. On the middle layer, create a circle that is all fill and no stroke. The fill color doesn't matter at all.
4. Select Frame 1 of the middle layer on the timeline and create a new frame. The new frame will appear at the Frame 2 position. Drag it out to Frame 90.
5. Place a keyframe at Frame 90. Select your newly created circle at Frame 90, and enlarge the circle until it is about twice as large as the stage. Make this layer a Shape Tweened layer in the Frame window. The middle layer now has an animation that shows the small circle becoming larger over time.
6. Place the playhead at Frame 65. Activate the top layer to make it current. Place a text block on that layer that reads Wilderness. Center it over the image. Click Frame 65, which is now a keyframe, and select Add a Frame. Drag this frame out to Frame 90. The text will appear at Frame 65 and stay until Frame 90.
7. Make the Image layer a masked layer and make the Wipe layer a mask layer. (Right-click on layer and select Mask from the contextual menu, or go to the main menus and select Modify ➪ Layer for both mask and masked layers.) The animating circle acts as a wipe, creating a transparent hole that enables you to see through to the layer below the image. Preview the animation, make any adjustments necessary, and save it to a disk. See Figure 22-1.

20 Min. To Go

The Shatter Wipe

Here's another wipe whose use is fairly common in broadcast video. It's a reveal that shows a top image or color background falling apart in order to display what is underneath. To learn more, complete the following steps:

1. Open a new Flash project. Create two layers, each with bitmap content. Select any two of your own images for this exercise. Place one image on each layer.

Session 22—Wipe F/X 253

Figure 22-1
Four frames from the radial wipe animation

2. Select the image on the top layer and go to Modify ⇨ Break Apart. The image will be broken into a selected editable shape, and appears with white dots over its surface.

3. Select the first keyframe of the top layer and select Add Frame. Move this frame to Frame 90 and create another keyframe there. Now it's time to shatter the image.

4. Go to Frame 20 on the top layer and create another keyframe there. At Frame 20, use the Polygon Select tool to create shards from the image and move the shards away from the rest of the image. *Shards,* as I use the term here, refers to sharp-edged slices of the image, created easily by outlining the shard shapes with the Polygon tool.. Each time you click and drag the Polygon tool, you create an edge. When you click on the first point again, the shard becomes a separated object. Do this until the image looks as if a projectile has shattered it. See Figure 22-2.

5. Go to Frame 45 and create another keyframe on the same layer. Add more movement to each of the pieces by pulling them further apart. Make sure they start to extend beyond the stage area. See Figure 22-3.

6. Repeat this procedure at Frame 60 and again at Frame 80, where the shards should be totally outside of the stage boundary.

7. Create a shape tween in the Frame Panel between every keyframe but not at the first frame. This enables the shatter to occur suddenly.

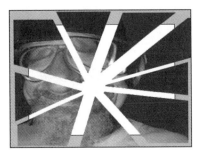

Figure 22-2
Move sections of the image to resemble a shattered piece of glass.

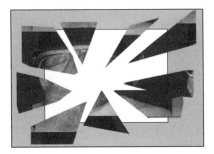

Figure 22-3
The pieces are on the move.

8. Make sure that the bottom layer also extends to Frame 90. Preview the animation and save it to a disk.

 A Flash shatter is interesting because the shattered pieces try to contain the whole image at times, resembling the reflections of solid glass.

10 Min. To Go

Creating an Animated Patterned Background

The following steps show you how to create a background that displays small, animated elements.

Session 22—Wipe F/X

1. Rename the default layer of a new Flash movie Timer. This will be a layer that helps set up the timing of an animation. With its first frame selected, place a tiny circle somewhere offstage in order to create an instant keyframe at position 1. Select Add Frame and drag that frame out to position 90. Now you have set up the general parameters for an animation.

2. Go to File ⇨ Open as Library and open the CH_07A.fla file from this book's CD-ROM. This is the flying bird created earlier in Chapter 7. Move the Bird symbol to your Project Library. See Figure 22-4.

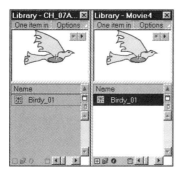

Figure 22-4
Move the Bird symbol to your own Project Library.

3. Create a new layer called *Bird 1* and place the Bird symbol from your symbol library on it.

4. Create a keyframe at Frame 10, and copy and paste another Bird symbol, moving it somewhere else in a flock. You should now have one instance of your bird at the first keyframe, and instances of it at the second. Insert another keyframe 10 to 15 frames later with another Bird symbol and move it to somewhere else in the flock. You will now have three birds at the third keyframe. Continue this process with more keyframes and pasted bird instances until you have created a larger flock. Load a background of your choice, preferably one with clouds. *Do not* create any tweens on the Bird layer. Animated symbols run without any need for tweening. See Figure 22-5.

Figure 22-5
As the animation progresses, animated birds appear in the flock.

Done!

This is really a wipe in reverse, focusing upon the capability to create interesting content from more than one Symbol.

REVIEW

In this session, you learned more about creating unique wipes and related effects. No doubt, working through these exercises has given you all sorts of ideas. Here's what was covered:

- Creating a wipe based upon mask and masked layers.
- Using the Break Apart operation to shatter a bitmap.
- Creating an array of animated symbols in order to generate a pattern effect over a background.

QUIZ YOURSELF

1. How is a radial wipe created?
2. How can a text block pop onscreen exactly where it is supposed to?
3. What is a shatter?
4. How is a bitmap shattered?
5. Should tweening be used with a layer of multiple symbols? Why or why not?

SESSION

It's About Time

Session Checklist

✔ Creating an animated clock
✔ Creating a digital symbol display
✔ Creating an hour glass

*30 Min.
To Go*

All of the exercises in this session are designed to heighten your awareness of how well Flash can be integrated with 3-D graphics. In this session, you'll learn how to create three different types of timepieces and how to animate them. Each of these three exercises integrate Flash with 3-D bitmap content.

All of the content (Clock_01.jpg, DigClk.jpg, and HrGls.jpg) needed for projects in this chapter can be found in the Resources folder of this book's CD-ROM.

Creating the Clock

When you think of a clock, you normally think of an object used to keep time, with the expected numerals 1 to 12 on its face. However, the design of a clock can incorporate any symbolic character, like this one, to remind you of what you are doing now. Do the following:

1. Open a new project, and load the Clock_01.jpg image from the Resources folder on this book's CD-ROM. This image was created by the author especially for this exercise in 3D Studio Max. Drag the image out of the library and drop it on the default layer. Name this layer Bkgrd. Resize the image as needed and center it on the stage. See Figure 23-1.

Figure 23-1
The Clock image is imported and positioned for Layer 1.

2. Select the first frame of the layer (which is now a keyframe) and select Add Frame. Drag the added frame to position 60 on the timeline. This sets the animation's length.

3. Create a layer above the Bkgrd layer, and name it Symbols. Create one more above that, and name it Hand.

4. Select the Symbols layer. Use the Text tool and type a line of text that says **FLASHWEEKEND**, making it all one word. Leave a space between each letter and use a 36-point type with your choice of font. Make it bold and italic.

5. With the text block selected, go to Modify ⇨ Break Apart. This enables you to select and move each letter independently. Select each letter and move it over the background clock until your image looks like the one displayed in Figure 23-2.

Figure 23-2
Move the letters until the image looks like this.

6. Now to create a timepiece hand. Select the Hand layer. Use the drawing tools to create your version of the graphic displayed in Figure 23-3.

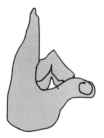

Figure 23-3
Use the drawing tools to create a hand.

7. Make the hand a symbol (Insert ⇨ Convert To Symbol) and name it Hand. Cut the original, and Paste it back on the appropriate layer, moving hand over the clock so that it points to the "F". See Figure 23-4.

Figure 23-4
Place the hand instance so it points to the "F".

8. Select the Hand and go to Rotate ⇨ Transform ⇨ Edit Center. You are going to move the center point of this particular instance of the hand so that it is roughly at the center point of the clock. When the center point becomes visible, move it to the center point of the clock. See Figure 23-5.

Figure 23-5
Move the center point of the hand to the center point of the clock.

9. Set a keyframe on the Hand layer at every five frames. Then move the playhead sequentially to each keyframe, and go to Modify ⇨ Transform ⇨ Rotate to rotate the Hand so that it address every keyframe by pointing in a clockwise direction to every letter on the clock. Preview the movie and save to disk. See Figure 23-6.

Figure 23-6
The hand rotates around the clock, reminding you that you are immersed in the Flash Weekend Crash Course.

Session 23—It's About Time

20 Min.
To Go

Creating a Digital Display

This strange device was found in a field in Indiana just moments after an alien craft vaporized into the atmosphere. It was later discovered to be an intergalactic clock, whose display always kept the travelers abreast of the time when their soap operas would be transmitted. To create the animated display in Flash, do the following:

1. File ➪ Import the DigClk.jpg file from the Resources folder on this book's CD-ROM. Resize as necessary to cover the entire stage on the default layer. Rename this layer Image. Go to Insert Frame and drag the added frame to the Frame 45 position. See Figure 23-7.

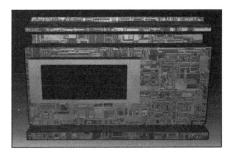

Figure 23-7
The DigClik.jpg image is placed on the bottom layer.

2. Use any symbol layer and create 4 lines of text in separate text blocks, using a graphical font. It can be Wingding, Dingbat, Astrology, or Hieroglyphic font, anything that looks a bit strange. Convert each of the 4 lines of text, one at a time, into a symbol (Insert ➪ Convert To Symbol). Name the text lines Symbol_1, Symbol_2, Symbol_3, and Symbol_4.

3. Delete the text from the stage. Place one instance of a text line on each of the four symbol layers, one per layer. Position each text block over the dark area of the bitmap image, which we'll be using for our screen area in this animation. Set varying lengths for the frames each text block resides in, and repeat this action randomly on the four layers, making sure that the frames don't overlap. Your final placements on the timeline will resemble something similar to Figure 23-8.

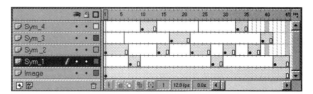

Figure 23-8
The instances of the symbolic font are placed on the timeline, repeated and staggered.

4. Preview the animation and you see strange messages posted on the screen of the alien device. See Figure 23-9.

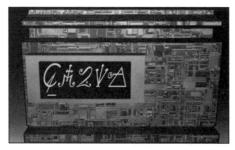

Figure 23-9
Perhaps the device is indicating that it's dinnertime.

 Tip **You could definitely enhance this effect by placing a *beep* sound event at every keyframe that appears on the symbol layers.**

Creating an Hour Glass

10 Min. To Go

This exercise underlines the importance of the connection between Flash and 3D graphics to create interesting animations. We will create an hourglass filled with animated sand that reacts to gravity. Do the following:

1. Import the image called HrGls.jpg from the Resource folder on this book's CD-ROM. Center and resize on the default layer. Name the layer Bkgrd. See Figure 23-10.

Figure 23-10
The Hourglass image is used as the background.

2. Insert a frame and drag it to position 60. This creates the animation's length.
3. Create two more layers, named Down and Up. Use a yellow fill to paint a shape on the Up layer (the top of the hourglass), which represents sand. See Figure 23-11.

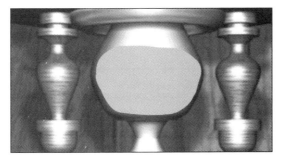

Figure 23-11
Paint some sand into the top of the hourglass.

4. Create a series of keyframes about every 20 frames. In each of the keyframes, as they progress, use the Arrow tool to select sections of the top of the sand pile for deletion.
5. Use shape tweening between all of the keyframes on the Up layer.
6. Go to the Down layer, and create keyframes for a series of larger and larger piles of sand by using the Paint tool. Use keyframes at the same points as you did for the Up layer.
7. Create one more layer called Stream. Use it to create a stream of sand from the Up layer to the Down layer, exploring your own design. Keyframe over time to give it some variance, and use a shape tween between each keyframe. See Figure 23-12.

Done!

Figure 23-12
A series of frames from the animation show the movement of the sand.

REVIEW

This session focused up some of the ways that Flash can be used in conjunction with 3-D graphics to create interesting movies. You learned to:

- Create a revolving object centered upon a background bitmap
- Create text objects that appear and vanish according to your needs
- Generate a shape-tweened animation that uses a background 3-D image as a reference

QUIZ YOURSELF

1. How can I move the center point of an image?
2. What fonts can be used to create an impression of alien text?
3. What type of tweening is used when the objects are to pop up on screen?
4. To create an easy flow of material like sand, what type of tweening do I use?

SESSION 24

Using Onion Skins

Session Checklist

✔ Understanding rotoscope editing

✔ Generating speed lines

✔ Using onion-skinned backgrounds

**30 Min.
To Go**

Onion skins have a long history of use in traditional animation endeavors. The term originally referred to the tracing paper an animator placed over her or his work in order to make the next rough cel (what now is referred to as a frame) refer to the cel drawn before it. Traditionally, animation uses four types of animators, each a master in their own right. The *keyframe animator* did just that and nothing else, creating the main keyframe art to define the story. The *tweener* (in-between animator) developed all of the drawings from one keyframe cel to the next. The *background artist* was and is usually a fine artist trained in traditional painting and illustration. The *colorist* applied color to the back of the mylar cel drawings to get them ready for the camera. Onion skins are used in Flash much as they are used in traditional animation.

Using Rotoscope Editing

Rotoscoping is the action of hand-drawing lines on a translucent surface placed over a photograph, frame of a movie, or any type of 3-D image. When a photo or other type of realistic image is rotoscoped, it *flattens out*, and the image looks more cartoon-like. If the image is a digital one, the rotoscoped image that results will also take far less disk storage space than the source image. When you use the bitmap to vector conversion capability in Flash, you are rotoscoping. There are times, however, when you want to place your own personalized style on the process; using the Flash onion-skinning process is perfect for such an operation. Complete the following steps:

1. Import a bitmap image sequence onto the default layer in a new Flash project. You can select any image sequence on your system or you can import the Face.jpg image sequence (three images) from the Seq folder inside the Resource folder on this book's CD-ROM. See Figure 24-1.

Figure 24-1
Import a bitmap sequence for a rotoscoping source and place it on the default layer in a Flash project. This is the first frame of the sequence of three images supplied on the CD-ROM.

This sequence was created in Adobe After Effects, using a *Bloat* filter.

2. Make sure View ➪ Snap To Objects is checked. Resize each of the three images to fit the stage.
3. Create another layer above the default layer, and name it Roto.
4. Rotoscoping is an animation operation. You can do the initial rotoscoping operation without using any onion skinning.

5. On the Roto layer, use the Pencil tool to trace each of the frames. Make your drawings loose, but try to close all distinct areas.

Note When you use the Pencil tool, uncheck View ➪ Snap To Objects. Also alternate between the Ink option and Smooth.

6. When you are finished drawing lines to represent the contours of the three images below, your drawings should look loose, as in Figure 24-2.

Figure 24-2
Your three drawings will look loose like this.

7. Make Layer 1 invisible and preview the animated results. What if you wanted to see the previous or next frames from any single keyframe, in order to edit any of the frames? How could you do that? That's where onion skinning comes in.

8. Go to the Onion Skin controls at the bottom of the timeline. See Figure 24-3.

Figure 24-3
The Onion Skin controls

9. Make sure that the background image is off, and then click the first Onion Skin control. This applies onion skinning to the movie. Notice that the Onion Skin markers are placed above the timeline. See Figure 24-4.

10. Switch to any keyframe and you can see all of the other frames, although they are ghosted out. See Figure 24-5.

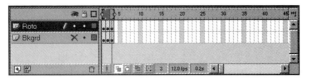

Figure 24-4
The Onion Skin markers are placed above the timeline.

Figure 24-5
With Onion Skin on, all of the frames are visible as an underlay.
The active frame appears most opaque.

11. Switching on the second control, Onion Skin outlines, creates thinner representations of the other frames and is useful when you want to edit the active frame in reference to the others. Preview and save your work. See Figure 24-6.

Figure 24-6
Thin lines represent the other frames when you switch on Onion Skin Outlines.

Session 24—Using Onion Skins

Please note that you will have to delete the background layer if you want to record a movie that shows only your rotoscoped work.

Creating Speed Lines

20 Min. To Go

Pass your hand quickly in front of your eyes. Can you see the images that trail behind your hand as it moves? In 3-D animation this is called a *motion trail*, but traditional cartoonists also use the older term *speed lines*. You can create speed lines in Flash. Do the following:

1. Create a ten frame animation that shows a filled circle traveling from one area of the stage to another. Use all the skills you have mastered so far to accomplish this.

2. Switch Onion Skin on. Click the last Onion Skin control, which is the Modify Onion Markers pop-up menu, and select Onion 5 from the list. This sets the number of ghosted frames at five.

3. Select a frame and move the red Onion Skin marker to that frame unless it moves automatically. Look at the frame five frames back from this one, and you see the onion skin effect. The onion skin effect is the same as a motion trail or a speed line.

4. To create a speed line animation, all you have to do is to select each frame and use a screen grab utility to grab the stage. A screen grab utility is a software program that allows you to freeze the screen, placing a copy of it in the Clipboard. As long as it remains there, it can be pasted down in any application that has a Paste command. Save each image with a corresponding sequential frame number (for example, MyImage_001.jpg). Put all of the single frames together in another Flash session and record as an animation. See Figure 24-7.

Please note that the previous exercise is not hinted at in the Flash documentation.

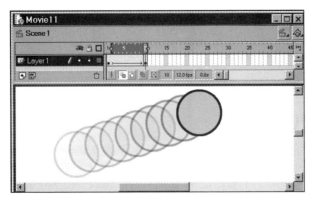

Figure 24-7
If you grab the screen with the Onion Skin option on, you can create frames for a speed-lined movie.

**10 Min.
To Go**

Creating an Onion Skin Background

Here's how to create a neat background treatment using the Onion Skin option, especially for logos. Do the following:

1. Create a text block that says **Acme Industries**. Using your accumulated knowledge, develop a ten frame animation that shows the text moving from the lower-left to the upper-right area of the stage. Use motion tweening to move the text block.

2. Turn Onion Skin on and select the last control (Modify Onion Markers); next, select Onion All from the list. Look at the last frame of your animation. It should resemble Figure 24-8.

Figure 24-8
Your image should resemble this image.

Session 24—Using Onion Skins

Done!

3. Use a screen grab utility to grab the image, and then save it to disk.
4. Quit the present Flash project and go to File ➪ New. Import the saved onion-skinned graphic and use it as a background. This works great as a Web page background.

REVIEW

In this session you covered the following:

- Applying the Onion Skin modifier
- Rotoscope editing with onion skinning
- Generating speed lines
- Creating a background from an Onion Skin operation

QUIZ YOURSELF

1. What is onion skinning useful for?
2. Where are the Flash Onion Skin controls located?
3. What are speed lines?
4. How can onion-skinned screens be used as backgrounds?

SESSION

Creating Strobes and Advanced Reveals

Session Checklist

✔ Creating strobes

✔ Understanding animated pull-on reveals

✔ Using eye zoom reveals

30 Min. To Go

This chapter has three exercises that further deepen your knowledge of Flash animation possibilities. You learn how to create strobes, animated pull-on reveals, and eye zoom reveals.

Creating Strobes

Many of you are familiar with the strobe effect used in dance clubs. *Strobing* is created by pulsing a light at succinct intervals. When used with no other light source, it can create a hypnotic, otherworldly feeling. The strobes we create in Flash are less intrusive, because they are used in an environment that is lighted by other means. Strobing is used on the Web to emphasize a small area of a page that surfers may miss if it is not called to their attention. Strobing is sometimes called *flashing* by Web designers, but aside from the fact that the term has some rather questionable connotations, it seems rather redundant to call this exercise "Flashing with Flash." The term strobing is also widely used by 3-D artists and animators, so it deepens your lexicon. Follow these steps to create a strobed object:

1. Place the text **NEW!** on the screen. Use any font you like, but make it about ⅔ as large as the stage. Remember that text objects support fill only (with no strokes). Make the fill color a bright blue.

A note about strobe colors. Strobes are all about calling attention through the use of a flashing effect. When the effect is based upon alternating one color with another, nothing works better than using one of the three pairs of complementary colors: red/green, blue/orange, or violet/yellow.

2. Set up a keyframe animation of 30 seconds at 10 frames per second (fps). Create keyframes every five frames. See Figure 25-1.

Figure 25-1
Your screen should look like this.

3. Make the letters a brilliant blue at frames 1, 10, 20 and 30, and a bright orange at frames 5, 15, and 25. These are all keyframe positions. Do not employ any tweening; just allow the letters to strobe. Preview the animation. You can save this as a GIF animation with background transparency on and apply it to a Web page, or use the same technique in your other Flash projects.

Session 25—Creating Strobes and Advanced Reveals

**20 Min.
To Go**

The Animated Pull-On Reveal

You have already been introduced to reveals in Chapter 15 of this book. This exercise shows you that animation components can also be used in more complex reveals. The following steps create an animation that pulls your message across the scene:

1. Open the CH_07A Library, found in the Projects folder on this book's CD-ROM. Drag the animated Birdy_01 symbol into your library, as shown in Figure 25-2.

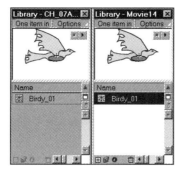

Figure 25-2
Drag the Birdy_01 symbol from the CH_07A Library to your library.

2. Draw two towing lines from the bird to a large rectangle being towed behind. Place some text, whatever message you want, in the rectangle. Use any font and size that fit the text.
3. Group everything into one group by using Modify ⇨ Group. Remember that all of this is taking place on just a single layer.
4. With Frame 1 selected, create an animation of 60 frames. Place a keyframe at the end, so that the timeline shows a keyframe at each end of the sequence.
5. Go to the Frame 1 keyframe, and drag the grouped graphic off to the left, so the bird's head is just entering the scene. See Figure 25-3.
6. Go to the keyframe at Frame 60. Move the grouped graphic off to the right so that nothing remains on the stage. See Figure 25-4.

Figure 25-3
At Frame 1, drag the graphic to the left so that the bird's head is just entering the scene.

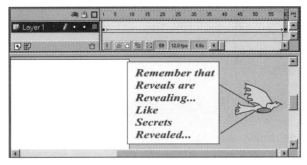

Figure 25-4
At Keyframe 60, move the grouped graphic off to the right of the stage as shown.

7. Hit the Play button on the Controller (which can be activated under Window ⇨ Controller if it is not already visible). Everything looks fine except for one detail . . . the bird's wings aren't flapping. Why? In order to see the animation in an animated movie-clip instance, you have to view a preview of the movie in Test Movie mode. Go to Control ⇨ Test Movie. The animated bird dutifully pulls the sign across the stage. Save your work.

 Anything can be used to accomplish a pull reveal . . . a rocket, a baby, a robot, or a rhino. Like the other exercises in this book, once you learn the concepts and tools, there are no creative limits.

The Eyes Have It!

**10 Min.
To Go**

The idea for this Flash project came from one of the old Bela Lugosi horror flicks. The camera zooms in on Dracula's eyes, where you can see animated bats in flight. The example we work out is a little less sinister, although you could do your own horror interpretation as well, if you created the right elements first. Follow these steps to create the effect of zooming in on an image and then viewing an animation inside the original image:

1. File ⇨ Import the Poser.jpg file from the Resources folder on the book's CD-ROM. The face was created in Curious Labs' Poser, an excellent addition to your Flash bag of handshaking tools (www.curiouslabs.com).

2. Resize the image until it fits your Flash stage. It is automatically keyframed at Frame 1. See Figure 25-5.

Figure 25-5
The Poser head fills the stage.

3. Name the layer Face. With Keyframe 1 selected, choose Insert Frame. Drag the new frame out to the Frame 160 position. Place another keyframe at position 90, but none after that. Move the timeline indicator to Keyframe 90.

4. With the keyframe at position 90 selected, go to Modify ⇨ Transform ⇨ Scale. You may wind up doing this a few times, depending upon the zoom and the screen resolution you are working at. Enlarge the face until the eyes fill the stage. See Figure 25-6.

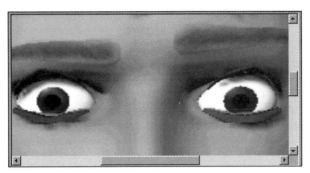

Figure 25-6
Enlarge the face until the eyes can't get any larger without going beyond the borders of the stage.

5. Now to complete the animation of the zoomed face. What we are seeking is the enlargement of the face (really, the effect will be that we are just zooming in on the face) to the point where the eyes can't really get any larger. Then we want the face to stay at that size for a while, to allow another part of the movie to take precedence. Create a motion tween from Keyframe 1 to Keyframe 90. Leave the rest of the frames, from 91 to 160, with no assigned tween. Control ⇨ Test Movie to see the results so far. If anything needs a little adjustment, do that now, and test again.

6. Create another layer called Eyes. Create a keyframe on that layer at the Frame 90 position. Lock the Face layer. Create another new layer and name it Birdy.

7. Choose File ⇨ Open As Library. Open the file named CH_25B.fla, which can be found in the Projects folder on this book's CD-ROM. Drag the Birdy_01 symbol from that library to your project's Symbol Library and copy it there. Close the CH_25B.fla library. See Figure 25-7.

8. On the Birdy layer at Frame 90, with the Face layer locked, use the Paintbrush or the Oval tool to draw a circle to replace the iris of the character's left eye. Place an instance of the BirdyA_01 symbol over it, and resize as necessary. Group the new eye and the bird into one grouped object. Control ⇨ Test Movie to see what it looks like. Edit as you see fit and retest. When you are satisfied with it, Edit ⇨ Copy and then Paste the eye-bird group and reposition it to create the other eye. See Figure 25-8.

Session 25—Creating Strobes and Advanced Reveals 281

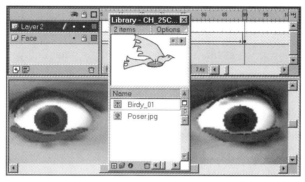

Figure 25-7
Copy the Birdy_01 symbol to your project's Symbol Library.

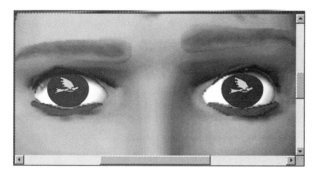

Figure 25-8
The finished eyes are placed in position at Frame 90 on the Eyes layer.

Done!

Tip

Obviously, you can place any animated symbol you care to in the eyes, and even create a slide show of different symbols and bitmaps. You could also place text in the eyes, perhaps for a Web banner display.

Review

In this session we focused on three advanced animation designs, enabling you to learn about:

- Creating strobes
- Generating pull reveals
- Placing an instance over a zoomed bitmap

Quiz Yourself

1. What are the main tools for creating strobes?
2. What can I do if I hit the Play button on the Controller, and an animated symbol instance does not display any animated attributes?

SESSION

Developing Nested Animations

Session Checklist

✔ Developing a nested animated symbol

✔ Creating a typewriter animated symbol

30 Min. To Go

You already created a nested animation without realizing it, when you completed the last tutorial in Chapter 25. A nested animation is an animation within an animation, and you can take this process down several more levels of complexity (an animation in an animation in an animation . . . and so on). Using the Symbol Library makes creating nested animations in Flash simple. Here are three examples that enable you to explore the options and the potentials of this technique.

Important! **Now that you have worked your way to this point, you will appreciate what this chapter points out, which is one of Flash's most valuable attributes — the creation of nested animations, based upon nested symbols. The way that the Symbol Library in Flash is hierarchically structured makes this feature possible.**

The two attributes of any Symbol Library that are important to keep in mind at all times are the following:

1. Instances from any Symbol Library can be used to create new symbols in Symbol Edit mode.
2. Each symbol in any Symbol Library can be composed of an unlimited amount of layers, each of which can contain another symbol or any other drawn, painted, or imported element.

The First Symbol

This exercise shows you how to embed animated groups within other animated groups. But first, follow these steps to set up an animated symbol to serve as the base of a nested symbol:

1. Open the file CH_07E.fla as a library, and drag the Fish_Group symbol to your library. See Figure 26-1.

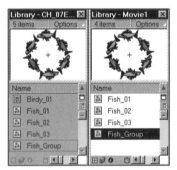

Figure 26-1
Drag the Fish Group to your library.

2. Drag an instance of the Fish_Group symbol to the stage.
3. Select Frame 1 of the Fish_Group instance on the timeline, and choose Insert ➪ Frame. Move the inserted frame to position 30 on the timeline.
4. Select Frame 30 and choose Insert ➪ Keyframe. Now you have keyframes at Frame 1 and 30.

5. Select Keyframe 30. Go to Window ➪ Panels ➪ Transform. With the Fish Group selected, type an angle of **–179** degrees in the Rotate area of the Transform panel. See Figure 26-2.

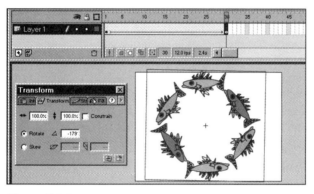

Figure 26-2
Type in a value of –179 degrees in the Rotate box.

6. Click the first keyframe and go to Window ➪ Panels ➪ Frame. Select the Motion tweening option from the pop-up menu.

7. Choose Activate Control ➪ Loop. Now the frames are set to loop in an on-screen animation playback (note that this is an authoring-only playback preview, and that the final animation will not loop based on the settings in the Control menu. An exported Flash Player .swf file plays and loops by default unless Action Scripts in the .swf override these behaviors). Hit the Play button on the Controller, and the fish should move in a counter-clockwise circle. With the animated fish selected, choose Insert ➪ Convert to Symbol. Name the new symbol Fish_01, and make sure it's a movie clip.

8. You can now delete the Fish_01 symbol instance from the stage. It remains in the Symbol Library as an animated symbol. We are in search of bigger fish.

20 Min. To Go

Building a Nest

Now that you have the initial symbol animated, the following steps teach you how to configure a more complex nested configuration.

Note: Remember that this process is very important, and goes straight to the heart of what Flash is all about.

1. With nothing on the stage (remember that your previously created fish-circle animation is in the Symbol Library), rename the default layer Timing. This layer will be used for a length of animation proxy only. Create a small circle somewhere far offstage so that the layer gets a keyframe at position 1 (color and position don't matter, because this circle will be hidden from the user). You are using this circle only to create a keyframe, so it remains off-stage. Choose Insert ⇨ Frame. Drag the new frame to position 60. At 12 frames per second (fps), this gives you a 5-second animation.

2. Go to Insert ⇨ New Symbol. Name the new symbol Fish_Group_02, and make sure it's a movie clip. Now you are in Symbol Edit mode, and anything you place on the stage becomes part of Fish_Group_2.

3. Drag the Fish_Group instance of the animated symbol you just completed to the stage. See Figure 26-3.

Figure 26-3
Drag the Fish_Group symbol instance to the Symbol Edit mode stage.

4. Go to Modify ⇨ Transform ⇨ Flip Horizontal. This flips the image horizontally.

5. Set up a keyframe animation of the Fish_Group_2 symbol for 30 frames. At frame 30, go to Window ⇨ Panels ⇨ Transform, and type in a Rotation of **179** degrees. This animates the Fish_Group_2 symbol clockwise. Close Symbol Edit mode, and you should see your new animated symbol in the Symbol Library, with a Play button next to it so that you can preview it. See Figure 26-4.

Session 26—Developing Nested Animations

Figure 26-4
The Fish_Group_2 symbol now resides in your Symbol Library.

6. Choose Insert ➪ New Symbol to create another symbol, the first nesting element. Name the new symbol Fish_Group_3, and make sure it's a movie clip.

7. In Symbol Edit mode, drag an instance of the Fish_Group symbol to the stage. Create another layer (leave the name at the default) and drag an instance of the Fish_Group_2 symbol to the stage. Resize the Fish_Group_2 instance so that it fits inside of the Fish_Group instance. Choose Edit ➪ Edit Movie to exit Edit Symbol mode and return to the main movie scene. If you look in your library, you now have an animated symbol with two concentric rings of fish, each circling opposite each other. Drag an instance of your final Fish_Group symbol from the library to the stage, and select Control ➪ Test Movie to see the final preview and save your work. See Figure 26-5.

Figure 26-5
The Fish_Group_3 symbol

8. Create another new symbol. This time, use two concentric Fish_Group_3 instances to compose it. You now have a unique symbol, consisting of four nested fish-circle animations, that can be used anywhere. See Figure 26-6.

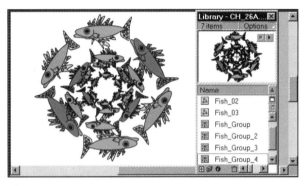

Figure 26-6
The Fish_Group_4 symbol

Creating a Typewriter Effect

10 Min. To Go

Here's a way to use these same ideas to create a typewriter effect, writing letters to the screen one at a time. Follow these steps to create a movie that spells out "Flash Weekend" across the screen:

1. Choose Insert ➪ New Symbol in a new Flash project. Name the symbol Typer, and make it a graphic symbol.
2. In Symbol Edit mode, name the default layer Timer. Draw a circle on it to create a filled keyframe at Frame 1. Hide this layer.

   When you create a timing layer in Symbol Edit mode, you cannot draw outside of the stage area. The timing layer used here is a device created by the author and does not appear as a term in the Flash documentation.

3. Choose Insert ➪ Frame and drag the new frame to position 120.

Session 26—Developing Nested Animations

4. Now create 12 new layers, one above the other. Name them F-L-A-S-H-W-E-E-K-E-N-D, with one letter for each layer. See Figure 26-7.

Figure 26-7
Your twelve "letter" layers should look like this in Symbol Edit mode.

5. Each of the letter layers will hold the letter that it is named after, starting with an "F." Each of the letters will be placed on a keyframe that is 10 frames advanced from the last letter, so the letters will occupy keyframes at positions 1, 10, 20, 30, 40, 50, 60, 70, 80, 90, 100, and 110. All of the layers should be configured so that their last frame is the same as the Timer layer's last frame: Frame 120. Delete the Timer layer. See Figure 26-8.

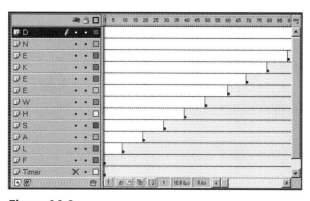

Figure 26-8
When finished, the Timeline inside the Edit Symbol mode should look like this.

6. You can adjust the timing of any of the letters as you like, and place the letters in any configuration you require. Quit Edit Symbol mode. Drag an instance of the new Typer symbol to the stage, choose Insert ➪ Frame, and drag the inserted frame to position 120. That's it. Preview by selecting Control ➪ Test Movie, and save. See Figure 26-9.

Figure 26-9
The finished animated symbol writes one letter at a time.

If you want to let the letters linger a bit longer, go back into Symbol Edit mode and adjust the length of the timelines for all of the letter layers.

Done!

Review

In this chapter, you learned the ins and outs of nesting processes, including the following:

- Flipping a symbol
- Creating nested symbols in symbols
- Creating new symbols
- Using the Transform panel to rotate selected elements
- Creating a nested, typewriter effect for a symbol

QUIZ YOURSELF

1. How can I flip (horizontally or vertically) any selected elements on the stage.
2. Why are nested symbols important?
3. What two attributes of the Symbol Library are important to keep in mind?
4. What is a typewriter effect?
5. Why are layers important to use in Edit Symbol mode?

PART V

Sunday Morning Part Review

1. What two attributes of the Symbol Library are very important to keep in mind?
2. What is the typewriter effect?
3. What are the three animated states of a button?
4. What is the fourth button state used for?
5. What is an object action?
6. How is a radial wipe created?
7. How can I get a text block to pop up at a specific place on the screen?
8. What is a shatter?
9. What are speed lines used to indicate?
10. How can onion-skinned screens be used as backgrounds?
11. What are the main tools for creating strobes?
12. What can I do if I hit the Play button on the Controller, and an animated symbol instance does not display any animated attributes?
13. How is a bitmap shattered?
14. Should tweening be used with a layer of multiple symbols? Why or why not?
15. How can the center point of an image be moved?
16. Which fonts can be used to create an impression of alien text?
17. What type of tweening do I use when I want the objects to pop on screen?

18. What type of tweening can I use to create an easy flow of material such as sand?
19. Why use onion skinning?
20. Where are the Flash Onion Skin controls located?
21. How can any selected element on the stage be flipped horizontally or vertically?
22. Why are nested symbols important?
23. How is a frame action different from an object action?
24. Why is it important to use layers in Edit Symbol mode?

PART VI

Sunday Afternoon

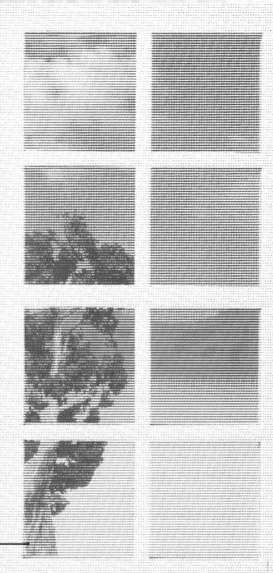

Session 27
Exploring Gradients

Session 28
Advanced Bitmap Techniques

Session 29
Understanding Instance Effects

Session 30
Exploring Flash 3-D

Session 31
Handshaking

SESSION

Exploring Gradients

Session Checklist

✔ Understanding and creating gradients

✔ Using gradients in animation

✔ Creating gradient backgrounds

*30 Min.
To Go*

Gradients give your Flash productions a little sparkle. They offer you smooth blends of color rather than just single color fills. In this chapter, you learn how to create gradients, how to animate them, and how to use them as background.

Creating Gradients

The tools for creating gradients in Flash are easy to use. Flash gradients are based upon two basic elements:

- Whether the gradient is linear or radial
- The makeup of the gradient's color palette

To explore gradient creation, do the following:

1. Open a new Flash project. Create a circle at the center of the stage, large enough to see the fill color clearly. Select and delete the stroke. Select the remaining circle fill. See Figure 27-1.

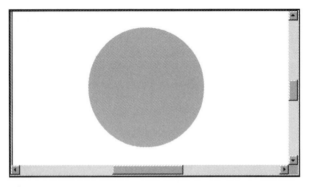

Figure 27-1
Start with a circle and remove its stroke.

2. Go to Window ➪ Panels ➪ Fill. The Fill panel appears. Select Linear Gradient from the list. See Figure 27-2.

Figure 27-2
The Fill panel with Linear Gradient selected

3. Note the makeup of the panel. To the left is a preview area that displays the way the current gradient will look when mapped to a selected object. At the center is the gradient spectrum, below which are color pointers. At the right is a color picker control. Move the color pointer on the right to the middle of the color spectrum bar, and see how that alters the gradient preview. See Figure 27-3.

Session 27—Exploring Gradients

Figure 27-3
Moving the color pointers alters the gradient's color space.

4. With the color pointer on the right moved to the center of the color spectrum bar, click below the bar on the far-right area of the Fill panel to add another color pointer. Click on the down arrow of the color picker to select the gradient color at that point. Look at the color preview area. See Figure 27-4.

Figure 27-4
Add another color pointer and set its color.

5. Click on the Arrow tool and select the circle. It is filled with the gradient. See Figure 27-5.

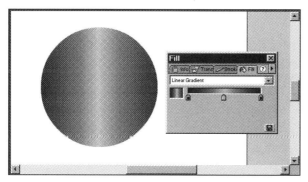

Figure 27-5
The selected object is filled with the gradient.

6. Select Radial Gradient from the list in the Fill panel. The selected circle is filled with the same gradient spectrum, but this time as a Radial Gradient. See Figure 27-6.

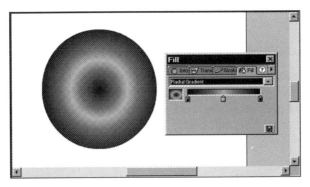

Figure 27-6
Switching between Linear and Radial Gradients is a snap.

You are now aware of the way that gradients are configured and controlled.

Animating Gradients

20 Min. To Go

Animated gradients represent the single, most eye-popping effect in Flash. You can create everything from explosions to pulsing stars and a range of other effects by using them. Do the following to create a basic animated gradient:

1. Open a new project. Place a circle on the stage, and remove its stroke.
2. This creates a keyframe at frame one on the default layer. Choose Insert ➪ Frame, and drag the inserted frame on the timeline to position 40. Go to Insert ➪ Keyframe at that point. Use shape tweening to animate between the keyframes.
3. Go to Window ➪ Panels ➪ Fill to open the Fill panel. With the circle selected choose the Radial Fill option. Your scene should now resemble Figure 27-7.

In a Radial Gradient Fill selection, the area to the left of the spectrum in the Fill panel represents the inside of the filled graphic, and the color on the right represents the outside.

Session 27—Exploring Gradients

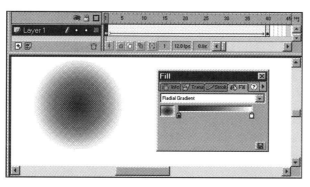

Figure 27-7
Your scene should look like this.

4. Note how the circle looks with the default radial fill applied at Keyframe 1. It is dark at the center and fades into the white background at the edge. Go to Keyframe 40 (the last frame) and select the circle if it becomes unselected. Alter the radial fill spectrum by transposing the color selector arrows in the Fill panel, so that the white one is at the left and the dark one is at the right. Another way to do this same thing is to alter the colors of each color marker but leave them where they are. Look at the circle. Now it has a bright center and a dark edge. Go to Control ⇨ Test Movie to see what happens. See Figure 27-8.

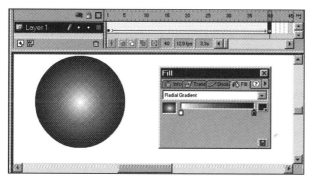

Figure 27-8
At the last keyframe, the color spectrum is reversed from what it was at Keyframe 1.

There are an infinite number of ways that you can configure gradient animations by working with the Fill panel in Flash. Here are a few pointers to observe:

- Gradients must have at least two colors to operate.
- Gradients can have no more than eight colors.
- Add more colors by clicking below the spectrum bar on the Fill panel.
- Colors can be deleted by selecting their color pointer and dragging them out of the Fill panel.
- The gradient you use at each keyframe can have its own number of color pointers, as long as there are at least two. This creates animations where colors gradually appear and disappear.
- To create a harder edge between colors, move their color pointers over each other at specific keyframes.

10 Min. To Go

A Gradient Background Project

In this small project, you'll create a gradient backdrop, and populate it with animated gradient text and pulsing stars. Do the following:

1. Drag out a rectangle that covers the stage. Remove its stroke. Name the default layer Backdrop. Create a 60 frame animation on the Backdrop layer. Your scene should now resemble Figure 27-9.

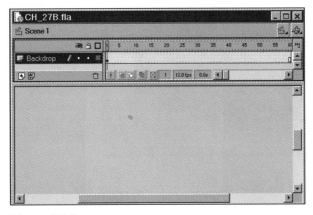

Figure 27-9
Your scene should look like this.

2. With the rectangle selected, open the Fill panel (Window ➪ Panels ➪ Fill). Choose Linear Gradient and configure a color scheme from light blue to black as shown in Figure 27-10.

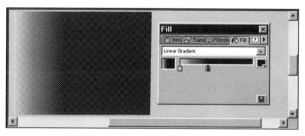

Figure 27-10
Configure a Linear Gradient fill from light blue to black.

3. Note that the rectangle gradient is facing left to right, and you need it to be up to down. To switch it around, go to the Transform panel by selecting Window ➪ Panels ➪ Transform. Click Rotate, and input **-90** degrees. Now you have to adjust the proportions of the rectangle so that it fits this new orientation. In the horizontal and vertical dimensions boxes, change the 100% readings to 75% and 140% respectively (you may have to alter these percentages somewhat, depending upon the size of your initial rectangle). The rectangle now fits the stage area, and the gradient fill is in the correct direction. See Figure 27-11.

Figure 27-11
This is how your scene should look now.

4. Create another layer and name it Text. Create a line of text for this layer that says "Cosmic" and make it large enough to dominate the sky; next, move it towards the top of the background. See Figure 27-12.

Figure 27-12
The Cosmic text is placed.

5. Select the text and choose Modify ⇨ Break apart. Now it is separated into filled objects with no stroke, perfect for applying a gradient, which is exactly what you are going to do. Insert a keyframe at the last frame of the Text layer.

6. Open the Fill panel with the text selected. Choose Linear Gradient at Keyframe 1 of the Text layer as shown in Figure 27-13.

Figure 27-13
This gradient has three colors, all bunched up at the left.

7. Configure the Linear Gradient selection at the last keyframe of the Text layer as shown in Figure 27-14.

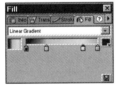

Figure 27-14
At the last keyframe, the Linear Gradient spectrum has four color pointers.

Move the timeline slider back and forth to preview the effect of the gradient moving across the text, causing changes in the text's visibility. Now for some pulsing stars.

Session 27—Exploring Gradients

8. Create another layer for a star; name the layer Star. If you want more stars later, create them on separate layers so you can vary their gradient effects. Place a circle where you want a star, and delete its stroke. Choose Radial Gradient in the Fill panel at Keyframe 1 for the star shape you just made, using a light blue at the center and fading to black at the outside. Place another keyframe at the middle of the Star layer's timeline, and one at the end. To pulse the star in a steady way, make the last keyframe the same gradient as the first. On the center keyframe, enlarge the amount of the spectrum taken up by the light-blue color by moving its pointer closer to the black color on the Fill panel. Use shape tweening to cause the star to pulse smoothly. Use no tweening to make it blink. When finished, preview the results. Fix as necessary and save to disk. See Figure 27-15.

Figure 27-15
Frames from the completed animation show a moving meteor created with the same process you used on the stars.

Done!

REVIEW

In this session, you have mastered the art of using gradient fills. Among the things you learned were:

- Configuring the Fill panel
- Choosing between Radial and Linear Gradients
- Using the color spectrum to animate gradients
- Creating a gradient background

QUIZ YOURSELF

1. What is the difference between a Linear and a Radial Gradient?
2. How can I change the color spectrum of a gradient?
3. How are gradients applied to objects?
4. How can I create a blink (pulse)?
5. What type of tweening should be used when animating a gradient fill?

SESSION

Advanced Bitmap Techniques

Session Checklist

✔ Painting and fills with bitmaps

✔ Internal bitmap editing

✔ External bitmap editing

✔ Creating tiled images

30 Min. To Go

Although Flash relies upon vector image data for most of what it accomplishes, that doesn't mean that bitmaps are left out of the picture. You have already explored some of the ways that bitmaps can be incorporated into your Flash projects in previous chapters in this book. This chapter expands your knowledge, giving you additional examples for your creative toolkit.

Using Bitmaps for Painting and Fills

Flash offers you the amazing capability to use bitmap images as content for paint and fill operations. Normally, in most other computer graphics applications, this is not allowed. Being able to accomplish this feat gives Flash more options as a creative tool. To learn more, complete the following steps:

1. Open a new Flash project. Select File ⇨ Import to import the Barn.jpg and Flwr_01.jpg images from the Resources folder on the CD-ROM that accompanies this book. Delete them from the stage because now they reside only in your project's Symbol Library. You'll use them later in this exercise. Figure 28-1 shows the barn and flower images.

Figure 28-1
The barn and flower images are imported.

2. Go to Window ⇨ Panels ⇨ Fill. You will see small thumbnails of the barn and flower images, as shown in Figure 28-2.

Figure 28-2
Your imported images appear as thumbnails in the Fill panel when Bitmap is selected.

3. Leave the Fill panel open. Select the Paintbrush tool with a medium-sized brush. Selecting first one image thumbnail and then the other in the Fill panel, paint a mix of the two images on the Flash stage, as you can see in Figure 28-3. You can accomplish this neat effect in Flash easier than in any other bitmap painting application.

Session 28—Advanced Bitmap Techniques

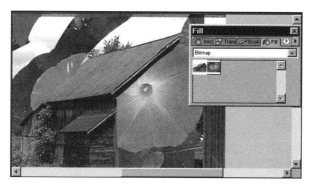

Figure 28-3
Interactively paint an image that is a blend of both imported images.

 Not only the Paintbrush, but any Flash drawing tool that works to create filled shapes can access this same bitmap painting attribute.

4. Click the Rectangle tool. Alternating between the barn and flower images, create a series of vertical strips. Your new painting should resemble Figure 28-4. You can even group it and save it to the library as a new graphic symbol by selecting Insert ⇨ Convert to Symbol.

Figure 28-4
A bitmap painting generated by using the Rectangle tool

20 Min. To Go

Internal Bitmap Editing

There are two ways to edit a bitmap image once it is inside of Flash: by breaking the image apart, or by doing vector conversion first. Each has its uses.

The Break-Apart method

You have already touched upon the Break-Apart operation, but now it's time to delve deeper. When you break apart a bitmap, you can use the Magic Wand to select parts of the image and create a bitmap/vector composite. To break apart a bitmap and create a bitmap/vector composite, follow these steps:

1. Import the barn image into a new Flash scene. Go to Modify ⇨ Break Apart. An array of tiny white dots appears on the bitmap, indicating that the original bitmap object was successfully broken apart and it is now a selected shape.

2. Use the Arrow tool and click outside of the image to deselect it. Click the Lasso tool. Click the Magic Wand Settings button at the bottom of the toolbar. The button is shown in Figure 28-5.

Figure 28-5
The Magic Wand Settings button

3. When the Magic Wand Settings window appears, set Threshold to 25 and leave Smoothing set to Normal. See Figure 28-6 for an example of how this window should look.

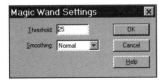

Figure 28-6
The Magic Wand Settings window

4. Click OK to select the settings. Click the Magic Wand button, next to the Magic Wand Settings button. See Figure 28-7.

Session 28—Advanced Bitmap Techniques

Figure 28-7
The Magic Wand button

5. Click the Magic Wand tool on the roof of the barn, which is a medium gray color. Most of the roof is selected. Click the Fill tool, and select a dark red color. Fill the selected roof by clicking the Paint Bucket tool in the area. Use the Magic Wand to select the grass in front of the barn and recolor it a darker green. See Figure 28-8.

Figure 28-8
Now the roof is a nice even red, and the grass in front is darker green.

The trace-based method

The drawback in tracing a bitmap image is that you are going to lose, or at least alter, some of the detail. The good news is that the traced areas are usually much easier to select with the Magic Wand tool because they will have already been transformed into more even-color blocks. With the right trace settings, you can even make a bitmap look like a watercolor painting. To create the look of a watercolor painting, follow these steps:

1. Open a new project. Place the Barn.jpg image in the scene so that it covers the stage.
2. Go to Modify ⇨ Trace Bitmap. When the Settings window appears, use the following values: Color Threshold, 50; Minimum Area, 40 Pixels; Curve Fit, Smooth; Corner Threshold, Few Corners. The resulting image takes on the appearance of a beautiful watercolor painting, as you can see in Figure 28-9.

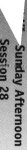

Figure 28-9
The traced image has been transformed into a painting.

10 Min. To Go

External Bitmap Editing and Tiled Images

Once an image has been imported into Flash, you can handshake (or communicate with another application through exchanging file format data) with any bitmap painting application on your system to edit it further. To edit a bitmap image with an external painting application:

1. Select a bitmap image in your Symbol Library that you want to alter by editing it externally. Right-click it (Windows) or Control+click (Macintosh). Select Edit With from the list. Select the bitmap image application you want to edit it with from the file folder on your system, for example, Adobe Photoshop. The image is immediately transferred to your selected editing application, as you can see in Figure 28-10.

2. Save the updated image after you have edited it. Next, update the imported image in Flash by selecting its name in the Symbol Library (open the library if it's not already open by selecting Window ➪ Library) and choosing Properties from the library's Options menu. Click the Update button on the right side of the Properties window. Figure 28-11 shows the edited image imported back into Flash.

Session 28—Advanced Bitmap Techniques

Figure 28-10
The image appears in Photoshop, where a distortion is applied to it.

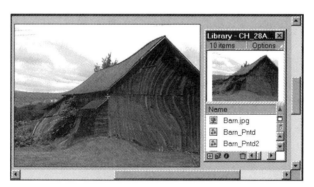

Figure 28-11
The edited image is imported back into Flash.

Creating tiled images

Creating tiled images for a Web page background is one of Web designers' favorite uses of images. Often, these tiled images are corporate logos, over which text and other content is placed. To created a tiled background, do the following:

1. Select File ⇨ Import to import the flower image (Flwr_01.jpg) into a new Flash project.
2. Go to Window ⇨ Panels ⇨ Transform to open the Transform panel and set the width/height parameters at 10 percent for the imported bitmap.
3. Create a rectangle that covers the stage. It will be filled with tiled images scaled proportionately to the height of your newly drawn rectangle. Figure 28-12 shows the tiled images filling the stage.

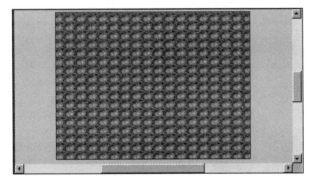

Figure 28-12
The tiled images fill the stage.

Done!

Review

In this chapter, you learned much more about manipulating and customizing bitmaps, including the following:

- Using the Paintbrush and other Fill tools to target a filled area with a bitmap
- Breaking a bitmap apart in order to alter its colors
- Transforming a bitmap into a painting

Session 28—Advanced Bitmap Techniques

- Handshaking with an external editing application
- Creating a page tiled with bitmap images

QUIZ YOURSELF

1. How do I access the Fill panel?
2. How do I fill a selected area with an imported bitmap?
3. How can I alter color areas of a bitmap in Flash?
4. How is a bitmap image in Flash given the look of a watercolor painting?
5. How can I access an external image editor while working in Flash?
6. How do I create pages tiled with bitmaps?

SESSION 29

Understanding Instance Effects

Session Checklist

✔ Creating instance fades

✔ Creating instance tints

✔ Understanding instance advanced effects

*30 Min.
To Go*

When you work with symbol instances, and place a number of the same instances in a scene, every instance of any one symbol does not have to be exactly the same as every other instance. You can alter each instance in some important ways to make it act unique in your Flash movies.

Learning about Instance Fade Effects

Fading a scene in and/or out can add a needed transition. Using fades on a symbol instance can help you add more viewer interest for a movie. To use fade effects on a symbol instance, follow these steps:

   1. Choose File ➪ Import and select the Barn.jpg file from the Resources folder on this book's CD-ROM. When it appears, resize it to fit the stage.

2. Select the barn image and select Insert ⇨ Convert to Symbol. Name the symbol BarnSym_01, and make it a graphic symbol. See Figure 29-1.

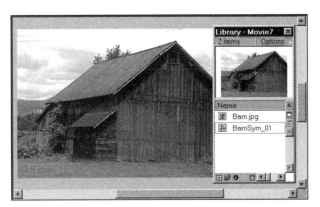

Figure 29-1
An instance of the BarnSym_01 symbol is placed on the stage.

3. Select View ⇨ Timeline, if the Timeline is not already open. Click the keyframe at position 1 on the default layer, and choose Insert ⇨ Frame. Drag the new frame out to position 60, and add another keyframe there. Add another keyframe at position 20, and yet another at position 40. Your Timeline should now resemble Figure 29-2.

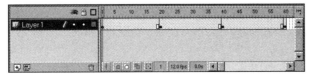

Figure 29-2
The Timeline with keyframes added

4. Select Keyframe 1. This selects the instance of your BarnSym_01 graphic on the stage at Frame 1. Go to Window ⇨ Panels ⇨ Effect to bring up the Effects panel. Select Alpha from the list. When the Alpha option appears, there is a percentage indicator next to it. Click the downward-pointing arrow next to the percentage indicator, and move the percentage slider down to 0%. See Figure 29-3.

Session 29—Understanding Instance Effects

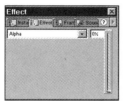

Figure 29-3
Move the percentage slider down to 0%, which sets the Alpha (opacity) value for the selected keyframe.

5. Click the X box to close the panel [for Mac users, this is the box in the upper-left corner]. The symbol instance on your stage should now be completely invisible. Set the same Alpha value for Keyframe 60 by selecting it in the Timeline — which in turn selects its contents on the stage — and repeating this procedure.

6. Repeat the procedure two more times, once each for Keyframes 20 and 40. This time however, set the Alpha percentage to 100 each time. At an Alpha setting of 100 percent, the instance is being told to become 100 percent opaque.

7. If you ran the animation now, you wouldn't get a Fade at all. Can you guess why? Exactly! The keyframes have no tweening set, so the image would just pop on and off. Go to Window ⇨ Panels ⇨ Frame, and set a motion tween for Keyframes 1, 20, and 40. Your Timeline now resembles Figure 29-4.

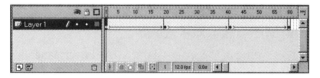

Figure 29-4
The finished Timeline

Run the animation, and the instance will fade in and out. Use a similar technique to fade any selected instance in and/or out. Just remember that you can only have one tweened instance per layer, but you can use as many layers as you want.

Tip: Place additional instances on their own layers so that you can use different fades at different times on selected instances of the same symbol.

Creating Instance Tint Effects

20 Min. To Go

To *tint* Flash images means one of two things:

- If the image was created in Flash, tinting means recolorizing the selected fill. This also holds true if the targeted area exists on a bitmap that you've either used Break Apart editing on or transformed into a vector image.
- If the image is an instance of a bitmap symbol, then tinting means what it says — that is, adjusting the entire symbol's overall hue, just as if you placed colored glass between your eyes and the object.

In this exercise, you'll tint an instance of a bitmap symbol. The following steps show you how:

1. File ⇨ Import the Barn.jpg file from the Resources folder on this book's CD-ROM. When it appears, resize it to fit the stage.
2. Select the barn image and go to Insert ⇨ Convert to Symbol. Name the symbol BarnSym_01, and make it a Graphic symbol.
3. View ⇨ Timeline, if the Timeline is not already open. Click the keyframe at position 1 on the default layer, and choose Insert ⇨ Frame. Drag the new frame out to position 60, and add another keyframe there. Add another keyframe at position 20 and two more at positions 30 and 40. Your Timeline should now resemble Figure 29-5.
4. Select Keyframe 1. Go to Window ⇨ Panels ⇨ Effect. The Effect panel appears. Select Tint from the list. When the Tint option appears, there is a percentage indicator next to it. Click the downward-pointing arrow next to the percentage indicator, and move the percentage slider to 50%. This enables you to see the bitmap instance through the tint. Adjust the RGB values, or select a hue from the color bar at the bottom of the panel. The image now has an even cast of the assigned tint placed upon it on the stage. See Figure 29-6.

Session 29—Understanding Instance Effects 319

Figure 29-5
The Timeline is ready.

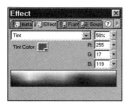

Figure 29-6
The Tint settings in the Effect panel

5. Set different hues for the Tint value at Keyframes 20, 30, and 40. At Keyframe 60, leave the percentage set to 100% and select a black color (or RGB = 0, 0, 0). This creates a solid black fill, inducing the effect called "Fade to Black."

6. Set up motion tweening at Keyframes 1, 20, 30, and 40. Your Timeline now appears as in Figure 29-7.

Figure 29-7
The finished Timeline

Preview the animation. You should see the bitmap image being effected by a series of different hues before fading to black.

**10 Min.
To Go**

Generating Instance Advanced Effects

Selecting the Advanced option in the Effect panel gives you more variable controls over Tints and Alpha settings. The following steps show you how:

1. File ⇨ Import the Barn.jpg file from the Resources folder on this book's CD-ROM. When it appears, resize it to fit the stage.

2. Select the barn image and Insert ⇨ Convert to Symbol. Name the symbol BarnSym_A1, and make it a Graphic symbol.

3. Select View ⇨ Timeline, if the Timeline is not already open. Click the keyframe at position 1 on the default layer and choose Insert ⇨ Frame. Drag the new frame out to position 60, and add another keyframe there. Add other Keyframes at positions 10, 20, 30, 40, and 50. Your Timeline should now resemble Figure 29-8.

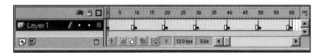

Figure 29-8
The Timeline is ready.

4. Select Keyframe 1. Go to Window ⇨ Panels ⇨ Effect to bring up the Effect panel. Select Advanced from the list. When the Advanced controls appear, a percentage indicator also appears next to the Red, Blue, Green, and Alpha (RGBA) channels. Click the downward-pointing arrow next to the R (Red) channel percentage indicator, and adjust the percentage slider range. You see that the range goes from –100% to +100%. Values below 0 remove red from the instance, and values above 0 force red to dominate the instance. If you prefer, you can also use the sliders that are next to the %R, %G, %B, and %A settings, which range from –255 to 255. These sliders give you a wider range of control over color and opacity. See Figure 29-9.

5. Set different RGBA percentages at all the keyframes on the Timeline. Make the alterations differ from each other by 15 percent, maximum, to create subtle shimmers of color. At Keyframe 60, select Brightness from the list, and move its slider to 100%. This creates a solid white fill, inducing the effect called "Fade to White".

Session 29—Understanding Instance Effects   321

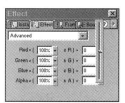

Figure 29-9
The Advanced settings in the Effect panel

6. Set motion tweening at Keyframes 1, 10, 20, 30, 40, and 50. Your Timeline now appears as in Figure 29-10.

Figure 29-10
The finished Advanced Effect Timeline

Done!

Preview the animation. You should see the bitmap being effected by different subtle hues before fading to white.

Review

In this session, you learned how to control the Tint and Alpha values for an instanced bitmap by using the Effect panel. This included:

- Setting the Tint parameters to create color washes
- Setting the Alpha percentage to create fades
- Using the Advanced control settings to create subtle color alterations in the instance

Quiz Yourself

1. How do I create a fade to black?
2. How do I create a fade to white?
3. Using the Advanced settings in the Effect panel, how can I create a tint that makes the instance look dominated by red?
4. When I test the animation, if the keyframes "pop" on instead of flowing evenly from one to another, what step have I omitted?

SESSION

Exploring Flash 3-D

Session Checklist

✔ Creating a traveling shadow

✔ Creating a 3-D scene

✔ Importing 3-D content

30 Min. To Go

By its very nature, Flash is a 2-D graphics and animation application. That doesn't mean, however, that you can't emulate a 3-D environment by its use. It just takes a little exploration and ingenuity, especially in manipulating layers that can make it seem as if objects are passing in front of or in back of each other. This makes it seem as if the objects exist in 3-D space, as the exercises in this chapter will show.

Creating 3-D with Shadows

The moment that an object casts a shadow, it is assumed that it exists in a 3-D environment. After all, at least three separate items are involved in 3-D space: the light source, the object, and the surface upon which the shadow is cast.

The following interesting and simple experiment demonstrates the relationship between these three items:

1. Open a new Flash project and place a rectangle on the stage that covers it. Rename the default layer Background.
2. Delete the rectangle's stroke. Select the Fill tool and then go to Window ⇨ Panels ⇨ Fill. With the Fill panel open, select Linear Gradient.
3. Configure the Linear Gradient with five colors, left to right: light brown, dark brown, dark brown, light pink, and light blue. Look at the way the color indicators are placed in the Fill panel by referring to Figure 30-1.

Figure 30-1
Configure the color indicators like this.

4. When you bunch up gradient colors, as displayed in Figure 30-1, you create a hard-edged separation, similar to a horizon line. Click the Transform tab to activate the Transform panel and type **–90** in the Rotate area to rotate your object –90 degrees. See Figure 30-2.

Figure 30-2
Rotate the rectangle counterclockwise by inputting a value of –90.

5. Look at the rectangle on the stage. Resize it (Modify ⇨ Transform ⇨ Scale) so that it fits the stage again. The result is a basic ground and sky background. See Figure 30-3.

Session 30—Exploring Flash 3-D

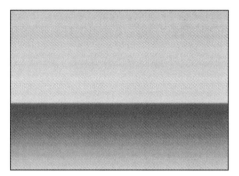

Figure 30-3
You will create this background.

6. Insert ⇨ Frame at Keyframe 1 and drag the new frame to position 60 on the timeline. Lock the layer. Now you have the basic structure for a 60-frame animation with a background in place.

7. Create another layer and name it Ball&Shadow. Hold down Shift, select the Circle tool, and drag out a perfect circle that fills about ⅕ of the sky area of the background. Go to Window ⇨ Panels ⇨ Stroke. Select the stroke around the circle and alter its size to 1 in the Stroke panel. See Figure 30-4.

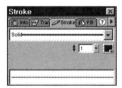

Figure 30-4
Alter the stroke to a size of 1.

8. Click the Fill tab in the same panel. Create a Radial Gradient fill for the circle that ranges from bright green to black. Exit the panel. Select the fill and stroke parts of your circle and group. The finished image is in Figure 30-5.

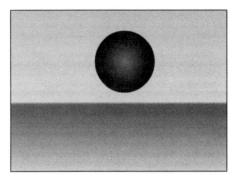

Figure 30-5
The finished ball sits against the background sky.

9. Create a gray oval on the "ground" under the ball that will act as the ball's shadow. Make it about the same size as the ball horizontally, but squash the height. Group the shadow with the ball so that they both move together. See Figure 30-6.

Figure 30-6
The ball now seems to cast a shadow on what appears to be a ground plane.

The 3-D effect is complete. If you move the ball the shadow follows. You can keyframe animate the ball-shadow group to fly across the stage, or start the ball and shadow small and enlarge them to create an animation that makes the ball and its shadow seem as if they are moving toward you. Save your work.

Session 30—Exploring Flash 3-D

**20 Min.
To Go**

Building a Magic Box with Layers

Layers are an important element in creating some 3-D scenes. The following scene uses layers to emulate the outside and inside of a magic box. Do the following:

1. Use the background from the last exercise, but delete the circle and its shadow by selecting the layer they are on and clicking the small Trash Can icon control at the lower-right area of the layers stack.
2. Create three layers above the background layer. Name them, from the bottom up, as BoxBack, Bird, and BoxFrnt.
3. Using the Line and Paint Can tools, create a half-cube object on the BoxBack layer like the one in Figure 30-7.

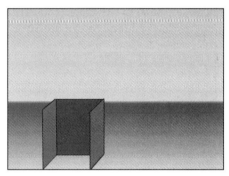

Figure 30-7
Create part of a box.

4. Skip the Bird layer for the moment and create the front of the box on the BoxFrnt layer. See Figure 30-8.

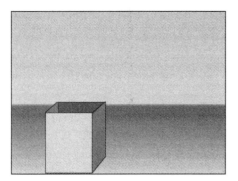

Figure 30-8
Create the front face of the box.

5. Lock the BoxBack and BoxFrnt layers. Go to File ⇨ Open as Library and open the CH_07A.fla file (on the book's CD-ROM in the Projects folder) as a library. Drag the Birdy symbol into your own library. See Figure 30-9.

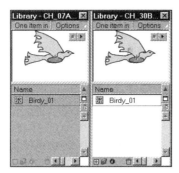

Figure 30-9
Drag the Birdy symbol into your own library.

10. Hide the BoxFrnt layer. Select the Bird layer to make it the current layer. Drag an instance of the Birdy symbol to the stage. Resize and rotate it so that it fits in the box, as shown in Figure 30-10.

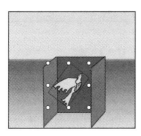

Figure 30-10
The Birdy instance is placed in the box.

11. Create keyframes at 25, 30, and 60. A keyframe at position 1 is already present. Make the Birdy instance fly out of the box on an animation path. At Frame 25, rotate the instance so that is starts to head for the right edge of the stage. At frame 30, complete the rotation. You can augment this animation in a million ways. You can add more birds to the box and have them leave at different times. You can add more birds in the sky, develop a more complex background, or even add more magic boxes with other creatures exiting for the clouds. You get the idea. Whatever you do, it'll be 3-D magic.

 You may even consider making the front of the box a button, which the viewer clicks to start the bird animation.

Importing 3-D Content

10 Min. To Go

One of the most exciting ways to develop 3-D movies in Flash is to import real 3-D content. This can be in the form of rendered image sequences from a 3-D application (such as 3D Studio Max, LightWave, Amapi, Hash Animation Master, Poser, or any other 3-D software that writes out files that Flash can interpret for import). It can also be any real-world digital footage. Once in Flash, you can transform the frames to vector data for a true Flash look, or break apart the bitmaps so that various elements can be deleted or customized. Let's look at one example. Do the following:

1. In a folder called Poserz, which is in the Resources folder on the CD-ROM, is a 30-frame JPEG (Joint Photographic Experts Group) image sequence generated in Curious Labs Poser software. It consists of a head going through some animated contortions.

If you select to import the first frame into Flash, you will be asked if you want to import all of the 30 frames. If you do so, all the frames come into Flash as separate keyframes, and you can preview the animation. For this exercise, however, you only need a single frame at the start, so when asked if you want to import all of the frames after selecting just the first one, reply NO. The first frame will be imported into Flash as a keyframe.

2. Select the frame and go to Modify ⇨ Trace Bitmap. Using the default settings, activate the Trace function. The bitmap image becomes a Flash vector image. Make it a symbol named Head_01. See Figure 30-11.

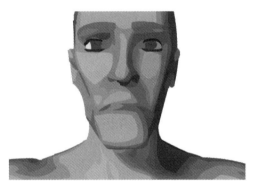

Figure 30-11
The first frame of the bitmap sequence is translated into a traced vector image.

3. Insert a new blank frame at Frame 2 and drag it out to Frame 70. At Frame 55, insert a new blank keyframe and import Frame 30 of the Poser sequence. Trace it on the stage.

4. At Frame 40, insert another blank keyframe and draw a large yellow circle. Configure the rest of the frames on the timeline as displayed in Figure 30-12. Frame 1 is keyframed at Frames 1 and 25 with no tweens. A shape tween connects Frame 26 to Frame 40, the circle. Frame 40 shape tweens to Frame 55, the last head image. Frame 55 lasts until Frame 70 with no tweens.

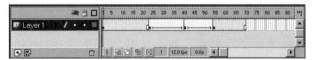

Figure 30-12
This Timeline displays the configuration of Frames 1 through 70.

Session 30—Exploring Flash 3-D 331

5. If you play this animation, the head morphs into a circle and morphs back into a head in the last frame. Some interesting line and fill transitions accompany the morph. See Figure 30-13.

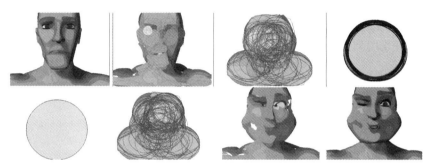

Figure 30-13
A series of frames from the morphed animation

The ANIMS folder in this book's CD-ROM contains AVI and QuickTime versions of this Flash movie.

Done!

Congratulations! You have completed the *Flash 5 Weekend Crash Course*! The last chapter contains handy reference information. You can always come back to this book to refresh your Flash knowledge.

REVIEW

In this session, you looked at the following ways in which 3-D content can be referenced and created in Flash:

- Creating shadows to simulate a 3-D environment
- Using layers to create a simulated 3-D object
- Importing 3-D content and using it to create a morphing animation

QUIZ YOURSELF

1. Why group an object's shadow with the object in a simulated 3-D environment?
2. How can I use layers to evoke a 3-D look?
3. How do I translate a bitmap image into vector content?

SESSION

Handshaking

Because you have already completed the Flash Weekend Crash Course, consider this chapter as a reference. *Handshaking* is Flash's ability to communicate with another application through exchanging file format data. Each month, more software applications are jumping on board the Flash bandwagon, adding the capability to export files in the Flash (.fla) and/or Flash Movie (.swf) format. This is good news for Flash users, because it provides much broader content development alternatives.

Macromedia Fireworks 3 and Dreamweaver 3 are high-priority applications when it comes to Flash handshaking, but they are not detailed in this book.

Macromedia FreeHand

With Flash, FreeHand users can employ any of the following handshaking methods:

- Choose File ➪ Export and select an animation from FreeHand in the Flash .swf format. The animation will play in Flash, or you can play it with any Web Browser that has the Flash plug-in installed.
- Display FreeHand artwork with the same high-quality anti-aliasing that Flash uses in order to preview what a Flash file will look like.
- Import and customize in a FreeHand or in an Illustrator 9 file headed for Flash use.

- Use FreeHand's more full-featured Tracing function on bitmaps headed for Flash display.
- Create text objects in FreeHand rather than Flash in order to use the superior warping and other effects. Then export the results to Flash.
- Use the FreeHand interface, which is designed to be as much like Flash as possible.
- Flash can read every FreeHand format version, making FreeHand the single most important content environment for Flash productions. See Figure 31-1.

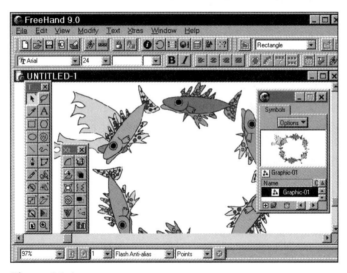

Figure 31-1
FreeHand's features and interface design resembles Flash, making handshaking easier to understand.

Adobe Illustrator

The Adobe Illustrator file format is the standard vector format, so Flash is wise to support it. Using Adobe Illustrator, you can create content for Flash in the .ai format. One thing to be careful of, however, is that while Illustrator gradients are supported, patterned gradients are not supported. See Figure 31-2.

Session 31—Handshaking

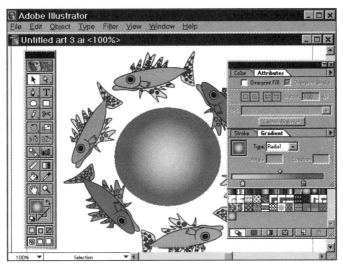

Figure 31-2
Illustrator imports are supported, but patterned gradients are not supported.

Corel Painter

Flash designer has many of the following advantages when using Corel Painter to develop Flash content:

- The Effects options in Corel Painter have the widest array of any bitmap application.
- Corel Painter's unique Image Hose enables you to spray graphic elements on an image.
- Corel Painter files can be used as Flash graphics content.
- Corel Painter enables you to work on single frame animation sequences, and it holds as many frames of the sequence as you have RAM memory to accommodate.
- Corel Painter saves out single-frame animation frames, including the Illustrator format.

See Figure 31-3.

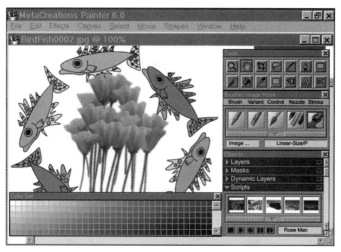

Figure 31-3
Corel Painter is an excellent bitmap option for developing Flash graphic and animation content.

Curious Labs Poser

In this author's opinion, Curious Labs Poser is an essential application for Flash users. Poser enables you to create both images and animations with anatomically correct human and animal models, and it all can be written out in bitmap formats that Flash can easily import. As of this writing, the software's version 4 was available. Version 5 should see a closer integration with Flash native formats. See Figure 31-4.

Discreet Logic's 3D Studio Max

3D Studio Max, the most widely distributed 3-D software in the world, is capable of addressing the Flash .swf format through a special plug-in called *Illustrate!* This plug-in offers the Max user superlative transformation of the 3-D graphics look into the flattened look that is so popular with professional animation for broadcast and film. Writing out to the .swf format assures both an integration with Flash, as well as an easy way to transmit Illustrate! animations to the Web via the Flash browser plug-in. Files can also be written out to the Illustrator form for integration into a Flash movie. See Figure 31-5.

Session 31—Handshaking

Figure 31-4
The Sketch Designer in Poser enables you to transform Poser's 3-D models into traditional media appearances, just right for Flash integration.

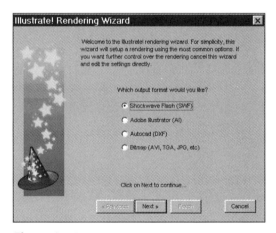

Figure 31-5
As Illustrate! is being configured, the first option is whether or not to write to the Flash .swf format.

Adobe After Effects

Adobe After Effects' future upgrades will address the Flash .swf format. Currently, you can enfold output from After Effects into Flash by importing files in the JPEG (Joint Photographic Experts Group), AVI (Audio Video Interface), or QuickTime formats. See Figure 31-6.

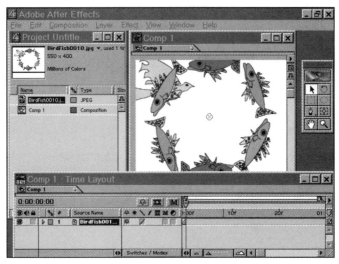

Figure 31-6
After Effects JEPG, AVI, and QuickTime output can be incorporated in Flash movies.

Adobe Photoshop

Every Effects developer around writes for Photoshop, making this a must-have application for all graphics and animation pursuits. Photoshop's capability to write to the GIF (Graphics Interchange Format), JPEG, and PNG (Portable Network Graphics) formats makes it a perfect Flash partner. Photoshop also reads the Illustrator format, so Illustrator image sequences can be modified and returned to Flash. See Figure 31-7.

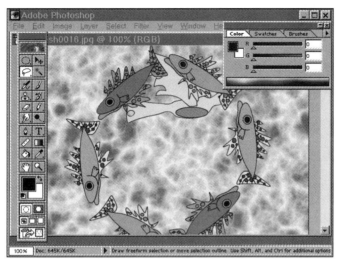

Figure 31-7
Photoshop is a perfect partner to Flash when it comes to image customization and modification.

These are only a few examples of software applications that can provide, modify, and display Flash files — offering you a far richer creative environment than Flash alone can provide. Dozens of other applications exist that could be added to this list, but what you have here gives you some idea of the wide array of possibilities present. Flash support is growing by leaps and bounds, gathering more developers all the time. Completing the *Flash 5 Weekend Crash Course,* and continuing to use Flash as a boundless environment for exploration, assures you a bright and creative future.

PART VI

Sunday Afternoon Part Review

1. Why group an object's shadow with the object in a simulated 3-D environment?
2. How can I use layers to evoke a 3-D look?
3. What is the difference between a Linear and a Radial Gradient?
4. How can you change the color spectrum of a gradient?
5. What type of tweening should be used when animating a gradient fill?
6. How do I access the Fill panel?
7. How do I create pages tiled with bitmaps?
8. How is a fade to black created?
9. How is a fade to white created?
10. How is a selected area filled with an imported bitmap?
11. How can color areas of a bitmap be altered in Flash?
12. How is a photographic bitmap in Flash translated into a painterly look?
13. How is an external image editor accessed in Flash?
14. Using the Advanced settings in the Effect panel, how can I create a tint that makes the instance look dominated by red?

15. When I test the animation, if the keyframes pop on instead of flowing evenly from one to another, what haven't I done?
16. What is the process for translating a bitmap into vector content?
17. How are gradients applied to objects?
18. How can I create a blink?

APPENDIX A

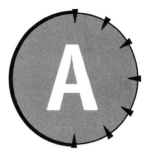

What's On the CD-ROM

The CD ROM that accompanies this book includes tutorial projects contained in the book, resources needed for tutorials, and demo software. It also includes libraries, and animations in both QuickTime and AVI (Audio Video Interface) formats for use in your Flash projects. It is also loaded with extras. Following is a brief description of the CD-ROM content:

Anims

In the Anims folder are some animations you may find of interest. These are in the QuickTime and Audio Video Interface (AVI) format. The Flash Movie (SWF) animations, however, are to be found in the Projects folder.

Libraries

In this folder, you find a small collection of libraries that you can use to transfer content to other Flash Symbol Libraries. Remember that you can also go to File ⇨ Load as Library and open any other Symbol Library from any available project.

Projects

This is the folder you use the most. It contains the project files (.fla) and their associated movies (.swf) referenced in this book. Some of the movies are not animated, however, because they await your development and work.

Resources

Whenever a tutorial calls for you to load something from the Resources folder, this is the place to go. Images in different formats are contained here for your interaction.

Demos

Look in this folder for a selection of demos. Try before you buy.

Amapi

Amapi for both Windows and Mac users is included on the CD. *Amapi* is a full-featured 3-D graphics and animation application that handshakes with a number of other 3-D file formats. Because it can write out Illustrator files, Amapi can help you develop 3-D content for Flash.

A super-fast 3-D modeler from Template Graphics Software, Inc. (TGS), Amapi helps you create both polygonal and NURBS (Non-Uniform Rational B-Splines) models. It exists both as a stand alone application (for PCs and Macs) and with a plug-in connection to 3D Studio Max. An interactive training CD for Amapi is available from Animhouse (www.animhouse.com). Following is the contact information for TGS:

    www.tgs.com/amapi
    Template Graphics Software, Inc.
    5330 Carroll Canyon Rd., Suite 201
    San Diego, CA 92121
    FAX: 858-452-2547

You can also go to any of the Web locations listed here to find out more about Amapi:

```
www.staigerland.com/amapi
www.17hours.com
www.chris-stocker.co.uk
www.smart3d.com
www.multimania.com/bretagnolle
http://perso.club-internet.fr/odrion/
www.deepcold.com
http://o.ffrench.free.fr/
www.martindeblois.com
```

Amapi on this CD

Here's a list of the Amapi files on this CD:

- Full version of Amapi 4.1
- Trial edition (TE) of the latest version, Amapi 5.15
- Large collection of 3-D models, materials, tutorials, and HTML documentation.

Using the Full version of Amapi 4.1

In order to use the full version of Amapi 4.1, do this:

1. Register online at www.tgs.com/amapi (look for "Register Online")
2. Enter this registration serial number: **A3D10694IDGF5**
3. When starting Amapi, you are prompted for a license password. Enter the following Amapi password (full license) to export and save: **20632f91316538c6f**

Completing the registration process gives you full access to Amapi 4.1 for free.

Using and Evaluating Amapi 5.15 TE

In order to evaluate the many new powerful features of Amapi 5.15, install and run the trial version of Amapi 5.15, which is included on this CD along with an extensive presentation of the new features, tutorials, documentation, and links to other Amapi users. When using Amapi 5.15 TE, you can operate in Demo mode (which is the default) for as long as you want without using a trial password.

Saving or exporting is disabled in Demo mode; however, all other features are enabled, such as rendering to image files, animation files (Audio Video Interface), and all modeling tools. You can therefore take your time and learn the new features of Amapi at your leisure without rushing into a buying decision. When you need to test the exports, or want to save your current 3-D model on disk, you'll need a trial password. In order to obtain a trial password, which is good for several weeks, complete the following steps:

1. Go to www.tgs.com/amapi.
2. Select PC Demo or Mac Demo.
3. Enter your registration info.
4. Make sure your e-mail address is correct. The trial password is sent automatically by the server via e-mail to that address.
5. After registration, a message including a temporary trial password is sent to your e-mail address. You then see a choice of sites from which to download the Amapi Demo (Trial Edition). You won't really need to continue at this point, unless a newer version of Amapi is available by that time.
6. After a few minutes, check your mailbox for an e-mail from TGS. It contains a trial password that is good for a few weeks.

What about the 3D Studio Max plug-in for Amapi?

You can find the installer for the 3D Studio Max plug-in to Amapi at this Web location:

    www.tgs.com/Support/Tutorials/Amapi/Amapi-3DMax.html

If the location has changed from the time of this printing, go to www.tgs.com/amapi and look for the Import/Export link, where you should be able to find a link to the 3D Studio Max plug-in. The plug-in installer (for Amapi 5.1) is available for Max versions 2.5 and 3. Amapi 4.1 works with the Max 2.5 plug-in only. For Amapi 4.1, the plug-in installer is provided on the CD.

Support

If you have questions on the use of Amapi, contact support@tgs.com (In Europe: support@europe.tgs.com). Other contact details are available at the main Web site at www.tgs.com.

APPENDIX B

Vendor Contacts

This appendix lists vendor contact information for the developers mentioned in this book:

Adobe Systems Incorporated

Products: After Effects, Illustrator, Photoshop
Web site: www.adobe.com

Corel Corporation

Product: Painter
Web site: www.corel.com

Curious Labs

Product: Poser
Web site: www.curiouslabs.com

Discreet

Product: 3D Studio Max
Web site: www.discreet.com

Macromedia, Inc.

Product: Flash, FreeHand
Web site: www.macromedia.com

Template Graphics Software, Inc.

Product: Amapi
Web site: www.tgs.com

APPENDIX

Exploring Macromedia Generator

Macromedia Generator was developed to support Flash users who want to use server-side interfacing to control Flash. The Developer edition of Generator 2 ships with Flash 5. Generator is also available in an Enterprise edition. Generator 2 features include the following:

- A new and improved Object palette that allows easy access to all Generator objects.
- Support for Flash 5, including the new Action Script and the Movie Explorer.
- Three new Generator objects: Multipage List, Radio Button, and Insert MP3.
- Generator SDK and API, which allow Java and other developers to add their own Generator objects.

Full documentation for the use of Generator 2 accompanies Flash 5.

APPENDIX

Answers to Part Reviews

Following are the answers to the reviews at the end of each part of the book.

Friday Evening Review Answers (Sessions 1-4)

1. Save the layout by choosing Window ➪ Save Panel Layout.
2. Click the line with the Arrow tool and, unless the point you click is a corner point, you can drag out a new, curved shape.
3. Click the segment with the Pen tool to create a new control point.
4. Use the Paint Bucket tool to add color to an enclosed shape.
5. Click the overlapping segments with the Arrow tool and select Edit ➪ Cut, or press the Delete key.
6. Go to Window ➪ Panels ➪ Stroke to change the color. An alternate way is to use the Ink Bottle tool with any color selected from the color palette.
7. Just click in the named area (Tools) and drag the Toolbar.
8. Snap segments together by choosing View ➪ Snap To Objects.
9. Go to Window ➪ Panels ➪ Stroke to set line style, line type and size.
10. Open the color palette and select a color.
11. Three symbol behaviors exist: movie clip, button, and graphic.
12. An instance is a copy of a symbol placed on the Flash stage.

13. Double-clicking the instance or going to Edit ⇨ Instance jumps you to Symbol Edit mode.
14. Modify the Brush tool by selecting from the size and shape lists in the Options section at the bottom of the Toolbar.
15. Click the Ink Bottle tool on the edge of the brushed line.
16. Edit the symbol in Symbol Edit mode. Get there by double-clicking the symbol instance, or by selecting the name of the symbol in the Library window and double-clicking it.
17. With the element on the stage selected, go to Insert ⇨ Convert to Symbol.
18. A Common Library is a Flash library that is not connected to a particular project, and can be used with any project.
19. Selecting the Arrow tool to reshape the intervening curves is the best way to edit a Brush-created line.

Saturday Morning Review Answers (Sessions 5-10)

1. Create a new layer by clicking the New Layer icon in the Timeline or by going to Insert ⇨ New Layer.
2. Go to Edit ⇨ Copy to copy one layer's elements and then go to Edit ⇨ Paste to paste them to the target layer.
3. Create content on each separate layer that is to be used for the background.
4. Double-click the layer name in the Timeline, and then type in the new name.
5. Deleting a layer removes all of its contents from the stage.
6. Move a layer by clicking and then dragging it to a new position.
7. Layers used in Symbol Edit mode apply only to that specific symbol.
8. The final design of the symbol can be made much more complex when you use symbol layers.
9. Choose Edit ⇨ Paste to paste content from one layer onto another.
10. Select the first frame and go to Insert ⇨ Frame. Drag the inserted frame to the end point that represents the last frame.

Answers to Part Reviews

11. Access the Controller by going to Window ⇨ Toolbars ⇨ Controller. Use it like a VCR Controller to navigate the Timeline.
12. Select the content and go to Insert ⇨ Convert To Symbol.
13. Place the instances on different layers at different points on the Timeline.
14. Preview a scene for playback by going to Control ⇨ Test Movie or Control ⇨ Test Scene.
15. Click the instance's Play button in the Symbol Library, or choose Control ⇨ Play Movie.
16. Go to Symbol Edit mode for the selected symbol and create duplicates of that symbol. Customize each as needed.
17. The library content in a Common Library can be used by other projects easily.
18. Just drag the symbols from the Common Library into the symbol list area in your project's Symbol Library.
19. A *mask layer* contains the content that applies to the *masked layer* below it.
20. Convert strokes to fills for editing purposes, and to remove the stroke.
21. Go to Modify ⇨ Shape ⇨ Convert Lines to Fills.
22. This is how the button appears when the mouse pointer is not over the button's active area.
23. This is how the button appears when the mouse pointer is over the button's active area.
24. This is how the button appears when the mouse is clicked down on the button's active area.
25. This is the area of the screen set aside as the button's active area.
26. Go to Control ⇨ Enable Simple Buttons, and RMB-click [Control+click] to bring up the menu options, and then select Actions.
27. Assign an action to a button state by selecting the appropriate Action Script.
28. Use layers so that any of the facial elements can be animated separately.
29. Shape tweening is indicated by a solid line with an arrow from keyframe to keyframe. Motion tweening is indicated by a dashed line from keyframe to keyframe. Shape tweening colors the Timeline green; motion tweening colors it blue.

Saturday Afternoon Review Answers (Sessions 11-16)

1. The three main options are font, size, and style.
2. Guide layers display stage content that needs to be referenced.
3. Separate layers can be edited separately.
4. Go to Modify ➪ Transform ➪ Scale and move the control handles.
5. Set the parameters by selecting File ➪ Publish Settings.
6. "Match Movie" is the most important item to consider. Unless you are an experienced HTML user, leave the rest at the default settings.
7. Exported formats have no connection to the Flash project file (.fla).
8. Highlight the selected text, and then select a new font from the Text menu.
9. Go to Modify ➪ Transform ➪ Scale and drag out the width control.
10. Select each letter individually by highlighting it, and then select the desired font.
11. The names of the three device fonts are sans, serif, and typewriter.
12. The text on a mask layer must be broken apart.
13. Set these options in the Frames panel.
14. DVE stands for "Digital Video Effect."
15. Create a text drop shadow by choosing Edit ➪ Copy, then Edit ➪ Paste in Place, and then grouping after placing the drop shadow where you want it.
16. The Alpha channel controls transparency.
17. By clicking the guide layer icon under the layers stack in the Timeline.
18. Break it apart and then move and rotate the letters.
19. Text is made of fills only, so it can be edited in the same way as any other filled object.
20. Access the Mixer panel by selecting Window ➪ Panels ➪ Mixer.
21. Progressive reveals cause image content to come into view by the slow removal of an overlayed graphic or mask.
22. Pop animations use keyframes without tweens.
23. Access the Frames panel by going to Window ➪ Panels ➪ Frame.

24. Export Flash images by going to File ⇨ Export Image and selecting the needed format.
25. The altered bitmap can be used as a background or as content for an animation.

Saturday Evening Review Answers (Sessions 17-20)

1. Amplitude is volume.
2. Create sound effects by adjusting the shape of the envelope(s).
3. Imported bitmaps can be scaled and rotated in the same way as any other content, by going to Modify ⇨ Transform ⇨ Scale and Modify ⇨ Transform ⇨ Rotate.
4. The vector translation of a bitmap is always different than the original image content, with the degree of difference based upon the settings used in the translation.
5. This Timeline process is called fading.
6. The SFX layer is used for event sounds.
7. Event sounds are used to mark specific events or sound effects.
8. Stream sounds are used to generate an overall sound track.
9. Access the Sound panel by selecting Window ⇨ Panels ⇨ Sound.
10. Looping repeats the sound as many times as you require.
11. Looping is not recommended for long stream sounds; use caution when using looping on event sounds as well.
12. To force any sound to stop at a specific frame on the Timeline, place a keyframe on the sound layer at that spot. Then go to the Sound settings panel and select Stop from the Sync list.
13. The global audio parameter controls are located within the specific file format pages in the Publish Settings window.
14. An animation that shows the content getting smaller and smaller is sometimes created by zooming out. The same effect can be created by scaling the image content to shrink over time.
15. The Sound Score layer is used for stream sounds.
16. Go to Modify ⇨ Break Apart and select the bitmap section you wish to alter.

17. Event sounds mark a keyframe event; stream sounds act like a soundtrack.
18. To fade out a sound, adjust the amplitude to zero in the sound's Edit envelope.

Sunday Morning Review Answers (Sessions 21-26)

1. First, instances from any Symbol Library can be used to create new symbols in Symbol Edit mode. Second, each symbol in any Symbol Library can be composed of an unlimited amount of layers, each of which can contain another symbol or any other drawn, painted, or imported element.
2. The effect of words appearing letter by letter in an animation is called a typewriter effect.
3. *Up*, *Over*, and *Down* are the three animated states of a button.
4. The fourth button state, *Hit*, enables you to select the button's active area.
5. An object action is a scripted direction applied to a button state.
6. A radial wipe is created by using a mask layer to delete parts of a circular mask over time.
7. Pop a text block to the screen by setting its initial keyframe on the Timeline at the frame position where you want it to suddenly appear.
8. A shatter is an effect that displays layer content falling away in shards.
9. Speed lines indicate that an object is moving through space.
10. Use these screens as backgrounds by using a screen grab utility to create an image of the onion-skinned layers.
11. The fill color of a selected object is altered to create strobes.
12. To see the animated symbol, choose Control ⇨ Play Movie or Control ⇨ Play Scene.
13. Shatter a bitmap by first using Break Apart editing, and then selecting and moving parts of the bitmap over time to fall out of the scene.
14. No. Tweening should only be used on one symbol layer at a time, unless you are striving for chaos. Animated symbols move internally without tweening.
15. Move the center point of any selection by going to Modify ⇨ Transform ⇨ Edit Center, and then move the center point.

16. Use a symbol font (Wingding, Dingbat, Astrology, or Hieroglyphic, for example) to create alien text.
17. Don't use any tweening when you want stationary objects to pop onscreen.
18. In this case, shape tweening is used.
19. Onion skinning allows you to see the other frames through the active one.
20. The Onion Skin controls are located in the Timeline window.
21. Choosing Modify ➪ Transform ➪ Flip Vertical or Flip Horizontal flips any selected element on the stage.
22. Nested symbols are important because they can create more complex symbol instances.
23. Frame actions target all the frames in a layer, not just those pertaining to a specific object.
24. Using layers in Symbol Edit mode keeps the content of a symbol separate so it can be edited without interfering with other content.

Sunday Afternoon Review Answers (Sessions 27-30)

1. Grouping the shadow with the object enables both object and shadow to move together, creating a more realistic 3-D effect.
2. Place content between two layers so the viewer gets the idea that depth is involved.
3. Linear Gradients look like a series of lines; Radial Gradients are constructed from an outer edge inward or from a center point outward.
4. Change the color spectrum by going to the Fill panel, selecting the gradient type, and altering the position and colors used in the gradient's spectrum.
5. Use shape tweening to animate a gradient fill.
6. Access the Fill panel by choosing Window ➪ Panels ➪ Fill.
7. In the Fill panel, select the Transform tab, and then set the width and height parameters for the imported bitmap. Create a rectangle that covers the stage and fill with tiled images set to the size you specify.
8. Choose black as the Tint value of the last keyframe.
9. Choose white as the Tint value of the last keyframe.

10. Select bitmap from the Fill panel list, and then choose the bitmap thumbnail that represents your choice.
11. Use a selected color fill on bitmap areas that have been broken apart.
12. Change the bitmap image to a vector image (Modify ⇨ Trace bitmap) with larger pixel area settings.
13. Select a bitmap image in your Symbol Library that you want to alter by editing it externally. Right-click [Control+click]. Select Edit With from the list. Select the bitmap image application you want to edit it with from the file folder on your system.
14. Set the green and blue values as low as possible and push red to the max.
15. If the keyframes do not flow evenly, you've neglected to use tweening between keyframes.
16. Go to Modify ⇨ Trace Bitmap and set the parameters according to the look you are trying to achieve.
17. Gradients are applied to objects as fills.
18. Create a blink by using no tweening between keyframes that display the object as visible and invisible.

Index

Symbols & Numbers
3-D applications, 329
3-D content
  bitmap, 259
  creating, 327–329
  importing, 329–331
  with shadows, 323–327

actors, 164
Adobe After Effects, 338
Adobe Illustrator, 334–335
Adobe Photoshop
  adding background gradient in, 200
  capabilities, 338
  as Flash partner, 338, 339
  handshaking, 338–339
  Illustrator format and, 338
  importing Flash files into, 199–200
advanced effects. See also instance effects
  in Effect panel, 321
  "Fade to White," 320
  finished Timeline, 321
  generating, 320–321
  RGBA percentages, 320
  Timeline, 320
Align panel, 212

Alpha channels, 179
animated background content. See also background content
  animated foreground content vs., 85
  cloud creation, 87–91
  creating, 85–91
  Timeline, 86–87
animated button character
  action assignment, 246–248
  animation creation, 244–245
  creating, 241–244
  Down state, 243, 244
  Hit state, 244
  in Library window, 243
  naming, 242
  "READY" text, 242
  stroke settings, 241–242
  Timeline window for, 245
  Up state, 243
animated foreground content
  animated background content vs., 85
  bird, 94–99
  creating, 93–104
  fish, 100–103
animated gradients
  configurations, 300
  creating, 298–300
  guidelines, 300
  radial fill, 298–299
  types of, 298
animated groups, embedding, 284

animated patterned background
 Bird symbol, 255
 creating, 254–256
 defined, 255
 illustrated, 256
animated pull-on reveal, 277–278
animated slide shows
 creating, 229–236
 defined, 229
 length of, 231
 number of images, 230
 slide placement, 233–234
 sound in, 234–236
 titles, 230–233
animated symbols
 creating, 284–285
 Fish_Group, 284, 286
 nesting, 285–288
animations
 button-driven, 244–245
 duration, 88
 GIF, 197
 length, 231
 logo title, 159–161
 nested, 283–291
 oval, 131–132
 on paths, 93–103
 playing, 88
 previewing, 99, 235
 text, 146–150
 variety, 146
animator(s)
 background artist, 267
 colorist, 267
 defined, 164
 keyframe, 267
 tweener, 267
ANIMS folder, 331
Anti-alias mode
 defined, 9
 distinguishing, 9
 illustrated, 10
 lines in, 18
arrow, 9
Arrow tool
 accessing, 20
 curves with, 174, 175
 defined, 20
 dragging on snapped node with, 21

 selecting image with, 45
 selecting overlapping elements with, 26
 selecting/separating curved elements with, 24–25
 using, 24–25, 159
audio (Flash). See also sound
 event, 213–216
 Publish settings for, 217–219
 streaming, 216–217
 understanding, 213–220
 working with, 221–227
Audio Video Interface (AVI) movies, 199, 331

B

background
 artist, 267
 colors, 231
 gradient, 300–303
 layers, 87
 onion skin, 272–273
 patterned, 254–256
 shadows project, 325
 single color, 81–82
background content
 animated, 85–92
 creating, 81–92
 stable, 81–85
Basic Actions. See also button actions
 definitions, 136
 double-clicking, 246
 FSCommend, Tell Target, If Frame is Loaded, 136
 Get URL, 136
 Go To, 135, 136, 246–247
 list of, 134, 246
 Load Movie, Unload Movie, 136
 On Mouse Event, 136
 Play/Stop, 136
 Stop All Sounds, 136
 Toggle High Quality, 136
behaviors
 button, 51, 120
 graphic, 51
 movie clip, 51
Bezier control points
 accessing, 46
 adding, 27–28
 creating, 46, 47
 defined, 24

Index

deleting, 47
moving, 50
Pen tool, 46
for resizing, 9
in sound amplitude, 226
using, 27
viewing, 26, 46
without border, 10

Bezier handles
defined, 22
manipulating, 24
moving, 47, 50
using, 25
viewing, 47

bird animation
Animated Bird symbol, 94
Bird_Body layer, 94, 95
BirdFly layer, 97–98, 99
Bird_Wing layer, 94, 95
creating, 94–99
flight path, 97–99
previewing, 99
wing movement, 95, 96

BirdFish Common Library, 117

bitmap editing
Break-Apart method, 308–309
external, 310–312
illustrated images, 309, 310, 311
internal, 308–310
trace-based method, 309–310

bitmaps
advanced techniques, 305–313
cautions, 206–207
cutting apart, 209–212
exploring, 205–212
external, editing, 310–312
files, 206
for fills, 305–307
flipping, horizontal, 206, 207
flipping, vertical, 206, 207
internal, editing, 308–310
for painting, 305–307
resolution dependence, 205
rotating, 206, 207
scaling, 206, 207
tracing, 208–209, 309
transformation time, 208
transforming, 205–208
translation to vectors, 208–209

vector-based graphics versus, 205

bitmap-to-vector translation, 153

branching projects, 129

Break-Apart editing
accessing, 56
defined, 56
internal bitmap, 308–309
text, 145

brush strokes
cloned, 39
connecting, 41–42
painting, 42–43

Brush tool
accessing, 35
defined, 35
fill color, 35
joining shapes with, 44
Options pop-up list, 36
Options section and, 35
Paint options, 36, 37
shapes, 38
Shift key with, 39
sizes, 36, 37
using, 38–45, 107

brushes
shapes, 38
sizes, 36

button actions
animated button character, 246–248
assigning, 132–136, 246–248
Basic Actions, 134, 136, 246
categories, 134
defined, 126
FSCommend, Tell Target, If Frame is Loaded, 136
Get URL, 136
Go To, 135, 136
introduction to, 129–137
list, 134
Load Movie, Unload Movie, 136
On Mouse Event, 136
Play/Stop, 136
Stop All Sounds, 136
Toggle High Quality, 136
types of, 246

button behavior, 51

button projects
designing, 129–132
Down state, 125
Eyes layer, 122

Continued

button projects *(continued)*
    Hit state, 126
    Mask_01 layer, 122, 123
    Mouth layer, 120, 121, 122
    oval animation, 131–132
    OvalAnim_01 layer, 130, 131
    Over state, 124–125
    previewing, 126
    Sun layer, 120, 124, 125, 126
    sun shape, 121
    Up state, 124, 126
button-driven animation
    actions, assigning, 246–248
    creating, 244–245
    frames, 245
    Timeline window for, 245
buttons. *See also button actions*
    activating, 126, 133
    animated, 241–245
    creating, 119–126
    defined, 119
    Down state, 125
    enabling, 133
    Hit state, 126
    magic box front, 329
    mask layer, 122–123
    naming, 242
    Over state, 124–125
    previewing, 126
    RMB-clicking, 133
    as symbols, 120
    Up state, 124
Buttons Library
    Arrow, 9
    Arrow Buttons icon, 8
    highlighted selection, 8
    illustrated, 8
    opening, 8

C

center point, moving, 262
character voices, 164
clock project. See also timepiece projects
    center points, 262
    creating, 260–262
    Hand layer, 260, 261
    Hand rotation, 262
    Hand symbol, 261
    hands illustration, 261
    image illustration, 261
    letters, 261
cloned brush stroke. *See also brush strokes*
    flipping, 40–41
    moving, 40, 41
    selecting, 39
Cloud clip, 90, 91
clouds
    animated, 87–91
    creating with Oval tool, 88
    duration, 88
color picker, accessing, 34
colorist, 267
colors
    gradient, 297
    highlight, 11
    movie background, 231
    opacity/transparency data, 179
    outline, 71
    Pen tool stroke, 48
    strobe, 276
    stroke, 48, 100
    through text, 176
Common Libraries
    BirdFish, 117
    Camera Shutter 3, 235
    creating, 59–60
    defined, 59
    editing symbols in, 60
    Flash library saved as, 51
    folder, saving projects in, 103
    listing, 60
    Sounds, 235
    submenu, 8
Control menu
    Enable Simple Buttons command, 126, 133
    Test Movie command, 99, 102, 103, 150, 175
    Test Scene command, 91
control points. See Bezier control points
Controller toolbar, 14
Controller window
    accessing, 86
    illustrated, 87
    Play button, 91, 98, 278
    Rewind button, 87
Corel Painter, 335–336
corner points, snapping lines to, 21

credits
- actors, 164
- alignment, 167–168
- animator(s), 164
- character voices, 164
- copyright and trademark symbols, 166–167
- creating, 163–171
- dedication, 164
- deep text controls, 168–171
- defined, 163
- director, 163
- fonts, 165–166
- global alignment, 168
- internal text alignment, 167
- listing, 163–164
- music & sound effects, 164
- narration, 164
- producer, 163
- story, 164
- text for, 165–171
- "Thanks," 164

Curious Labs Poser, 336, 337
curved lines. See also lines
- Bezier handles, 22
- Break Apart command on, 77
- creating, 21–22, 26
- Sub-Select tool with, 22

curves
- common, removing, 24
- editing, 24, 46
- grouped, 25
- reshaping, 47

D

dedication, 164
deselection, 41
device fonts, 171, 175
digital display. See also timepiece projects
- beep sound event, 264
- creating, 263–264
- illustrated, 263, 264
- symbolic font instances, 264

Digital Video Effects. See also text animation
- creating, 188–190
- defined, 188
- illustrated, 190

director, 163

Discreet Logic's 3D Studio Max, 336–337
diver's suit. See also head animation
- creating, 112–117
- drawing face, 115
- Face Mask layer, 113, 115
- illustrated, 116
- painting, 115
- Suit layer, 113
- as symbol in Project Library, 116–117
- Tanks layer, 115

Down state. See also buttons
- activating, 125
- animated button character, 243, 244
- defined, 125

drawing tablet, 31
drop shadows (text). See also text; text effects
- creating, 176–177
- defined, 176
- illustrated, 177

DVEs. See Digital Video Effects

E

Edit Envelope window
- accessing, 225
- Custom option, 226
- Effect list, 225–226
- Fade Left to Right option, 225
- illustrated, 225, 226, 227
- score sound fade out, 234
- sound waveform display, 225

Edit menu
- Clear command, 18, 19, 20
- Copy command, 39, 77, 78, 149, 157
- Copy Frames command, 224
- Cut command, 186
- Duplicate command, 74
- Edit Movie command, 59, 97, 126, 287
- Paste command, 186, 189
- Paste Frames command, 224
- Paste In Place command, 39, 77, 78, 116, 149
- Preferences command, 7, 32
- Select All command, 18, 19, 20

Edit Movie mode, 157
editing
- Break-Apart, 56, 145, 308–309
- curves, 24, 46

Continued

editing *(continued)*
    external bitmap, 310–312
    instances, 55–58
    internal bitmap, 308–310
    layer content, 78
    layers, 154
    with Pen tool, 48–50
    rotoscope, 268–271
    score sound, 236
    sound envelope, 224–226
    text, 145–146
Editing tab (Preferences window)
    Drawing Settings area, 33
    illustrated, 32
Effect panel
    accessing, 316, 318, 320
    Advanced option, 320
    Alpha percentage slider, 317
    illustrated, 317, 319
    RGB values, 318
    RGBA percentages, 320
    Tint option, 318
event sounds. See also sounds
    beep, 264
    creating, 213–216
    defined, 213
    download of, 216
    duration, 215
    files, 213–214
    looping setting, 224, 235
    streaming sounds versus, 216
Export Movie window, 198
exporting
    defined, 193
    Flash movies, 198–201
    publishing versus, 193
external bitmap editing, 310–311
eyes project
    Birdy layer, 280
    creating, 279–281
    defined, 279
    Eyes layer, 280
    face enlargement, 279–280
    finished illustration, 281
    poser head for, 279

fade effects. See also instance effects
    defined, 315
    with different fades, 318
    "Fade to White," 320
    finished Timeline, 317
    running, 317
    Timeline, 316
    using, 315–317
fades, 188
Fast mode
    defined, 9
    distinguishing, 9
    illustrated, 10
    lines in, 18
file extensions, missing, 206
File menu
    Close command, 6
    Export command, 198
    Export Image command, 198, 199
    Export Movie command, 198
    Import command, 214, 222, 263
    New command, 6, 82, 105, 120
    Open As Library command, 194, 280
    Open command, 255, 328
    Publish command, 196, 198
    Publish Preview command, 198
    Publish Settings command, 218
    Save As command, 29, 34
files
    Barn.jpg, 306, 315
    Bic_Anim_01.fla, 194
    bitmap, 206
    CH_07A.fla, 255, 328
    CH_07E.fla, 284
    CH_11.fla, 154
    CH_16A.fla, 194
    CH_16B.fla, 196, 198
    CH_17Tower.fla, 214
    CH22_01.jpg, 252
    CH_25B.fla, 280
    Clock_01.jpg, 259, 260
    DigClk.jpg, 263
    event sound, 213–214
    FHandTrace_02.swf, 209
    Flwr_01.jpg, 306
    HrGls.jpg, 259, 264

Index

imported, 194
MyFace_02.fla, 46
Poser.jpg, 279
saving, 194
slide show image, 233
transferring, between libraries, 195
WAV, 234

Fill panel
accessing, 33, 296, 306
color spectrum bar, 297, 298
gradient animations and, 300
illustrated, 35, 296
imported images in, 306
Linear Gradient option, 296, 301, 302, 324
Radial Gradient option, 158, 298, 303, 325

fills
bitmaps for, 305–307
gradient, 297
head animation, 105
radial, 158, 159
selecting, 35
text creation with, 175
types of, 33

fish animation
developing, 100–103
fish instances, 102
Fish layer, 100
Fish_Group symbol, 102
FishJump layer, 101
symbol, 100–101
testing, 102

Flash
function of, 5–6
importing into, 200–201
interface, 6
opening, 6

flashing. See strobes

flipping
bitmaps, 206, 207
cloned brush stroke, 41
horizontal, 40, 206, 286
vertical, 91, 96, 206, 207

fonts. See also text
credit, 165–166
defined, 142
device, 171, 175
illustrated, 142
list, 165
sans-serif, 143, 171

selecting, 165
serif, 142, 143, 171
size, 165–166
typewriter, 171

Frame Actions window
accessing, 247
defined, 247
illustrated, 248
Stop action, 247, 248

Frame panel
accessing, 89
Easing area, 189
illustrated, 89, 147, 190
Motion option, 98, 146
Rotate area, 190
Scale checkbox, 189
Tweening option, 89, 98

frames. See also keyframes
for button-driven animation, 245
copying, 90, 224
Down, 120, 125
dragging, 223, 286, 316, 320
Hit, 120, 126
in-between, 98
inserting, 90, 223
moving, 88
multiple, selecting, 90
Over, 120, 124–125
pasting, 224
Up, 120, 124

FSCommend, Tell Target, If Frame is Loaded action, 136

G

General tab (Preferences window)
Highlight Color option, 11–12
Undo Levels input area, 7

Get URL action, 136
GIF animations, 197
Go To action, 135, 136

gradient background project
Backdrop layer, 300
COSMIC text placement, 302
creating, 300–303
defined, 300
finished illustration, 303

Continued

gradient background project (continued)
  linear gradient fill configuration, 301
  Star layer, 303
  Text layer, 301
gradients
  animating, 298–300
  bunching up, 324
  color selections, 297
  color space, 297
  creating, 295–298
  defined, 295
  elements, 295
  fills, 297
  linear, 296
  previewing, 296
  radial, 298
  spectrum, 296
  working with, 295–304
graphic behavior
  assigning, 154, 157
  as behavior type, 51
graphic elements
  dragging, 277, 278
  grouped, dragging, 277, 278
  logo, 157–159
  scaling, 189
Grid settings window, 13
Grid submenu. See also View menu
  Edit Grid command, 12
  Show Grid command, 168
  Snap to Grid command, 168
grids
  illustrated use of, 168
  settings, 12–13
  snapping to, 12–13, 168
  viewing, 11–12, 168
grouped elements
  defined, 25
  drawing and, 185
  embedding, 284
guide layer. See also layers
  creating, 148, 154
  defined, 70, 148
  invisible, 150
  naming, 148
  working with, 148–150

H

handles. See Bezier handles
handshaking
  Adobe After Effects, 338
  Adobe Illustrator, 334–335
  Adobe Photoshop, 338–339
  Corel Painter, 335–336
  Curious Labs Poser, 336, 337
  defined, 333
  Discreet Logic's 3D Studio Max, 336–337
  Macromedia FreeHand, 333–334
head animation
  adding shading to, 107
  animating, 112
  basic head illustration, 111
  Brows layer, 108, 109
  creating, 105–112
  with diver's suit, 112–117
  eye shape creation, 109
  Eyes_01 layer, 109, 110
  Eyes_02 layer, 110
  Face layer, 107, 108
  Face Mask layer, 113
  fill color, 105
  instance, 112
  layer creation, 106
  layer shapes, altering, 113
  Mouth layer, 111
  pupils creation, 110
head morph project
  AVI and QuickTime versions, 331
  defined, 329
  first frame, 330
  frame series, 331
  importing, 329–331
  Timeline display, 330
Highlight Color option (Preferences window), 11–12
Hit state. See also buttons
  animated button character, 244
  area, creating, 126
  defined, 126, 243
hot area, 243
hour glass. See also timepiece projects
  creating, 264–266
  defined, 264

Down layer, 265
illustrated, 265
sand movement illustration, 266
Stream layer, 265
Up layer, 265
Hypertext Markup Language (HTML), 197

I

Illustrate!. See also handshaking
configuration, 337
defined, 336
images
bitmap, 251
changing size of, 9
importing, 306
moving, 23
scaling, 9
selecting, 45
in slide shows, 230, 233
tiled, 312
importing
3-D content, 329–331
bitmap image sequence, 268
into Flash, 200–201
into Photoshop, 199–200
Ink Bottle tool
options, 31
selecting, 49, 83
using, 177
input devices, 31
Insert menu
Add Frame command, 223
Convert to Symbol command, 56, 72, 79, 90, 106, 116
Frame command, 284, 286, 288
Keyframe command, 132, 284
Layer command, 68, 82, 83
Layer Name command, 87
New Symbol command, 52, 94, 100, 120, 154, 157
instance effects
advanced, 320–321
fad, 315–318
tint, 318–319
understanding, 315–322

instances
defined, 54
deleting, 77
dragging/dropping, 73, 74
editing, 55–58
placing, 54, 57
rescaling, 54
resizing, 55, 133
rotating/scaling, 55
selecting, 54, 77
Symbol Library, 284
interactive buttons. See also button actions
activating, 126, 133
creating, 119–126
design, 130–131
Down state, 125
Hit state, 126
mask layer, 122–123
Over state, 124–125
Up state, 124
internal bitmap editing, 308–310

J

Joint Photographic Experts Group (JPEG), 196

K

Kern option, 169
keyframe animator, 267
keyframes. See also frames
alterations, 113
animating between, 298
copying, 224
creating, 99
indicators, 112
inserting, 89, 95
selecting, 96
at sequence ends, 277
stopping sounds at, 217

L

Lasso tool, 210
layer content. *See also* **layers**
  deleting, 72
  editing, 78
  hidden, 76
  illustrated, 73
  management, 72–79
  marquee around, 72, 77
  moving, 75–76
  naming, 72
  as outline, 70
  selecting, 77
Layer Properties window
  accessing, 71
  illustrated, 71
  Layer Height option, 72
  Lock checkbox, 71
  Name box, 71
  Outline Color swatch, 71
  Show checkbox, 71
  Type buttons, 71
layers. *See also* **layer content**
  adding, 68
  background, 87
  Cloud, 91
  default, 230
  deleting, 70, 78
  displaying contents of, 70
  editing, 154
  guide, 70, 148–150
  height, 72
  insertion location, 68
  joining shapes on, 44
  locked, opening, 70
  locking, 70, 82, 107, 154, 174
  magic box with, 327–329
  mask, 122–123
  moving, in layer stack, 74
  naming, 107, 154
  outline color, 71
  progressive reveal, 184, 185
  renaming, 71, 72
  scene, 95
  selecting, 68, 69
  shapes, altering, 113
  shapes, selecting, 116
  symbol, 95
  on Timeline, 88
  timing, 288
  working with, 67–80
Layers window. *See also* **Timelines**
  guide layer in, 148
  illustrated, 68, 69
  Insert Guide Layer control, 70, 71
  Insert Layer control, 70, 71
  Lock icon, 70
  opening, 67–68
  Outline mode, 70, 75
  selecting layers in, 68, 69
  Square icon, 70
  Trash icon, 70
letters
  deselecting, 178
  finished, 157
  illustrated, 155
  rotating, 156
  selecting, 156
  strokes around, 179
libraries
  Buttons, 8
  Common, 51, 59–60
  creating, 51–55
  defined, 51
  loading content to/from, 8–11
  navigating, 58–59
  placing objects in, 56–57
  Project, 60
  saving, 51
  Symbol, 283, 284
  symbols, creating, 52–55
  transferring files between, 195
  working with, 51–60
Library preview window
  graphic appearance in, 52, 53
  Play button, 90
Library window
  Delete icon, 59
  Folder icon, 58–59
  icons, 58
  Library Options list, 57
  New Symbol icon, 59
  opening, 51–52
  Options list, 243
  sound files in, 215, 222

Index

Line tool
  accessing, 17, 18
  drawing with, 18–23
  Shift key with, 23
linear gradients. See also gradients; radial gradients
  configuring, 301, 324
  in Fill panel, 296–297
  spectrum pointers, 302
lines
  constraining, 23
  control points, viewing, 47
  curved, creating, 21–22
  drawing, 18
  editing with Pen tool, 50
  grouped, 25
  sizes, illustrated, 19
  sizing, 18, 19
  snapping, 20
  styles, 20
Load Movie, Unload Movie action, 136
logo design project
  CircleGuide layer, 156
  creating, 153–161
  finished, 160
  finished Text layer, 157
  letters illustration, 155
  letters manipulation, 156
  letters selection, 156
  LogoBkgrd symbol, 157, 158
  LogoFinal symbol, 159
  LogoText symbol, 154
  SeaSnake symbol, 158
  steps, 154–157
  TextGuide layer, 154
logos
  creating, 153–161
  graphics, 157–159
  importance of, 153
  separating elements of, 160
  as symbols, 154
  text, 153–157
  in title animation, 159–161

M

Macromedia Dreamweaver 3, 333
Macromedia Fireworks 3, 333
Macromedia FreeHand
  features/interface design, 334
  handshaking methods, 333–334
magic box project. See also 3-D content
  Bird layer, 328
  Birdy symbol, 328, 329
  box creation, 327–328
  BoxBack layer, 328
  BoxFrnt layer, 327, 328
  building, 327–329
  button, 329
  defined, 327
Magic Wand Settings window
  accessing, 308
  illustrated, 308
  Smoothing option, 308
  Threshold option, 308
Magic Wand tool
  accessing, 308
  illustrated, 309
  using, 309
Magnification submenu. See also View menu
  Frame command, 11
  Show All command, 11
Main toolbar, 14
mask layer. See also layers
  defined, 122
  down-arrow icon, 123
  effects, 123
  fill content on, 122
  illustrated use of, 123
  as mask target, 123
  selecting, 122
  text, 173–176
  using, 122–123
media, in Flash library, 51
Mixer panel
  accessing, 178
  Alpha box, 178, 179, 180
  components, 178–179
  illustrated, 179
  Mixer icon, 178
  R, G, B boxes, 178, 180

Modify menu
    Break Apart command, 56, 77, 145, 155, 158
    Group command, 25, 45, 149, 158, 176, 277
    Layer command, 154, 173, 252
    Movie command, 230
    Shape command, 131
    Trace Bitmap command, 208, 309, 330
    Transform command, 9, 40, 146, 207
    Ungroup command, 25
motion trail. See speed lines
Motion Tweening. See also tweens
    creating, 144
    distinguishing, 112
    for moving text block, 272
    selecting, 146
    setting, 147
movie clip, 51
Movie Properties window
    accessing, 231
    Background Color, 231
    Frame Rate value, 231
    illustrated, 231
    Width/Height Dimensions, 231
movies
    AVI, 199, 331
    background color, 231
    exporting, 198–201
    length calculation, 230
    QTVR, 198
    QuickTime, 197–198
    size, 231
MP3 sounds, 214
music & sound effects, 164

N

narration, 164
nested animations. See also animations
    based on nested symbols, 283
    defined, 283
    developing, 283–291
    Fish_Group_2 symbol, 286–287
    Fish_Group_3 symbol, 287
    Fish_Group_4 symbol, 288
    nest building, 285–288
    symbol animation, 284–285
    Symbol Library for, 283

nested symbols, 283
nonmoving background content. See also
    background content
    composite, 82
    creating, 81–85
    single color, 81–82
    Sky layer, 82–85
    types of, 81

O

Object Actions window
    accessing, 133, 246
    Basic Actions list, 134
    bottom half of, 135
    function of, 134
    illustrated, 133, 246
    Object Actions list, 134
On Mouse Event action, 136
Onion Skin controls
    accessing, 269
    illustrated, 269
    Modify Onion Markers menu, 271, 272
    outlines, 270
onion skins
    background creation, 272–273
    defined, 267
    history, 267
    markers, 269, 270, 271
    in rotoscoping, 268–271
    in speed lines, 271–272
    using, 267–273
Outline mode
    defined, 9
    illustrated, 10
oval animation
    creating, 131–132
    modifying shape of, 132
    OvalAnim_01 layer, 131
    playing, 131
    Timeline, 132
Oval tool
    accessing, 17
    cloud shape creation with, 88
    overlapping circles with, 23
    Shift key with, 23
    using, 23–25, 109, 113

ovals
  constraining, 23, 155
  overlapping, 88
  Sub-Select tool on, 106
Over state. *See also buttons*
  area, creating, 124–125
  defined, 124
overlapping elements
  assumption, 24
  removing, 26
  selecting, 26

P

Paint Bucket tool
  accessing, 29, 34
  using, 36, 43
Paintbrush tool
  accessing, 306
  using, 306–307
painting, bitmaps for, 305–307
panels
  Align, 212
  default, 15
  Effect, 316–320
  Fill, 33, 296
  Frame, 89, 98, 146–147, 189–190
  layouts, saving, 15
  list of, 14
  Mixer, 178–180
  Sound, 215–216, 224–225
  Stroke, 46, 241–242
  Text Options, 168–171
  Transform, 285, 286
Panels submenu. *See also Window menu*
  Effect command, 316, 318, 320
  Fill command, 33, 296, 298, 301, 306, 324
  Frame command, 89, 95, 131, 146
  Mixer command, 178
  Panel Sets command, 14
  Sound command, 215, 223
  Stroke command, 18, 20, 46, 100, 109, 130, 177
  Transform command, 285, 286
path animation. See also animations
  bird, 94–99
  defined, 93
  developing, 94–103
  fish, 100–103

  use of, 93
patterned background, animated, 254–256
Pen tool
  accessing, 27
  for adding control points, 27–28
  Bezier control point creation, 47, 84
  Bezier control points, 46
  defined, 46
  editing with, 48–50
  joining shapes with, 44
  using, 46–50
Pencil tool
  access, 32
  Ink option, 33
  joining shapes with, 44
  Line Thickness option, 241
  LMB with, 33
  Smooth mode, 94
  Snap To Objects command and, 269
  Solid Stroke option, 241
  using, 68
Photoshop. See Adobe Photoshop
Play/Stop action, 136
Polygon tool, 253
pops, 188
Poserz folder, 329
Preferences settings window
  Drawing Settings area, 33
  Editing tab, 32
  General tab, 7
  Highlight Color option, 11–12
  opening, 7
  Undo Levels input area, 7
producer, 163
progressive reveal. See also text animation
  defined, 183
  illustrated, 187
  layers, 184, 185
  steps, 184–187
  variations, 186
Project Libraries
  Cloud clip, 90
  creating, 72
  Diver, 117
  dragging files to, 195
  editing symbols in, 60
  face symbol, 116
  importing, 194

Continued

Project Libraries *(continued)*
    opening/closing, 75
    saving, 117
    suit symbol, 116–117
projects
    animated button character, 241–244
    animated patterned background, 254–256
    animated slide show, 229–236
    bird animation, 94–99
    branching, 129
    button, 120–132
    button-driven animation, 246–248
    clock, 260–262
    digital display, 263–264
    eyes, 279–281
    fish animation, 100–103
    gradient background, 300–303
    head animation, 105–112
    head morph, 329–331
    hour glass, 264–266
    loading, 194–195
    logo design, 153–161
    magic box, 327–329
    nonmoving background content, 81–85
    oval animation, 131–132
    saving, 103
    screens, starting new, 6
    shadows, 323–326
    timepiece, 259–266
Projects folder
    CH_07A.fla, 328
    CH_07A Library, 277
    CH_11.fla, 154
    CH_16A.fla, 194
    CH_25B.fla, 280
Publish Settings window
    accessing, 196, 218
    Alpha setting, 197
    Flash tab, 196–197
    Formats tab, 196
    GIF tab, 197
    HTML Alignment setting, 197
    HTML tab, 197
    illustrated, 196, 218
    JPEG Quality slider, 196
    Layers setting, 197
    Playback settings, 197–198
    Quality setting, 197
    QuickTime tab, 197–198
    RealPlayer tab, 219
    Scale setting, 197
    Type options, 218
    Use Default Names setting, 196
    Window Mode setting, 197
publishing
    defined, 193
    exporting versus, 193
    Flash content, 196–198
pull-on reveal
    Birdy_01 symbol, 277
    creating, 277–278
    grouped graphic, 277, 278
    testings, 278

Q

QuickTime
    control parameters, 218
    morph animation movie, 331
    Publish settings, 198
    Virtual Reality (QTVR) movies, 198

R

radial fill, 158, 159
radial gradients. See also gradients; linear gradients
    creating, 303, 325
    in Fill panel, 298
radial wipe. See also wipes
    bitmap images, 251
    creating, 252
    defined, 251
    frame illustration, 253
    layer, 252
RAM, 7
RealAudio parameters, 219
Rectangle tool
    accessing, 17, 26, 307
    bitmap painting generated by, 307
    dragging, 26
    Shift key with, 23
    using, 26–29, 307
rectangles
    borders, curved, 174
    constraining, 23
    creating, 82

Index

overlapping, 26–27
random, multicolored, 174
registration symbol, 166, 167
Resources folder
   Barn.jpg, 306, 315
   CH22_01.jpg, 252
   Clock_01.jpg, 259, 260
   DigClk.jpg, 263
   FHandTrace_02.swf, 209
   Flwr_01.jpg, 306
   HrGls.jpg, 259, 264
   Poser.jpg, 279
   Poserz folder, 329
   slide images, 233
reveals
   progressive, 183–187
   pull-on, 277–278
rotating
   bitmaps, 206, 207
   clock hand, 262
   editing handles, 150
   with Frame panel, 190
   instances, 55
   logo letters, 156
rotoscoping
   as animation operation, 268
   background layer and, 271
   defined, 268
   using, 268–271
rulers, viewing, 11–12

S

sans-serif fonts
   for credits, 165
   defined, 143
   as device font, 171
   smaller typefaces and, 189
Scale and Rotate window, 206, 207
scaling
   bitmaps, 206, 207
   curved lines, 74
   in eyes project, 279
   graphic elements, 158, 189
   handles, 158
   images, 9
   instances, 54, 55
   text, 146

scenes
   3-D, creating, 327–329
   previewing, 91
score sound. See also sound
   editing, 236
   fade out, 234
   in Score layer, 234
screen grab utility, 271, 273
script actions, operations for, 246
scrolls. See also text animation
   creating, 187–188
   defined, 187
selecting
   with Arrow tool, 24–26, 45
   control points, 47
   fills, 35
   fonts, 165
   Ink Bottle tool, 49, 83
   instances, 54, 77
   keyframes, 96
   layer content, 77
   layers, 68, 69
   letters, 156
   line styles, 20
   mask layer, 122
   multiple frames, 90
   overlapping elements, 26
   sound files, 214
   text, 145, 166, 176
serif fonts. See also fonts
   choosing, 145
   for credits, 165
   defined, 142
   as device font, 171
   use of, 143
shadows project. See also 3-D content
   3-D environment assumption, 323
   background, 325
   Ball&Shadow layer, 325
   creating, 323–326
   finished ball, 326
   shadow, 326
   stroke size, 325
Shape submenu, 131
Shape Tweening, distinguishing, 112
shapes
   editing, 79
   joining, 44
   layer, altering, 113
   layer, selecting, 116

shards, 253
shatter wipe. See also wipes
    creating, 252–254
    defined, 252
    shattered pieces, 254
single color backgrounds, 81–82
skewing, 55
slide shows. See animated slide shows
sound envelope
    defined, 224
    editing, 224–226
    warble effect, 227
sound files
    formats, 214
    importing, 214–215
    in Library window, 215, 222
    selecting, 214
sound layers
    adding, 248
    creating, 222
    multiple, 221–223
Sound panel
    accessing, 215, 223
    Edit button, 224, 225, 234
    illustrated, 215
    Loops setting, 215, 223
    Stop option, 217
    Stream option, 216, 217
    Sync list, 216, 217
sounds. See also audio
    amplitude, 226
    applying, to animations, 229–236
    bi-channel panning effects, 226
    duplicating, on Timeline, 223–224
    event, 213–216
    MP3, 214
    previewing, 215, 222
    slide show, 234–236
    streaming, 216–217
    warble effect, 227
speed lines. See also onion skins
    creating, 271–272
    defined, 271
    illustrated, 272
Status toolbar, 14
Stop All Sounds action, 136
story, 164

streaming sounds. See also sounds
    creating, 216–217
    defined, 216
    event sounds versus, 216
    looping and, 216
    start of, 216
strobes
    colors, 276
    creating, 275–276
    defined, 275
Stroke panel
    accessing, 46, 241
    illustrated, 46, 242, 325
    Line Thickness option, 241
    Stroke type, 46, 241
strokes
    around letters, 179
    brush, 39, 41–43
    color, 48, 100
    fill, 49
    size, 177
Sub-Select tool
    clicking curve with, 46
    on curved-line drawing, 22, 23
    defined, 22
    for moving images, 23
    selecting control points with, 47
    for showing Bezier control points, 26
    using, 22–23, 25
    on vertical oval, 106
.swf file format, 196
Symbol Edit mode, 158
Symbol Edit window
    accessing, 52, 94
    illustrated, 53
    Timeline in, 96
Symbol Library
    attributes, 284
    instances, 284
    in nested animations, 283
    symbols, 284
Symbol Properties window
    accessing, 52, 58, 59
    Behavior options, 52
    Button option, 242
    Graphic option, 100
    illustrated, 52
    playing animated symbol in, 96

Index

symbols
- buttons as, 120
- center point, 52
- center point proximity relationship, 53
- cloned, 54
- creating, 52-55, 94
- edited, placing in library, 56-57
- editing, 57-58
- graphic, 154
- layers, 95
- logos as, 154
- naming, 56, 286, 287
- nested, 283
- Symbol Library, 284

T

text
- alignment, 167-168
- animated slide show, 230-233
- animating, 146-150
- bold, 230
- breaking apart, 145
- color through, 176
- credits, 165-171
- drop shadows, 176-177
- enlarging, 232
- font, 142-143
- global alignment, 168
- internal, alignment, 167
- logo, 153-157
- modifying, 145-146
- moving, 176
- rotating, 150
- scaling, 146
- selecting, 145, 166, 176
- size, 144
- style, 144-145
- tools and options, 142-145
- transparent, 177-180
- typing, 143

text animation
- creating, 146-150
- DVEs, 188-190
- fades, 188
- options, 183-191
- pops, 188
- progressive reveal, 183-187
- scrolls, 187-188

Text cursor, 155, 165

text effects
- creating, 173-181
- drop shadows, 176-177
- text masks, 173-176
- transparent text, 177-180

text masks, 173-176

Text menu
- Align Center command, 167
- Font command, 143, 165
- Size command, 144, 165, 230
- Style command, 144, 230

Text Options panel
- accessing, 168
- Character tab, 168-171
- Dynamic Text option, 171
- Font Size slider, 168, 169, 177
- Input Text option, 171
- Kern option, 169
- Paragraph tab, 168, 169
- Static Text option, 171
- Text Options tab, 168, 169
- Tracking option, 177
- Zoom indicator, 170-171

Text tool
- accessing, 143
- activating, 165
- using, 165, 230

tiled images, 312

Timelines. See also frames; Layers window
- accessing, 86, 120
- Add Frame option, 86, 253
- advanced effects, 320, 321
- animated background content, 86-87
- animated button character, 245
- BirdFly layer, 99
- Bird_Wing, 96
- for button-driven animation, 245
- fade effects, 316, 317
- filling in, 86
- fps box, 230
- Frame Indicator, 88
- Frames area, 86
- head morph project, 330

Continued

Timelines *(continued)*
  illustrated, 68
  instance fade effects, 316
  keyframes, 89
  Motion Tweening, 112
  Onion Skin controls, 269–271
  Onion Skin markers, 269, 270
  oval animation, 132
  playhead, 89
  Shape Tweening, 112
  sound duplication on, 223–224
  in Symbol Edit mode, 96
  tint effects, 319
  typewriter effect, 289
  using, 86–87
timepiece projects
  clock, 260–262
  digital display, 263–264
  hour glass, 264–266
  overview, 259
timing layers, 288
tint effects. *See also instance effects*
  creating, 318–319
  finished Timeline, 319
  settings, 319
  steps, 318–319
  Timeline, 319
tinting, 318
title animation
  creating, 146–150
  length, 231
  slide show, 230–233
  testing, 232
  zoom out, 232
titles. *See also text*
  creating, 141–151
  logos in, 159–161
  modifying, 145–146
  positioning, 146
  serif fonts, 143
  setting tone, 142
  tools and options, 142–145
Toggle High Quality action, 136
toolbars
  Controller, 14
  Main, 14
  Status, 14

Tools window, 13
  Arrow tool, 20–21
  Brush tool, 35
  color swatches, 28, 48
  defined, 13
  free-floating, 13
  illustrated, 18
  Lasso tool, 210
  Line tool, 18
  opening/closing, 13
  Oval tool, 23
  Paint Bucket tool, 29
  Paintbrush tool, 306
  Pen tool, 27, 46
  Pencil tool, 32
  Polygon Select tool, 253
  Rectangle tool, 26, 307
  selection arrows, 20
  Sub-Select tool, 22–23
Trace Bitmap settings window
  accessing, 208, 309
  illustrated, 208
  settings, 309
trademark symbol, 166
Transform panel
  accessing, 285, 286, 301
  horizontal/vertical dimensions boxes, 301, 312
  illustrated, 285
  Rotate box, 285, 301, 324
Transform submenu. *See also Modify menu*
  Edit Center command, 262
  Flip Horizontal command, 40, 206, 286
  Flip Vertical command, 91, 96, 206
  Rotate command, 54, 101, 150, 156, 210
  Scale and Rotate command, 206
  Scale command, 9, 10, 54, 74, 132, 146, 158
transparent text. *See also text; text effects*
  creating, 177–180
  illustrated, 180
  Mixer panel and, 178–179
tweener, 267
tweens
  creating, 98
  defined, 98
  Motion Tweening, 112, 144
  Shape Tweening, 112

Index

typewriter effect
  creating, 288–290
  illustrated, 290
  letter layers, 289
  letter timing, adjusting, 290
  Timeline, 289
  Timer layer, 288
  Typer symbol, 288
typewriter fonts, 171

Undo Levels setting (Preferences window), 7
ungrouping, 25
Up state. See also buttons
  animated button character, 243
  defined, 124

vector-based graphics
  bitmaps versus, 205
  translating bitmaps to, 208–209
View menu
  Anti-alias command, 9, 38, 171
  Fast command, 9, 33
  Grid command, 11–12, 33, 168
  Guides command, 33
  Hide Edges command, 10
  Magnification command, 11
  Outlines command, 9
  Rulers command, 11–12
  Show Grid command, 184
  Snap To Lines command, 21
  Snap To Objects command, 20, 268
  Timeline command, 67, 120, 316, 318, 320
  Zoom In command, 10
  Zoom Out command, 10

warble effect, 227
Web sites, appearance speed, 5–6
Window menu
  Actions command, 246, 247
  Cascade command, 15
  Close All Panels command, 15
  Common Libraries command, 8, 60
  Controller command, 278
  Library command, 51, 72, 310
  Panels command, 14–15, 20, 33, 46
  Save Panel Layout command, 15
  Tile menu, 15
  Toolbars command, 14, 86
windows, cascading/tiling, 15
wipes
  defined, 251
  radial, 251–252
  in reverse, 256
  shatter, 252–254
work space
  customizing, 11–15
  highlight color preference, 11
  view options, 11–13
  Window menu options, 13–15

zoom out, 232
zooming
  in/out, 10
  percentage, 11
  in Text Options panel, 170–171
  using, 10–11

IDG Books Worldwide, Inc. End-User License Agreement

READ THIS. You should carefully read these terms and conditions before opening the software packet(s) included with this book ("Book"). This is a license agreement ("Agreement") between you and IDG Books Worldwide, Inc. ("IDGB"). By opening the accompanying software packet(s), you acknowledge that you have read and accept the following terms and conditions. If you do not agree and do not want to be bound by such terms and conditions, promptly return the Book and the unopened software packet(s) to the place you obtained them for a full refund.

1. **License Grant.** IDGB grants to you (either an individual or entity) a nonexclusive license to use one copy of the enclosed software program(s) (collectively, the "Software") solely for your own personal or business purposes on a single computer (whether a standard computer or a workstation component of a multiuser network). The Software is in use on a computer when it is loaded into temporary memory (RAM) or installed into permanent memory (hard disk, CD-ROM, or other storage device). IDGB reserves all rights not expressly granted herein.

2. **Ownership.** IDGB is the owner of all right, title, and interest, including copyright, in and to the compilation of the Software recorded on the disk(s) or CD-ROM ("Software Media"). Copyright to the individual programs recorded on the Software Media is owned by the author or other authorized copyright owner of each program. Ownership of the Software and all proprietary rights relating thereto remain with IDGB and its licensers.

3. **Restrictions On Use and Transfer.**

    (a) You may only (i) make one copy of the Software for backup or archival purposes, or (ii) transfer the Software to a single hard disk, provided that you keep the original for backup or archival purposes. You may not (i) rent or lease the Software, (ii) copy or reproduce the Software through a LAN or other network system or through any computer subscriber system or bulletin-board system, or (iii) modify, adapt, or create derivative works based on the Software.

    (b) You may not reverse engineer, decompile, or disassemble the Software. You may transfer the Software and user documentation on a permanent basis, provided that the transferee agrees to accept the terms and conditions of this Agreement and you retain no copies. If the Software is an update or has been updated, any transfer must include the most recent update and all prior versions.

4. **Restrictions on Use of Individual Programs.** You must follow the individual requirements and restrictions detailed for each individual program in Appendix A of this Book. These limitations are also contained in the individual license agreements recorded on the Software Media. These limitations may include a requirement that after using the program for a specified period of time, the user must pay a registration fee or discontinue use. By opening the Software packet(s), you will be agreeing to abide by the licenses and restrictions for these individual programs that are detailed in Appendix A and on the Software Media. None of the material on this Software Media or listed in this Book may ever be redistributed, in original or modified form, for commercial purposes.

5. **Limited Warranty.**

    (a) IDGB warrants that the Software and Software Media are free from defects in materials and workmanship under normal use for a period of sixty (60) days from the date of purchase of this Book. If IDGB receives notification within the warranty period of defects in materials or workmanship, IDGB will replace the defective Software Media.

    (b) **IDGB AND THE AUTHOR OF THE BOOK DISCLAIM ALL OTHER WARRANTIES, EXPRESS OR IMPLIED, INCLUDING WITHOUT LIMITATION IMPLIED WARRANTIES OF MERCHANTABILITY AND FITNESS FOR A PARTICULAR PURPOSE, WITH RESPECT TO THE SOFTWARE, THE PROGRAMS, THE SOURCE CODE CONTAINED THEREIN, AND/OR THE TECHNIQUES DESCRIBED IN THIS BOOK. IDGB DOES NOT WARRANT THAT THE FUNCTIONS CONTAINED IN THE SOFTWARE WILL MEET YOUR REQUIREMENTS OR THAT THE OPERATION OF THE SOFTWARE WILL BE ERROR FREE.**

    (c) This limited warranty gives you specific legal rights, and you may have other rights that vary from jurisdiction to jurisdiction.

6. **Remedies.**

    (a) IDGB's entire liability and your exclusive remedy for defects in materials and workmanship shall be limited to replacement of the Software Media, which may be returned to IDGB with a copy of your receipt at the following address: Software Media Fulfillment Department, Attn.: *Flash 5 Weekend Crash Course*, IDG Books Worldwide, Inc., 10475 Crosspoint Blvd., Indianapolis, IN 46256, or call 1-800-762-2974. Please allow three to four weeks for delivery. This Limited Warranty is void if failure of the Software Media has resulted from accident, abuse, or misapplication. Any replacement Software Media will be warranted for the remainder of the original warranty period or thirty (30) days, whichever is longer.

(b) In no event shall IDGB or the author be liable for any damages whatsoever (including without limitation damages for loss of business profits, business interruption, loss of business information, or any other pecuniary loss) arising from the use of or inability to use the Book or the Software, even if IDGB has been advised of the possibility of such damages.

(c) Because some jurisdictions do not allow the exclusion or limitation of liability for consequential or incidental damages, the above limitation or exclusion may not apply to you.

7. **U.S. Government Restricted Rights.** Use, duplication, or disclosure of the Software by the U.S. Government is subject to restrictions stated in paragraph (c)(1)(ii) of the Rights in Technical Data and Computer Software clause of DFARS 252.227-7013, and in subparagraphs (a) through (d) of the Commercial Computer — Restricted Rights clause at FAR 52.227-19, and in similar clauses in the NASA FAR supplement, when applicable.

8. **General.** This Agreement constitutes the entire understanding of the parties and revokes and supersedes all prior agreements, oral or written, between them and may not be modified or amended except in a writing signed by both parties hereto that specifically refers to this Agreement. This Agreement shall take precedence over any other documents that may be in conflict herewith. If any one or more provisions contained in this Agreement are held by any court or tribunal to be invalid, illegal, or otherwise unenforceable, each and every other provision shall remain in full force and effect.

my2cents.idgbooks.com

Register This Book — And Win!

Visit **http://my2cents.idgbooks.com** to register this book and we'll automatically enter you in our fantastic monthly prize giveaway. It's also your opportunity to give us feedback: let us know what you thought of this book and how you would like to see other topics covered.

The IDG Books Online Web site is your online resource for tackling technology — at home and at the office. Frequently updated, the IDG Books Online Web site features exclusive software, insider information, online books, and live events!

10 Productive & Career-Enhancing Things You Can Do at www.idgbooks.com

- Nab source code for your own programming projects.
- Download software.
- Read Web exclusives: special articles and book excerpts by IDG Books Worldwide authors.
- Take advantage of resources to help you advance your career as a Novell or Microsoft professional.
- Buy IDG Books Worldwide titles or find a convenient bookstore that carries them.
- Register your book and win a prize.
- Chat live online with authors.
- Sign up for regular e-mail updates about our latest books.
- Suggest a book you'd like to read or write.
- Give us your 2¢ about our books and about our Web site.

You say you're not on the Web yet? It's easy to get started with IDG Books' *Discover the Internet*, available at local retailers everywhere.

CD-ROM Installation Instructions

The CD-ROM located inside the back cover of this book can be used on Macintosh and on Windows 95/98/NT/2000 systems. The CD-ROM includes artwork and tutorial projects featured in the color section of the book and product demos.

To gain access to the CD-ROM contents, follow these steps:

Macintosh/Windows

1. Insert the CD-ROM in your CD-ROM drive and wait for the CD-ROM icon to appear on your screen.
2. Double-click with the left mouse button [Mac users double-click] to open the CD-ROM.
3. Double-click on the content to load it, or place the selected content on your hard drive for future access.

Note that you can access project content directly from Flash by loading the project on the book's CD-ROM.